For Mohammed Zafar

With Best Wishes
Compliments & ...
S.F. Ahm...
March 21, 2014

God, Islam, and the Skeptic Mind

A Study on Faith, Religious Diversity, Ethics, and the Problem of Evil

by

SAIYAD FAREED AHMAD
SAIYAD SALAHUDDIN AHMAD

Blue Nile Publishing
Berlin • Kuala Lumpur

First published by Blue Nile Publishing in 2004
bluenilegroup@yahoo.com.sg

Saiyad Fareed Ahmad & Saiyad Salahuddin Ahmad

All Rights Reserved

Except for the quotation of short passages for the purposes of criticism and review, no part of this publication may be reproduced without the express permission of the authors and publisher.

ISBN 983-41294-1-6

National Library Malaysia Cataloguing in Publication Data
A catalogue record for this book is available from the National Library

Printed by

Polar Vista Sdn. Bhd.
15, Jalan 6/118C, Desa Tun Razak,
56000, Kuala Lumpur, Malaysia

*To my
children and grandchildren,
Zainab, Hasan, Zahra and Husain-
who will be the harbinger of
Islam in the new age.*

Contents

Preface i
Introduction iii

1 Does God Exist and How Do I Know Whether God Exists?   1

1.1	Parameters of the Question	2
1.2	The Design Argument	3
1.3	The Cosmological First Cause Argument	8
1.4	The *Kalam* Cosmological Argument	9
1.5	The Cosmological Necessary Being Argument	11
1.6	The Ontological Argument of Anselm	12
1.7	The Moral Argument	13
1.8	The Argument from Consciousness	14
1.9	Experiencing God	15
1.10	God According to God- The Divine Names & Attributes	19
1.11	Knowing of God in Islam	26

2 Is God Compatible with Science & Reason and Can I be Certain of God's Existence?   41

2.1	Sizing Our Senses- The Blindness of Empiricism	42
2.2	God & Science	46
2.3	The Bounds of Reason	51

2.4	Spiritual Certainty Versus Blind Reason	54
2.5	Islam & Knowledge	59
2.6	Islam, Reason & Science	61
2.7	The Qur'an & Prophethood	65
2.8	Unveiling & Inspiration	68
2.9	The Heart of Certainty	71

3 Why Does God Allow Evil and Suffering? 81

3.1	What are Evil & Suffering?	82
3.2	The View of Logic	84
3.3	The Purpose of Mankind in Relation to Evil	86
3.4	Lessons of Affliction	89
3.5	With Justice for All	101
3.6	Are My Actions Free or Determined?	107
3.7	What is the Role of Satan?	114

4 How Can We Understand Religious Diversity? 125

4.1	Approaches to Religious Diversity	126
4.2	The Primodial Religion Peaceful Submision	130
4.3	The Key to Salvation	136
4.4	The People of the Book	139
4.5	Eastern Religions	154
4.6	The Beauty of Islam	158
4.7	The Wisdom of Religious Diversity	168

5 Does Morality Require God? 181

5.1	Is Morality Relative or Absolute?	183
5.2	Secular Ethics - Hedonism and Perfectionism	186
5.3	Secular Humanism	188
5.4	Religious Ethics	196
5.5	The Foundation of Islamic Ethics	198
5.6	Does God Command Immoral Acts?	199
5.7	The Trust of Moral Responsibility	201
5.8	The Real World	205
5.9	What Is Unique About Islamic Ethics?	209

APPENDIX 225

The Ninety-Nine Attributes of Allah

INDEX 229

Preface

The present work grew out of a series of lectures delivered in North America and Malaysia between 1997 and 2003. Part of the material incorporated in the book was used as teaching material in response to questions posed by students in a course on "Islamic Ideology and Muslim Society" at the International Islamic University Malaysia. The core content of the book stems from questions and answers based on extensive interactions between Saiyad Salahuddin and prison converts, Muslim youth groups as well as non-Muslims in Dallas, USA. Materials were added as the writing progressed to make the book more comprehensive and suitable for publication. The questions that form chapter headings have basically been retained as they were originally posed during these interactions. We pray that the book will provide answers to those who are sincerely searching along the path of knowledge and devotion.

We would like to express our gratitude and indebtedness to a number of persons who have been responsible for the editing and publication of the book. We deeply appreciate the help and encouragement offered by Professors Syed Raza Kazmi, Department of English, and Mohamed Ajmal Abdul Razak Al-Aidrus, Deputy Dean of International Institute of Islamic Thought and Civilization (ISTAC), both affiliated with the University. The book has immeasurably benefited from their deft, adroit and skillful editing. We wish to thank Brother Subhan al Latif for his constructive criticisms and patient, cheerful preparation of the book through its various phases of publication.

Last but not the least, we wish to acknowledge our deep sense of gratitude to our wives – Nakhat Ahmad and Uzma Ahmad for sacrificing the time which was rightly theirs while writing the book. And finally, we fall short of words to express our thanks to Dr. Saiyad Nizamuddin Ahmad for his inspiration, comments and the computer time that he so generously devoted without which the book would remain incomplete.

We bow down to Allah and thank Him for His mercy and blessings and seek His forgiveness for any errors.

Saiyad Fareed Ahmad
Saiyad Salahuddin Ahmad
Kuala Lumpur, Malaysia

Introduction

It was in the twilight years of the nineteenth century that Friedrich Nietzsche proclaimed in stentorian tones that "God is dead." Much earlier, the "Age of Enlightenment", the scientific findings of Copernicus and Newton, and the philosophical critiques of Hume and Kant had already cracked the very edifice of Christianity and set the stage for the Divine Funeral. Once declared dead, it was left to Thomas Hardy to preside over His burial which he celebrated in a poem entitled "God's Funeral", declaimed to the world sometime between 1908 and 1910. This was meant to be a new dawn casting light on a new world. Gone was the dark shadow of the stern and inscrutable deity banished forever from the human consciousness by the new and improved Man of the twentieth century.

Science, progress, technology, modernization, industrialization, and secularism were to form the catechism of the new materialist dispensation. As the highly evolved man of the twentieth century approached his one-hundredth birthday, he was to celebrate his enormous achievements and mark the birth of a new millennium. On the eve of the so-called Y2K, media outlets eagerly provided round-the-clock coverage of the dawning millennium from Australia to Wyoming. As the clock struck midnight in each time zone, geriatric journalists were resuscitated to offer sagacious sound bites on the great moments and figures of the "American century". The apotheosis came when the clock struck twelve in Times Square with all eyes transfixed on a huge metallic ball as it was dropped from the top of the Times Tower. Images after images of drunken, dancing mobs bathed in champagne were played across the television screen. Such were the rituals of the highly evolved and civilized modern man, who could celebrate unprecedented material and technological progress without being aided or encumbered by ancient deities.

Yet, for the astute and discerning observer, the battle to bury God and religion was far from over. Even during the hey-day of skepticism and agnosticism, the seeds of conviction and what Sartre called the "God-shaped hole in human consciousness" had far from vanished. In America, the Protestant Fundamentalist movement was taking hold during the late nineteenth century in the form of pre-millenialism[1], led by John Darby (d. 1882) and Dwight Moody (d. 1899), and Scientific Protestantism[2], promoted by the New Light Presbyterian Seminary in Princeton, New Jersey. Judaism witnessed the birth of Zionism, which spurred a vehement reaction from Orthodox Jewry as demonstrated by the adherents of Habad Hasidism and Kabbalism, the followers of Rabbi Yitzak Kook (d. 1935) and Rabbi Isaac Reines (d. 1915), and later the Neturei Karta[3], which all understood the desire to establish a Jewish homeland in Palestine, but not at the price of compromising Judaic law. Islam also saw a reaction to centuries of colonialism and the fall of the Ottoman Empire with the emergence of reformist movements led by Jamal Ad-Din Al-Afghani (d. 1897), Muhammad Abduh (d. 1905), the puritan Rashid Rida (d. 1935), and "Sir" Syed Ahmad Khan. With the horrendous massacre of over 70 million people during World War I and II and the emergence of communism, people across the world were second-guessing the harsh consequences of alienation from God and questioning whether their newly found skepticism had failed them.

While the body bags continued to stream in from the "collateral damage" of war, social, psychological and environmental problems remained rampant, despite the promise of the scientific and technological revolution that had remarkably embellished the material quality of life for a precious few. These were the side effects of progress: problems such as the enormous gap between the rich and the poor, widespread crime, drug and alcohol abuse, sexual assault and aggression, widespread depression and anxiety, suicide, massive decimation of forests, and pollution of our atmosphere and water, were all continuing to climb (see Chapter 5). It should not be surprising, then, that the religious movements begun several decades earlier led to still greater reactions to modernity among all three Abrahamic faiths, especially in the1970s. The fundamentalist Protestant Right of Jerry Falwell and Pat Roberts, the Orthodox Jewish movement in Israel and the Islamic Revolution in Iran were all significant signs of a religious revival that still affects the world today. Finally, less than two years after the millennium mayhem, on Sep. 11, 2001, the world literally witnessed the horrific downing of the American icons of power. While we may never know the truth behind the cause of these attacks, they were presented, among other things, as a terrorist plot against modernity, capitalism, American imperialism, freedom, secularism and/or Christianity.

It is in this context and against this backdrop that we bring up timeless philosophical and theological questions concerning God. It is our contention that the issues discussed in this book, such as the role of science and reason, understanding evil and suffering, religious diversity, and the source of morality and ethics, were not only of importance to past times, but are of even greater significance to the present predicament of modern man. Ignoring them will only serve to worsen the most challenging problems of our times. Regardless of where one may stand with respect to such issues, answers and different perspectives must be sought, not only to provide peace of mind and direction in our lives, but also for the greater benefit to society-at-large. We can no longer assume that science and technology and the status quo will ensure the progression of mankind and rid it of all ills and nuisances. In addressing these issues, it is also our hope to make clearer their relevancy and importance to our daily lives.

Part of the reason why such questions are not addressed more frequently is the very way modern societies have been "designed". Besides the separation between church and state, the modern industrial man is forced to focus on maximizing his contribution to the "gross domestic product" and whatever free time remains is usually devoted to highly dissipating activities like watching television or guzzling beer at the neighborhood bar. The modern world leaves precious little time even for one's family and friends, let alone the spiritual contemplation of major philosophical questions.

Even when answers are sought, the Western world has largely focused on philosophical and "Judeo-Christian" responses. Islamic perspectives concerning theology have mostly been neglected or over-simplified with the vast majority of popular and academic discourse dominated by penetrating analysis of "political Islam". Hence, it is not only part of the purpose of this book to introduce teachings of Islam concerning God and our relationship to Him, but also some of its distinguishing characteristics. For instance, Islam's view of science, religion, ethics, human nature, economics and politics is unique in relation to other religions and has enormous practical implications.

It is often difficult for non-Muslims to understand that for a Muslim there is no aspect of personal or collective life unaffected by God or his or her religion. In fact, Islam's concept of worship is so broad and comprehensive that a Muslim can theoretically spend his or her entire life in worship. No Muslim worthy of the name can eat, drink, sleep or converse without beseeching Allah, the all-encompassing Arabic word for God. Nonetheless, Muslims, like any other group of people, are not immune to the globalization of modernity. With the increasing education of Muslims in Western institutions, Muslims too are increasingly asking the most fundamental of questions pertaining to God. Unfortunately, most Muslim institutions do not readily address questions such as the existence of God and evil, pre-destination versus free-will, religious diversity, or the underlying basis for ethics. We do not believe the reason for doing so to be deliberate, but rather based on a failing assumption that answers to such questions are already known to Muslims or are unimportant. In today's world, such presumptions cannot be made, nor can it be taken for granted that future generations will simply rely on and follow the belief system of our parents and religious leaders.

Nor should it be assumed that questioning the basis of one's faith is categorically detrimental or "bad". While it is true that meaningless and endless questioning can obviously be unproductive, sincere questioning can lead to considerable strengthening and understanding of belief in God. In fact, whether it is admitted or not, all "believers" have gone through periods of questioning and answering tenets of their faith.

The objective of this book is, thus, basically to provide an introductory Islamic perspective to common questions concerning God. The questions addressed would mostly be considered part of the study of the philosophy of religion. Certainly, a vast number of works have been composed that investigate such matters in minute detail. This book, however, has at least three distinctions. Firstly, by presenting an Islamic perspective, it presents an angle which has been largely ignored in the Western world. Secondly, there are few books in English covering issues concerning God while targeting a Muslim audience with a "modern mind-set." As noted earlier, Muslims too have begun to question their beliefs and principles and their concerns must be addressed. Thirdly, its language and style are intended to be relatively easily understood by the common reader, unlike the highly complex and technical jargon of most philosophical works. Its style is not so simplistic so as to compromise content, yet not so difficult that it would rival academic dissertations.

As secondary objectives, it is likely that even though the book is primarily addressed to a Muslim audience, non-Muslims as well as recent converts to Islam will also find great value therein. The events of September 11, 2001 have highlighted the importance and need for re-examining our most fundamental beliefs and understanding alternative views. It is also our view that, given the rich heritage of Islam and the historical role of Muslims in addressing the challenges of their times, Muslims should be at the forefront of answering such questions. The larger community of mankind can only benefit from such exchange of views on questions of common interest.

It is also worthwhile to understand what this book is not. It is not intended to be a completely comprehensive review of the questions at hand from either a philosophical or an Islamic perspective. Given the vast array of views expressed by both Muslim and non-Muslims, philosophers and laymen, theists and atheists, we can, at best, only provide introductory information. Although we have largely relied on the Qur'an and, to a lesser extent, on agreed upon sayings of Prophet Muhammad (SAW), we do not claim to represent the "official" Islamic position, if there is such a thing; but we do claim to offer an informed Islamic perspective.

In Chapter 1, we begin with a discussion of the most fundamental and paramount question of the existence of God. In it, the most well-known arguments from Western philosophy for the existence of God are summarized and tested, followed by an introduction to the classical view of the nature and knowledge of God in Islam. Chapter 2 examines the overall role of science and reason, the related question of their compatibility with faith in God, and an Islamic perspective of knowledge and certainty. The most common argument of skeptics, atheists, and agnostics alike, the question why God allows evil and suffering, is next addressed in Chapter 3. Within it, the popular question of pre-destination versus free-will is also confronted. The fourth chapter deals with the question of religious diversity: why does it exist, what does it mean, how can religions be evaluated, how does Islam view other religions, and what distinguishes Islam? Finally, Chapter 5 closes with a discussion of various views of whether morality requires God and provides an overview of Islamic ethical principles and some of their unique aspects.

It is our sincere hope that, if by reading this book, our readers are strengthened in their faith, inspired to make positive changes in their lives, or at the least, gain a greater appreciation for Islamic teachings concerning God, then we will have been successful, by His Will and Mercy.

Notes

1 A Protestant movement that envisaged Christ returning to earth before the millennium due to the increasing corruption of the modern world.
2 A Protestant movement that appealed to reason in reconciling the faith of Christians while insisting that every verse of the Bible was absolutely true and binding.
3 The Neturei Karta ("the guardians of the city") is a form of Orthodox Judaism whose followers maintain that the modern state of Israel is in complete violation of Jewish Law and forbid any participation in politics or support of state-sponsored activities

| Chapter 1

Does God Exist and How Do I Know Whether God Exists?

To see a World in a grain of sand
And a Heaven in a wild flower
Hold Infinity in the palm of your hand
And Eternity in an Hour

William Blake, Auguries of Innocence, 1808

In ancient Sumeria, an incantation priest was called upon to exorcise the Dimme demoness, believed to be responsible for, among other things, the murder of infants. Dimme, was thought to be the daughter of Anu, god of the heavens, who was banished from heaven for her evil. The exorcism's recited incantation formulae were typically based upon dialogues between the god Enkin and his son, Asalluhi, in which help was requested from the father to combat demons and evil spirits.[1]

The habit of belief in the Unseen is as old as the habit of civilization. Whether at the very cradle of civilization at Uruk in ancient Mesopotamia, the banks of the Nile, the Indus valley, the Yucatan peninsula, or the Huang Ho river, we encounter hymns to the gods and goddesses of Innana, Osiris, Sarswati, Quetzalcoatl, and the enigmatic Tao. From the beginning of human history, faith in unseen forces was not only common, but part and parcel of the daily lives of people across the world. Belief in not only God, but also ghosts, spirits, demons, life after death, reincarnation, and concepts like the ether[2], mana[3], qi[4], and prana[5] has existed across multiple cultures, civilizations and all eras.

The question of God's existence is arguably the most fundamental and important question that can be asked. Even atheists admit that the idea of God is intimately linked with human history and "has made more of a difference to human life on this planet, both individually and collectively, than anything else ever has."[6] Theists, atheists and agnostics alike have all discussed and debated God's existence for ages and will continue to do so. In fact, many would argue that human beings have a natural and inherent yearning to understand God and other metaphysical ideas, including a fundamental understanding of where they came from and why they and the universe exist.

Challenging the existence of God, however, has become increasingly fashionable in recent times with the onslaught of notions like secularism, materialism, scientism, evolutionism, and other modern ideologies. Such ideologies are generally considered to have their origins in seventeenth century Europe, where the scientific worldview was beginning to take hold and the Church began to face a challenge it is yet to recover from. Christian scripture was found to conflict with major findings, beginning with the Copernican theories of the sun as the center of the universe, and later Darwin's theory of evolution. Add in the influence of atheistic thinkers like Hume, Kant, Marx, Freud and Nietzsche and the marketing glitz of the current Western political and economic domination of the globe, and we have the result that it is now common to encounter those who believe God and religion no longer have any real relevance in their lives and feel that the human condition can better progress without such "unproven" and "nebulous" ideas.

1.1 Parameters of the Question

When addressing the question of God's existence, several related questions must be asked:
    (1) What is meant by "God"?
    (2) If God exists, can and how do I know He exists?, and
    (3) How certain is my knowledge and can it be proved?

Questions 1 and 2 are addressed in this chapter, while question 3 along with the related questions of compatibility of God with science and reason in the next.

Before addressing these questions from an Islamic perspective, it is worthwhile to examine the view of Western philosophy. In this regard, a vast number of arguments and so-called proofs have been offered by many thinkers, philosophers and believers throughout the course of history. Some of them are exercises in pure reason, while others appeal more to our senses and the world that surrounds us. Another argument does not rely on rational abilities nor the senses, but instead argues that God is a being to be experienced. Some theists also hold that belief in God is in no need of rational proofs given the guidance provided by Divine Revelation or Scripture.

In any case, in the process of arguing for the existence of God, these arguments inevitably touch on various aspects of Divine qualities or attributes, such as that of Creation, Omnipotence, Being and Justice. A comprehensive definition for God, however, cannot be found given that God is immaterial and inherently beyond the limitation of words or confinement. Nonetheless, a common Western, monotheistic understanding of the term "God" has been summarized by Richard Swinburne as "a person without a body, present everywhere, the creator and sustainer of the universe, a free agent, able to do everything, knowing all things, perfectly good, a source of moral obligation, immutable, eternal, a necessary being, holy, and worthy of worship."[7] Without immediately going into the merits or flaws of such an understanding, the concept of God is addressed in more detail from an Islamic point of view in Sec. 1.11.

Let us begin, however, by examining some of the most common arguments in favor of the existence of God.

1.2 The Design Argument

The popular argument from design asserts that the delicate order, consistency and precise design observed in the universe must be attributed to a supreme, omnipotent, intelligent and purposive force and not to mere chance, "mother nature", natural selection or evolution or any other worldly force. There are two key aspects to this argument: one that relates to design in the sense of purpose, and the other that relates to design in the sense of order, regularity and consistency.

One of the most famous thinkers to argue for design in the sense of purpose (the teleological argument) was William Paley (1743-1805). He used the analogy that if a clock were discovered by someone and asked where it came from, it would be absurd to argue that the clock was found simply because it had existed forever. The clock exists because it has a maker who made it for a distinct purpose. In this case, the clock has several intricate parts that are put together and framed and adjusted to produce motion, which in turn is regulated to provide a relative measure of time. Similarly, he claimed that the universe and its many parts, which are far more complex than a clock must have intelligent design and purpose. As a simple example, anyone who has studied the human eye would be foolish to think that it has been created (or "evolved" as some would have it) without purpose or intelligent design.

Other kinds of design arguments relate to order, regularity and an underlying unity in nature, have received increasing support in modern scientific fields such as quantum physics, astronomy and biochemistry. An emerging group of scientists has recently argued for the existence of God from this angle.[8]

For instance, scientists are continually affirming that the universe is a very finely tuned system with a delicately balanced harmony of fundamental constants or cosmic singularities[9]. These constants are numerical values assigned to various processes in nature such as gravity, the rate of expansion of the universe and nuclear forces. With respect to the formation of the universe, astronomers have estimated that the balance of matter to antimatter had to be accurate to one part in ten billion for the universe to even arise. Had it been larger or greater by one part in ten billion, no universe would have arisen. Similarly, the universe wouldn't have arisen if the rate of expansion of the Big Bang had been one billionth of a percent larger or smaller[10].

...the universe wouldn't have arisen if the rate of expansion of the Big Bang

had been one billionth of a percent larger or smaller.

Hoyle and Wickramasinghe[11] have calculated the probability of the random formation of a single enzyme from amino acids anywhere on the earth's surface as being one in 1020. To complicate matters further, human beings have around 2000 enzymes, which makes the chance of obtaining them all randomly only one in 1,040,000. If that wasn't enough, you must consider that enzyme formation is only one step necessary for life and says nothing of the more complex processes like the formation of DNA, the transcription of DNA to RNA or mitosis and meiosis, etc. In the end, they conclude that the probability of life resulting from random ordering of organic molecules is in effect zero.

The harmony and design demonstrated by these and other features cannot be attributed to mere chance. According to Paul Davies, theoretical physicist at Cambridge University, "… the seemingly miraculous concurrence of these numerical values must remain the most compelling evidence for cosmic design."[12] A number of other arguments from fields of modern science supporting the existence of God are considered in more detail in Chapter 2 while discussing the compatibility of God with science.

Despite the strength of these arguments, a number of criticisms of the arguments from design have been made, the most prominent of which came from Immanuel Kant (1724-1804) and David Hume (1711-1776), and claim, among other things, that:

(i) the design or order we perceive is actually "mind-imposed" rather than "God-imposed",[13]

(ii) it is an unacceptable extrapolation to go from saying there is order in the universe to saying that God exists,

(iii) if there is order, then why can't it be attributable to human beings or mere chance?

(iv) if we are consistent with the idea of order and design, then something must have designed God, and

(v) unexplainable disorder and evil also exists.[14]

Let us then briefly offer some potential counterarguments:

1. If the order were purely "mind-imposed" and not "God-imposed" then the whole system of scientific and empirical inquiry should be considered "mind-imposed" and lacking any objectivity. While it is recognized that there are limitations and subjectivity associated with modern scientific methods, this does not mean that there are absolutely no objective learnings to be had. The many mathematical equations that describe various processes in nature are not mere figments of imagination and have been proven to be excellent approximators of reality. If order were mindimposed, does this mean that there was really no order when human beings were not present on earth or that all semblance of order would suddenly vanish if the human race were to be wiped out?

2. If it is acknowledged that there is some order that is imposed by something other than the universe, then it is reasonable to suppose that this being is powerful, purposive, incorporeal, immaterial, and has will. Though this is an incomplete description of God, these qualities are, nonetheless, important attributes of God, which all theists cling to and which most atheists deny.

3. As detailed in "The Cosmological First Cause Argument" below, the Cause of all causes, including order and design, must be other than this world, otherwise it too will be like matter and subject to the law of causation. In addition, the likelihood of the universe arising by mere chance is essentially zero as indicated by modern calculations discussed earlier.

4. If it is implied that Darwinian evolution or natural selection can be used as an alternative to Divine order, then this too is blatantly false. Other writers, such as M. Behe[15], D. Dewar[16] and K. Ward[17] have offered a thorough discussion of the fallacies in interpreting Darwinian evolution. Suffice it to say, however, that even if one were to accept Darwinian evolution, this does not in any way explain the cause or source of such evolution. In fact, such evolution can be used to strengthen the theistic

argument of Divine providence and intelligent design. Darwin, himself expressed some of his doubts when he wrote in a letter that "the belief in natural selection must at present be grounded entirely on general considerations...when we descend to details...we cannot prove that a single species has changed, nor can we prove that the supposed changes are beneficial, which is the groundwork of the theory".[18]

5. As will be detailed below in the First Cause, Kalam and Necessary Being arguments, God cannot be caused or designed by another being. If the implication of the original criticism is that multiple gods could also be responsible for design, then there is no logic in such a thought. Multiplicity only applies to finite beings. For example, if the world we occupy is finite in space, multiple worlds can easily be envisioned; but if the world is infinite in space there cannot be but one world. Similarly, there can only be one Infinite, Supreme Being- anything more would contradict the concept of infinity. It is also worthwhile to reference the famous principle known as "Occam's Razor", which has even been defended by Hume himself. This principle, which has been supported by numerous philosophers and scientists, whether theistic or atheistic, states that "entities are not to be multiplied beyond necessity". The implication is that if a single, supreme God can be said to be responsible for intelligent design in the universe, then there is no reason to posit multiple gods just for the sake of argument. Still further, there is the problem of potential conflict and division of power among multiple deities that must be dealt with.

> ... there can only be one Infinite, Supreme Being- anything more would contradict the concept of infinity.

6. Even if one were to accept the idea of disorder, one has to explain the order that does exist. Nonetheless, to address the criticism, it should be realized that disorder is also a subjective term that can be misperceived. The modern study of fractals in mathematics is a clear example of order being found where others had only perceived random disorder and irregularity. Many patterns in nature, including everything from the

branches of a tree, the winding path of a river or coastline, the distribution of galaxy clusters, the branching of blood vessels to even the Brownian motion of molecules and particles have been described by the concept of fractals that are generated by geometric equations that repeat at very small scales to produce amazing shapes and surfaces on a larger scale.[19] Hence, just because Hume or Kant does not perceive order does not mean order does not exist (for disorder in the sense of evil and suffering, refer to Chapter 3 for a more detailed investigation).

1.3 The Cosmological First Cause Argument

One of the earliest thinkers to promote this argument was the famous Greek philosopher, Aristotle (384-322 B.C.). It was later supported and modified by Thomas Aquinas and countless other thinkers, philosophers and laymen alike. Most theists and believers support this argument, though many clarify that God is continuously sustaining the universe, not just initiating it. Others support the argument of emanation.[20] Aristotle related God as the "Unmoved Mover" or "Prime Mover" who causes all causes and activity in the universe since everything and every occurrence must be traced back to an original cause or source based on the law of causality. God is the eternal Prime Mover who moves all things while He remains stationary. To use the analogy of the wheel, every part of it moves or rotates except the very center, which remains motionless.

Of course, skeptics are quick to claim faulty logic since the argument results in an infinite series of causes and the original cause must also be caused. However, the Prime Mover or Cause of all causes is different from secondary causes in that it is immaterial and spiritual in nature, and hence, is not subject to the laws governing matter. In addition, the Prime Mover is an agent that must be free to do as He pleases since this is the only way that a temporal universe could arise from an eternal cause. He is also considered infinitely powerful in order to create something out of nothing. Some have also specified that the First Cause must be timeless and unchanging since if there is no actual change, there is no change in time (others do not consider this an essential part of the argument). Time can only pass in connection with movement or change and is also a creation of God.

David Hume has taken issue with the law of causality saying that the ideas of cause and effect are distinct, and that it is possible for something to arise without a cause.[21] In fact, he argues that there need not be any explanation whatsoever for the universe- it simply is the way it is. Hume basically says that because we can imagine a being of existence without any cause, then it follows that a being can exist without any cause or at least it must be proven that a being cannot exist without cause. However, this argument is very weak and has been refuted by a number of philosophers who argue that the mere imagining of a being does not entail existence without cause.[22] Imagining that a chicken came into being without cause does not mean that the chicken can actually exist without cause. If all objects and events have causes, why should only the cosmos be expected to exist without cause?

Critics also question why there cannot be an infinite series of causes. This question is answered in the next argument.

1.4 The *Kalam* Cosmological Argument

Though cosmological arguments have been posited by numerous philosophers and thinkers, this particular form of the argument was developed and supported by medieval Muslim philosophers such as Al-Farabi (b. 870), Al-Ghazali (b. 1058) and Ibn Rushd (Averroes, b. 1126).[23] The Kalam argument basically states that our current existence and universe has to be finite and with a beginning because it would be impossible to arrive at the present moment if the past were infinite and uncreated. It argues that it is impossible to cross an actual infinite. Simply stated, no one can ever count to infinity, so we cannot be living in an eternal universe. It should also be remembered that the conditions which apply to the First Cause argument also apply here- namely that the First Cause is immaterial, free, and timeless.

The crux of the argument hinges on whether or not there can be an infinite set of actual things or persons or events. While some have argued that an infinite series can be crossed, in actuality, only a potential infinite can be crossed and not an actual infinite.[24] Without getting into the mathematical minutiae of the debate, it is obvious that arriving at the present moment involves more than just the issue of counting from zero to infinity, it also requires a start or an impetus. This is analogous to trying to jump out of a bottomless pit.

Some have claimed that modern science, particularly the Second Law of Thermodynamics and the Big Bang theory, supports the idea of a beginning to the universe.[25] The Second Law of Thermodynamics states that in a closed system the amount of energy to do work is always decreasing, which when applied to the universe as a whole, means it is constantly being expended and will eventually cease to exist. This implies that the universe cannot be infinite, otherwise it would have already reached an equilibrium end state. The Big Bang theory developed in the 20th century basically states that everything, including matter, energy, space and time, were all compacted into a single point with no dimensions which exploded to form the universe. Regardless of whether one believes in this theory or not, the theistic implication is that the universe arose from what has been described as nothingness.[26]

Others, like Stephen Hawking, have considered the possibility that the universe is neither finite nor infinite and could, instead, be finite but unbounded in time.[27] This theory is supposedly based on quantum mechanics and Einstein's general theory of relativity. Nonetheless, accepting or rejecting this theory in our view does not undermine the theistic stance.

Some skeptics object that showing that the universe had a beginning doesn't actually prove the existence of God or the continuance of the universe. It is, however, an important step in pointing to God's attribute as Creator, as well as having implications for Divine purpose and Necessary Being, as we will discuss later.

In any case, the Kalam cosmological argument is a powerful one that even its detractors struggle with to this day.

1.5 The Cosmological Argument of Necessary Being

One of the early formulators of this argument was the Muslim philosopher, Ibn Sina (Avicenna, 980-1037), and later Gottfried Leibniz (1646-1716) and countless other thinkers have lent it further support. It starts with the premise that everyone and everything is dependent on someone or something else. Restated, everything in the world is contingent, and by inference, the world itself is contingent. If one were to continue this series of contingency and causality as far back as we can go, we still have an infinite contingent series. Thus, to reach the present moment and for us to exist today, there must be a non-dependent necessary being. In other words, there must be a sufficient reason *for* the world which is *other than* the world. In this sense, this argument is similar to the earlier First Cause argument. At the same time, it is distinct because it argues that the essence of The Necessary Being must inherently include existence, which bears some similarity to the ontological argument of Anselm as we will see below. Hence, this argument not only says that God exists, but that God must exist to solve this dilemma of contingency. Unlike the Kalam argument, it posits God's existence without needing to debate the question of an infinite or finite universe.

> *...there must be a sufficient reason for the world which is other than the world.*

Of course, critics question the necessity of a "necessary being" and question how we know that everything is contingent. While they would agree that objects and events are contingent, they claim it is false extrapolation to say that the whole universe must be contingent.[28] In response, it should be said that it has been established by consistent observation, since the beginning of human history, that all matter requires causation, without exception, so it is logical for the universe, as a whole, to require causation. God, on the other hand, is immaterial and transcends space and time, and therefore does not require causation by necessity. Recall also Hume's objection to causality in which he somehow tries to argue that it is possible for something to arise without a cause. This point was rebutted earlier under "The Cosmological First Cause Argument".

1.6 The Ontological Argument of Anselm

Though there are a number of variants of the ontological argument, the most prominent is that of Anselm of Canterbury (1033-1109 A.C.). It is one of the most clever examples of philosophical logic ever produced and has many ardent supporters to this day. It starts with the argument that anyone, even a "fool", can believe that something exists, at least in understanding, for which nothing greater or more perfect can be conceived. The second part of the argument is that something for which *nothing greater can be conceived* cannot exist in understanding alone, for existence in reality is greater than relative existence in the mind, and that something is none other than God.

This elusive but clever argument had its detractors as one might expect and some of their objections were as follows:

1. It is impossible to conceive of a "being than which nothing greater can be conceived" since it would boggle the mind to think of something infinitely perfect.[29]

2. If the argument were valid, then the mere imagination of an object, such as a perfect island, would entail its actual existence.[30]

3. Just because God is being defined as something that must exist does not mean that the concept of God is real. In other words, if there is God, He must exist, but how do we know there is God in the first place?[31]

Anselm replied thus, firstly, if you can understand the phrase the "most perfect being" then you have already conceived of such a being. Secondly, there is nothing in the definition of objects (or islands) that necessarily entails perfection, whereas the definition of God entails perfection. Yes, it is true that somebody could imagine a perfect island and this would not entail its existence. However, there is no such thing as a truly perfect island because I could always argue that there could always be more coconuts or trees or parrots or levels of perfection ad infinitum. God, on the other hand, is defined by His perfection of attributes and there is nothing or no one *more perfect than* He. Thus, since it is more perfect to exist than not, God must exist.

As for the third objection, many critics incorrectly assume that Anselm is merely defining God to include existence. What he is really questioning is whether something for which nothing greater can be conceived can exist only in our understanding or intellect. Others like Norman Malcolm have interpreted Anselm's statements in his "3rd Proslogion" as not assuming existence as a perfection but instead, arguing that God must exist because He is Necessary Being[32]. In other words, God exists not because existence is a perfection, but because His existence is necessary (the Necessary Being Argument).

1.7 The Moral Argument

Though it is uncommon to use morality as a primary basis in arguing for the existence of God, it is nonetheless a popular line of thought that morality requires a God who is an objective source of moral and ethical commands and possesses the power to enforce these commands by rewarding and punishing acts, thereby allowing justice to prevail in the end. Immanuel Kant however, used the goals of morality to argue for the existence of God. In his view, other rational arguments, such as the ontological and cosmological ones, cannot provide sound proof for the existence of God. He asserts that the aim of morality is what he calls the "Highest Good" and ultimately, happiness for self and society. In other words, perfect virtue must be rewarded with perfect happiness. The catch, however, is that human beings cannot perfectly achieve this Highest Good or virtue in this world, nor is there proportional reward of happiness for virtuous persons. Hence, there is a dilemma with a Highest Good that seems unattainable, but is, nonetheless, a necessary end result of morality. To resolve the dilemma, he argues that God must exist in order to reward fidelity to moral commandments and fully realize the Highest Good. Hence, without God the Highest Good cannot be realized

Critics of Kant deny that there must be a correlation between morality and happiness and argue that someone may, hence, desire to be virtuous only for the sake of happiness rather than for its own sake. They also use Kant's own claim that rational arguments are futile in trying to prove God's existence to say that the moral argument is simply another kind of rational argument. However, what Kant claimed was that one has the right to believe in God, not as a metaphysical or rational truth, but as a *practical* and moral necessity. Another criticism surrounds the question of why we should believe in the ultimate prevalence of justice, for Kant seemingly infers the existence of God from what would happen if God existed.

Other kinds of moral arguments assert that one can infer the existence of God from moral commands. These commands imply the existence of a moral commander or law-giver since each command should have a commander. Others point to the moral conscience or sense of responsibility and guilt that people often naturally feel with respect to moral duties. John Henry Newman (1801-1890) wrote, "If, as is the case, we feel responsibility, are ashamed, are frightened, at transgressing the voice of conscience, this implies that there is One to whom we are responsible, before whom we are ashamed, whose claim upon us we fear."[33] Atheists are quick to claim that moral conscience can be authoritative in itself and does not require answering to a Higher Being. Correspondingly, they claim that moral conscience is merely an outgrowth of parental, societal and institutional influences instead of a Divine gift.

Still others claim that morality does not require God or religion, but that being moral is a consequence of believing in God. We are morally obliged to enact moral duties because God wills that we do so. Hence, whatever God wills is the right thing to do simply because God wills it (the question of whether God is necessary for morality is discussed further in Chapter 5).

1.8 The Argument from Consciousness

John Locke (1632-1704) used the argument from consciousness as his central argument for the existence of God. It basically uses the premise that consciousness cannot arise from matter alone. He relatedly claims that there must be an eternal cogitative being or eternal mind from which consciousness and the ability to think arise. Hence, he assigns God, among other things, the attribute of an eternal, perfect mind.

Atheists tend to challenge the assumption that consciousness cannot arise from matter (and are helped by the fact that Locke himself conceded that God could, if desired, bestow consciousness and the ability to think to material objects). They point to modern scientific evidence, such as the complex electrochemical pathways in the brain that can affect consciousness, with the implication that if something material can affect consciousness, then it is conceivable that matter could be conscious or give rise to consciousness. The idea is that science may eventually determine that the immaterial can arise from the material. However, Swinburne has counter-argued that science has never been able to provide a viable explanation for consciousness based on matter alone, and is unlikely to be able to, and that it is much more probable that consciousness is the product of a Higher Being with intelligent design.[34] Keith Ward has also eloquently supported this view: "The existence of minds can only be explained, if explained at all, in terms of the intrinsic values that they can create and apprehend. The ultimate explanation of a plurality of dependent minds, which have originated through a long process of development in a material universe, lies in the existence of a mind that does not depend on such processes of development or on anything else whatsoever. It will be itself of supreme value, and thus self-justifying or self-explanatory, and it will generate finite minds for the sake of the goodness they can realize."[35]

1.9 Experiencing God

This argument has intentionally been separated from others since it is not a so-called rational proof for the existence of God. Rather, it is a compelling view that holds that belief in God does not require any evidence based on reason and instead, should rely on personal experience of Him. Implicit in this argument is the assumption that personal experience is a valid form of knowledge or epistemology. Everyone, whether we realize it or not, utilizes personal experience as a source of knowledge. Who can deny the experience of tasting a mouth-watering dessert, the thrill of racing on a roller-coaster, suffering the agony of defeat, or the jubilation of a child playing in the park?

One cannot experience the depth and feel of the ocean without plunging one's self into it. Rational methods cannot prove, beyond any doubt and to the satisfaction of all, either the existence or even absence of God. Just as a male cannot fully understand the pangs of childbirth without experiencing it, so too an atheist cannot comprehend the experience of a mystic without "tasting belief". The "experiencing of God" does not necessarily imply that you become equal or one with God or that He talks to you at night, but that you, at the very least, realize *His Presence*. Of course there are an infinite number of degrees of experience, and the exact nature of the experience often cannot be described by words, for it is unlike any other.

> *One cannot experience the depth and feel of the ocean without plunging one's self into it.*

Throughout human history, there have been countless proponents of the experiential argument with the most common being the mystics, theologians and faithful adherents of various religious traditions. In fact, William James has claimed the role of religious experience to be so important that he believes all organized religion and theology is actually a secondary outcome of primary, solitary experiences of God[36].

There are a number of different ways to categorize experience. For example, hearing a description of fire, seeing a fire and actually touching a fire are all different levels of experience. One method classifies the circumstances of the experience under:

(1) religious experience
(2) natural experience, and
(3) personal, non-religious experience as discussed below.

These roughly correspond to the primary ways that God reveals Himself to human beings, i.e. through Divine scripture and the message of the Prophets, the natural world, and through what is "within", i.e., the human spirit and its connection to the Divine.

Religious Experience:

Although the distinct forms of worship that characterize each religion are unique in many ways, they also share a common thread in their goal to connect and become "closer" to God by obeying His commandments. In the course of this worship, one can come to experience God. Whether it is the davening of Jews, the baptism of Christians, the *puja* of Hindus, the *ngondro* of Tibetan Buddhists or the *salat* of Muslims, adherents of all religions claim at least some form of experiencing God through worship. Though significant differences exist between religions with respect to truth-claims, theology and practices (see Chapter 4), the experiencing of God is not limited to any single religion- for God can manifest Himself to any He pleases. Most religions consider their forms of worship to be not just rituals rewarded with seats in Paradise, but also loci of experience, intended to provide a glimpse of God in this world.

The mystics of each religious tradition, more than any other group, seek to "touch God" during their earthly existence and have formulated the closest thing to a detailed methodology for experiencing and approaching God. These methods are often based on an asceticism with intense devotional practices and the idea that God, who is wholly spiritual and immaterial can be experienced if we allow our own spiritual nature to flourish and minimize our worldly and material nature. This involves the prescription of various spiritual exercises for controlling an individual's particular vices and minimizing temptations.

Within the religious tradition there is also something to be said for experience by "way of knowledge". A number of believers describe a sense of experiencing or realizing God as they learn more about Him, whether through scripture, the message of Prophets or saints or personal inspiration. As will be discussed in Chapter 2, the more we sincerely seek knowledge of God, the more God bestows knowledge upon our hearts.

Natural Experience:

Who hasn't at one time or another gazed at the stars in the night's canopy, smiled at the sight of a lion feeding its cub or marveled at the grandeur of mountain peaks, and as a result, pondered the Beauty, Compassion and Majesty of the Lord? This is experiencing God at its simplest but most beautiful level. It is in such moments that people can experience Divine epiphanies and realize the dependence of the finite on the Infinite and Transcendent.

Earlier, we had discussed the compelling design and order observable in the universe. Although this order can readily be realized by a layman, it is most deeply studied by the scientist. As described under the Design Argument, a number of scientists have realized the connection between the universe and its Creator despite the ongoing efforts of the establishment to secularize modern science and rid it of its Divine source. Here the Attributes of God most readily realized are His Power to exert order and control over the universe and His Creation and fashioning of countless forms of life, which includes not only the initial creation of the universe but also its continuous sustenance.

Personal Experience:

This type of experience is characterized by a deeply personal experience of God that is not associated with specific religious ritual or worship, but involves everyday events that awaken the spirit within. It could be triggered by a single event, be sudden and miraculous in nature, or be a more gradual awakening spanning many years. For example, we have all heard of someone who is miraculously healed from a life-threatening disease, one who awakens from a dream that transforms his or her life's purpose, one who is dramatically rescued from a raging house fire, one who experiences telepathy or extrasensory perception (ESP), one who observes a levitating saint, one who meets a child prodigy, or someone who has a near death experience. All such examples illustrate one commonality: a dramatic, out-of-this-world experience whereby one distinctly perceives the presence of a Higher Being.

The experience, however, could also be more gradual in nature, as is the case with some who reflect on past events and experiences that have shaped their lives and distinctly perceive Divine pattern, guidance, compassion and wisdom. Here, when we step back to take an external and objective view of our lives, we realize there is Divine purpose in every occurrence and there is no such thing as luck or randomness.

Of course, it is easy for skeptics to dismiss such experiences as delusionary and wishful thinking, but that is not the point. The fact is that experiencing such events can be utterly conclusive and demonstrative of God for those who experience them. The case for religious experience is also made more compelling by the fact that people from all wakes of life, all periods of history, and all corners of the globe continue to report this kind of experience and will continue to do so.

1.10 God According to God —The Divine Names and Attributes

Recall how we opened the chapter with the posing of two questions:
(1) What is meant by the term "God"? and
(2) If God exists, how do I know He exists?
(3) Mana is a supernatural force thought to dwell in certain persons or sacred objects

Let us start with a discussion of the first question from an Islamic perspective before discussing methods of knowing Him.

God is as God has described Himself. He has not left humanity without guidance and has chosen to reveal what we need to know about Him and obeying Him through His Divine Books and Messengers and creation of the universe. If one believes in God, then it is logical to seek knowledge about the nature of God from God Himself. In Islam, this information has been provided directly in the form of the written and recited word in the Qur'an. The sayings of Prophet Muhammad, called *ahadith* in Arabic, provide further amplification of our knowledge of God based on the revelation that he received. Every aspect of Islamic law and spirituality revolves around God, as the worship of Him is the very goal of existence.

When discussing God, it is important to remember that God's essence is unknowable, for He is Infinite and we are finite; He is Pure Spirit and we are not.[37] Does this mean, however, that we are incapable of perceiving and knowing anything about God? No, because God Himself has made us capable of attaining *relative* or *limited knowledge* of His Attributes as manifested in creation and in ourselves. This concept is confirmed in the Qur'an: "They cannot comprehend anything out of what He knows save what He wills" (2:255).

> ...God Himself has made us capable of attaining relative or limited knowledge of His Attributes as manifested in creation and in ourselves.

Our ability to think and use our intellect is a Divine gift that derives from the Creator who possesses these attributes before they are reflected in the mirror of creation. Why else would God appeal to mankind in the Qur'an to use their intellect, reflect, think and understand over 125 times in the Qur'an? Thus, those who do not use their God-given faculties are condemned in the Qur'an: "The worst of creatures in the sight of God are those persons who are deaf and dumb and do not reflect" (8:22).

God describes Himself in the Qur'an according to various Attributes or Divine Names which serve to provide a limited understanding of Him. Islamic scholars and theologians have summarized these Divine Attributes under categories such as Oneness, Mercy, Justice, Life, Power, Knowledge, Will, and Speech. These comprise different attributes of God, not different gods. "Allah" is the all-inclusive Arabic word for God which summarizes and unifies all these attributes. "Allah" is a unique term that cannot be modified in the sense that the term "god" can be modified into forms such as "godly", "godless", or "godfather", and is neither masculine nor feminine (the terms "He" or "Him" are occasionally used in this text to represent God, not because God is male or more male-like, but only as pronouns for practical, linguistic purposes). Nor does Islam accept any Christian references to God as the "Son", "Father" or "Savior". The Qur'an and sayings of Prophet Muhammad contain ninety-nine Names or Attributes of Allah, though in principle, there is an infinite number of Attributes (see Appendix A).

These Attributes of Allah (SWT) are also referred to repeatedly in the Qur'an in verses such as the following:

> He is Allah, the One other than Whom there is no god, the Knower of the hidden and the manifest, the Compassionate, the Merciful. He is God, the one other than Whom there is no god, the Commander, the All-Powerful,

> Pure and Without Defect, the Bestower of Safety, The Protector, The Precious, The Mighty, The Sublime, The Most Elevated. Exempt and purified be He from the partners which they ascribe to Him. (59:22-23)
>
> Say: 'Call upon Allah or call upon the All-Merciful; whichever you call upon, to Him belong the Most Beautiful Names.' (17:110)
>
> He is the First and the Last, the Manifest and the Non-Manifest, and He has full knowledge of all things. (57:3)
>
> He taught Adam The Names, all of them, then He placed them before the angels, and said, 'Tell Me The Names of these if you are right… (2:31)

The famous testification of faith in Islam, *la ilaha illallah*, or there is no god but Allah is a supreme synthesis of its worldview known as *tawhid*. The statement is firstly, a summary of belief and doctrine because it points to the unity of the Divine Being while rejecting all false deities, including all that is external or material, as well as that which is internal, such as our own ego, passion, arrogance and knowledge. Thus, all beauty is from the Beauty of Allah, all reality is from the Reality of Allah, all knowledge is from the Knowledge of Allah, all power is from the Power of Allah, all love is from the Love of Allah, all mercy is from the Mercy of Allah, all justice is from the Justice of Allah, and all that is good is from the Goodness of Allah. The unity of Allah is reflected in the unity that pervades the universe.

Secondly, the statement is meant not merely to be said and believed, but also enacted. Thus, all worship and spirituality is to be directed towards Him alone. Different levels of spirituality and perfection are based on different levels of realization of this statement. True enactment of the statement is to be conscious of God in every single act and as Prophet Muhammad (SAW) has said, "to worship Allah as though you did see Him"[38]. Hence, in terms of reliance, it is to "Know for sure that if the entire community has gathered in order to benefit you by something, they cannot benefit you by anything unless Allah has written it for you; and if all of them have gathered to cause you evil, they cannot except according to what has been written by Allah. The pens have been lifted and the ink is dry."[39]

While it is beyond the scope of this chapter to discuss the essential Attributes of God at length, it is important to understand the Islamic belief in the Supreme Unity of God, or *Tawhid*, that is central to all Islamic beliefs and practices. It is this Unity that has been compromised in all other religions, as we shall discuss in detail in Chapter 4. Why has Islam emphasized this concept repeatedly? Putting aside for a moment the value in correcting the corrupted notions of God that have developed in other religions (see Chapter 4), there are additional reasons:

Firstly, associating partners with God makes no sense from either a logical or scientific perspective. It is simply illogical and inconceivable for there to be a multiplicity of Infinite and Supreme Beings, for this would violate the very definition of infinity. Multiplicity only applies to finite beings. For example, if the world we occupy is finite in space, there can be multiple worlds; but if the world is infinite in space there cannot be but one world. Furthermore, numerous arguments from the modern world of science all point to an underlying unity that pervades the universe, as we shall discuss in Chapter 2. Earlier we also introduced the famous principle known as "Occam's razor", which states, among other things, that "entities are not to be multiplied beyond necessity." Clearly, if a single, supreme God can be reasonably posited as the source of the universe, then there is no reason to posit multiple deities just for the sake of argument. Belief in multiple deities is also problematic with respect to potential conflict and division of power among the deities.

Secondly, worshipping or submitting to any entity other than God is fruitless and meaningless since it is only God, in His Essence, who can respond to such devotion. In more mystical terms, it is only God who is Absolute Being while all other creation is relative being—hence, that which is Real and Existent must be worshipped. The modern gods and demagogues of money, power, fame, democracy, capitalism, materialism, socialism, scientism, progress, and the like have been granted fleeting and illusory power, while all true power emanates from God alone. On a more mundane level, when we are ill and wish to get better, we ask a doctor for help, not the moon or a monkey, nor for that matter, an engineer or teacher. From an Islamic point of view, we should primarily beseech God, and secondarily ask the doctor for help since all healing is ultimately from God. This amounts to realizing that God utilizes secondary causes, i.e. the doctor and the medicine in this case, but that secondary causes cannot be confused with the primary cause.

> *The modern gods and demagogues of money, power, fame, democracy, capitalism, materialism, socialism, scientism, progress, and the like have been granted fleeting and illusory power, while all true power emanates from God alone.*

Finally, worshipping the One and Only God is for our own good. Just as God has made certain laws that govern the natural world, He has made laws that govern worship, faith, morality and behavior. Through the course of history, man has increasingly benefited from studying the laws that govern the natural and material realm, but has increasingly failed to realize the benefits of complying with the laws that govern the spiritual realm. God has decreed that felicity, both in this world and the next, lies in obeying these laws. Through His Mercy and Love, He only wishes what is best for His creation, whether we realize it or not. Just as parents only wish what is best for their children, so too with God and His creation. Thus, worshipping other than God not only throws it into disarray, but is also detrimental to achieving enduring happiness and satisfaction.

Besides Unity, Islam recognizes the importance of preserving the perfect balance between His Transcendence (beyond space, time and limitation) and Immanence (closeness to creation). Most religions have compromised Divinity by either overemphasizing or underemphasizing transcendent and immanent aspects. Christian theology, for example, compromises transcendence by maintaining belief in Divine incarnation in human form and that God has "begotten a son". Modern Hinduism and various tribal religions also maintain belief in Divine incarnation in human, animal and inanimate forms. Islamic theology does not allow for any Divine incarnation or indwelling, nor can God be considered male or female, for this is all regarded to be below His majesty and too delimiting for the Supreme Being. On the other hand, certain people like Isaac Newton and religions like Deism[40], which was a Christian sect originating in the 17th century, held that

God was a Heavenly father who designed the world and then left it to be without involvement, which compromises the immanence or closeness of God to creation. Here again, Islam holds no such belief in the disinterest or aloofness of the Lord.

Spirituality involves not only experiencing God as being above and beyond all things but also in seeing His signs in all things and within us. Recognizing His signs in all creation, however, is very different from equating God with creation or any form of anthropomorphism. The exoteric dimension of Islam represented by the Shari'ah or Law emphasizes the transcendent aspect, while the esoteric dimension of Islam, represented by Sufism (the science of self-purification), emphasizes the immanent. As noted in the previous passage from the Qur'an, Allah (SWT) is simultaneously both The First and The Last; The Outwardly Manifest and The Hidden or Non-Manifest. He is Transcendent because He stands infinitely beyond creation in the perfection of His Attributes, and at the same time, He is Immanent because He manifests His Attributes through creation.

> *He is Transcendent because He stands infinitely beyond creation in the perfection of His Attributes, and at the same time, He is Immanent because He manifests His Attributes through creation.*

A few examples from the Qur'an that emphasize the transcendent nature of God are as follows:

Nothing whatsoever is like Him… (42:11)

… it is He who has Power over all things. (5:120)

… and Allah has Knowledge of all things. (4:176)

No vision can grasp Him, but His grasp is over all vision- He is above all comprehension yet is acquainted with all things. (6:103)

They do indeed blaspheme who say: 'Allah is Christ the son of Mary.' But said Christ: 'O Children of Israel! Worship Allah, my Lord and your Lord'... (5:72)

Although God is not considered to be anthropomorphic or like human beings, He is nonetheless considered to be "near" His creation and always available to those who have the yearning to be "near" to Him. While many non-Muslims allege that the God of Islam is cruel and stern, the reality is that "Allah's Mercy prevails over His Wrath"[41] and is so close to His creation that we do not even realize it. This immanence or nearness is reflected in passages such as:

We are nearer to Him than the jugular vein. (50:16)

When My servants ask you concerning Me- I am indeed close (to them). I respond to the call of the caller when he calls on Me... (2:186)

To Allah belong the East and the West: whithersoever you turn, there is the face of Allah... (2:115)

...And He is with you wherever you may be and Allah sees well all that you do. (57:4)

His simultaneous transcendence and immanence, or incomparability and similarity is summarized in the following verse where God is considered incomparable, and yet, He is perfect and infinite in His attributes of Hearing and Seeing: "Nothing whatsoever is like Him and He is The Hearing, The Seeing" (42:11).

While we have introduced certain essential attributes, it is also just as important to know what God is not. As introduced earlier, Allah (SWT) purifies Himself from all forms of polytheism, which includes not only worship of false gods such as the sun, moon, stars, universe, animals, holy persons, and physical idols, but also modern idols such as money, sex, power, fame, and arrogance, as well as from all kinds of anthropomorphism, such as attributing to Him a son or daughter, or sleep and slumber. Islam considers it blasphemous to think of God having rested on the seventh day of creation or that He wrestled with Satan. It is also important to realize that the Qur'an does not explicitly mention atheism, for it is actually just another form of polytheism that often involves self worship through the arrogance and pride of considering one's own knowledge to be sufficient and considering one's own power to act to be limitless. Just a few passages of the Qur'an in this regard are:

> Have you seen him who has chosen for his god his own lust? (25:43)

> Verily, those whom you call upon besides Allah are servants like yourselves: call upon them and let them listen to your prayer if you are truthful! (7:194)

> Say, 'Will you worship besides Allah, something which has no power either to harm or benefit you? It is Allah who is The Hearing and The All-Knowing. (5:76)

> These (idols) are nothing but names which you have devised—you and your forefathers—for which Allah has sent down no authority. They follow only conjecture and the caprice of their souls... (53:23)

> Or have they (polytheists) taken for worship gods besides Him? Say, 'Bring forth your proof!" This is the message of those with Me and the message of those before Me. But most of them (polytheists) know not the Truth, and so turn away. (21:24)

Thus, we have seen that Islam considers Allah the One and Only God who is worthy of worship and who possesses perfection with respect to all Attributes described unto Himself, such as those of unity, transcendence, immanence, power, life, compassion, knowledge, justice, hearing, seeing, and creation.

1.11 Knowing of God in Islam

Having introduced the subject of the nature of God, it is now appropriate to discuss how we begin to know of God's existence from an Islamic perspective.

First, it must be understood that human beings basically acquire knowledge using the following means:
(1) the rational faculty or reason
(2) the five basic senses[42], and
(3) intuition or knowledge associated with the heart and spirit.[43]

Our sources of knowledge are basically three-fold as well:
1. The universe, including the heavens, the earth and the natural world.
2. Man—including what is within ourselves, i.e. the above-mentioned faculties, as well as that taught by Prophets and other people, both present and past.
3. God's Revelation in the form of scriptures and inspiration to individuals. In this regard, Allah (SWT) states in the Qur'an:

> We will show them Our signs upon the *horizons and in themselves*, until it is clear to them that He is the Real. Is it not enough that your Lord does witness all things? (41:53)

God is known in the world through manifestations of His Attributes as discussed earlier. Each created entity manifests God in varying intensity. Thus, for example, a rock manifests latent power, plants manifest life and animals manifest life, knowledge, power, and will to a certain degree. Of all creation, however, human beings have the most potential to reflect or manifest all Divine Attributes and with the greatest intensity. Thus, for example all forms of love, knowledge, forgiveness and justice demonstrated between individuals or on a societal level, are manifestations of Divine Love, Knowledge, Forgiveness and Justice.

To know of God, the Qur'an appeals to mankind in a number of different ways that correspond to the three methods of acquiring knowledge mentioned above. The Qur'an does not provide intricate and abstract "theological proofs", but rather uses concrete examples, parables and historical precedents to appeal to our faculties of reason, sense-perception and intuition in recognizing the Giver of these faculties and the multitude of Divine signs all around and within us. In this section, we will focus on appeals to our faculties of reason and sense perception since we have already introduced various arguments relating to these faculties from a Western philosophical viewpoint. Other kinds of Qur'anic appeals to knowledge of God, such as those associated with intuition, the heart and submission will be reserved for Chapter 2, where these subjects will be treated in greater detail. The role of Divine scriptures and the Message of the Prophets in knowing God will also be discussed therein.

Overall, the Qur'an and sayings of Prophet Muhammad (SAW) present an underlying theme and message that belief in God is reasonable, logical and self-evident for anyone who uses their intellect, and whose heart is sincere in desiring the Truth. The sincerity of the heart is an essential ingredient often found missing in modern discourse about God (see Chapter 2). Sincerity and submission are normally pre-requisites for any serious knowledge of God. We know God only to the extent that He bestows such knowledge upon our hearts. In Islam, it is not merely belief in the existence of God that is required, but rather a sincere commitment to obey and submit to God.

> ...belief in God is reasonable, logical and self-evident for anyone who uses their intellect, and whose heart is sincere in desiring the Truth.

It must also be kept in mind that Qur'anic appeals to our reason and senses are not like the philosophical arguments discussed earlier. As we will find, the Qur'an uses language and parables that are simple, beautiful and to the point, whereas philosophical arguments tend to be more complicated and engaged in an endless and nebulous cycle of debate and counter-debate. This is why academic and philosophical debate over God and various minutiae do not usually result in any meaningful change and are often rooted in arrogance. The atheist's or agnostic's argument is analogous to one who observes a series of footprints in the desert sand and concludes that the wind must have blown abnormally and randomly formed them, instead of concluding that they have been formed by a passing being!

Before studying some of the Qur'anic appeals to knowledge of God, it is necessary to understand that Islam considers all human beings to have acknowledged Allah as our Lord, or *rabb* in Arabic, before we were created. In fact, disbelief amounts to a conscious denial of our original nature. Allah (SWT) says in the Qur'an,

> "When your Lord drew forth from the children of Adam from their loins—their descendants and made them testify concerning themselves (saying), 'Am I not your Lord'. They said, 'Yes, we do testify!', lest you should say on the Day of Judgment, 'Of this we were never mindful.'" (7:172)

> "And call in remembrance the favor of Allah unto you, and His covenant, which He ratified with you when you said, 'We hear and we obey': and fear Allah for Allah knows well the secrets of your hearts." (5:7)

Hence, we have all already testified that Allah is our *rabb* (which is usually translated as Lord and is most closely associated with the Attributes of Creator and Sustainer) and that we will obey Him before our physical existence in this world. Prophet Muhammad (SAW) also stated regarding the purity of creation, "Every child is born according to primordial nature *(fitra)*, then his parents make him a Jew, Christian, or Zoroastrian."[44] Thus, unlike the Christian belief in original sin, Islam believes that all human beings have been born "pure", and that when we acknowledge God's existence, we are actually recollecting or returning to our original nature. This should not come as a great surprise given that our spirit and intelligence derive from the Divine Spirit and Intellect (see Chapter 2). The greatest proof for God's existence, then, is already within you!

...disbelief amounts to a conscious denial of our original nature.

Having said that, let us study some of what the Qur'an has to say when considering the earlier discussed categories of arguments. Certain Qur'anic statements can be said to roughly correspond to the Design, Cosmological First Cause, Necessary Being, Moral and Experiential Arguments, though the Qur'an is believed to be in no need of having to conform to philosophical arguments. The following are just some of the pertinent verses in the Qur'an related to these topics (inclusion of all the sayings of Prophet Muhammad in this regard would be beyond the scope of this work) and are intended to provide a glimpse of the variety of appeals presented in the Qur'an.

Design and Order:

> Your God is but One God. There is no other god other than Him, Compassionate and Merciful. In the creation of the heavens and the earth, in the alteration of night and day, in the ships that ply the seas to the benefit of man, in the water sent down from the heavens to revive the earth after its death, in the different species of animals scattered across the earth, in the rotation of the winds, in the clouds that are subordinate to God's command between heaven and earth—in all of this, there are signs for men who use their intellects. (2:163-164)

> Tell men to reflect with care and see what things the heaven and the earth contain. (10:101)

> Were there a creator in the heavens and earth other than the One God, their order would vanish and the world would be destroyed. (16:79)

> Surely We have created everything in measure. (54:49)

> (Pharaoh) said, 'Who, then is your Lord, O Moses?' He said 'Our Lord is the One who endowed all things with a particular form of creation and then gave it guidance.' (20:49-50)

> Do they not look at the birds in the heavens and see how the skies have been subjugated to them? It is God alone Who keeps them aloft, and in this there is an evident sign of God's power for the people of faith. (16:79)

> It is not permitted for the sun to overtake the moon, nor can the night outstrip the day; each swims along in its own orbit. (36:40)

> O mankind! If you have doubt about the Resurrection, consider that We created you out of dust, then out of sperm, then out of a leech-like clot, then out of a morsel of flesh, partly formed and partly unformed, in order that We may manifest Our Power to you; and We cause whom We will to

rest in the wombs for an appointed term, then do we bring you out as babes, then foster you that you may reach your age of full strength; and some of you are called to die, and some are sent back to the feeblest old age, so that they know nothing after having known much. And further you see the earth barren and lifeless, but when We pour down rain on it, it is stirred to life, it swells and it puts forth every kind of beautiful growth in pairs. (22:5)

Or who has created the heavens and the earth? And who sends you down rain from the sky? Yea, with it We cause to grow well-planted orchards full of beauty and delight- it is not in your power to cause the growth of the trees in them. (Can there be another) god besides Allah? Nay, they (unbelievers) are a people who swerve from justice. Or who has made the earth firm to live in; made rivers in its midst; set thereon mountains immovable, and made a separating bar between the two bodies of flowing water? (Can there be another) god besides Allah? Nay, most of them know not. Or, who listens to the distressed one who calls on Him, and who relieves the suffering and makes you (mankind) inheritors of the earth? (Can there be another) god besides Allah? Little is it that you heed! Or, who guides you through the depths of darkness on land and sea, and who sends the winds as heralds of glad tidings, going before His mercy? (Can there be another) god besides Allah?- High is Allah above what they associate with Him! (27:60-63)

First Cause and Creation:

He is the First and the Last, the Manifest and the Non-Manifest, and He has full knowledge of all things (57:3)

Did man emerge from non-being through his own devices? Was he his own creator? Did mankind create the heavens and earth? Certainly they do not know God
(52:35-36)

We created man out of an essence of clay, then We established him in a firm place in the form of sperm. Then We made the sperm into coagulated

> blood, and then into a formless lump of flesh. Then We made it into bones and then clothed the bones with flesh. Finally We bought forth a new creation. How well did God create, the best of all creators! (23:12-14)

> We created not the heavens and earth ... save through the Real. (15:85)

Necessary Being:

> O Men, it is you who stand in need of Allah. As for Allah, He is above all need, worthy of praise. (35:15)

> O Messenger, say: 'He is God, the One, the God Who is free of need for all things and of Whom all beings stand in need. No one is His offspring, and He is not the offspring of anyone, and He has no like or parallel.' (112:1-4)

Moral Argument:

> Do those who commit evil deeds suppose that We shall make them as those who believe and do good deeds, while their life and death is just the same? Bad is their judgment! And Allah has created the heavens and the earth with truth, and that everyone may be repaid what he has earned. And they will not be wronged. (45:21-22)

> ...The promise of Allah is true and sure. It is He who begins the process of creation and repeats it, that He may reward with justice those who believe and work righteousness; but those who reject Him will have draughts of boiling fluids and a grievous penalty because they did reject Him. (10:4)

> By the soul and the proportion and order given to it, and its enlightenment as to its wrong and its right, truly he succeeds that purifies it and he fails that corrupts it... (91: 7-10)

Experiential:

> We will show them Our signs upon the horizons and in themselves, until it is clear to them that He is the Real. Is it not enough that your Lord does witness all things?(41:53)

To Allah belong the East and the West: whithersoever you turn, there is the face of Allah... (2:115)

...And He is with you wheresoever you may be and Allah sees well all that you do. (57:4)

And serve your Lord until there come unto you the certainty. (15:99)
Be God-fearing and God will teach you. (2:282)

Say: 'If you do love Allah, follow Me, Allah will love you and forgive your sins... (3:31)

Although these statements from the Qur'an represent but a few examples of various means of knowing of God based on earlier arguments, any serious study of the Qur'an would make it clear that there are an infinite number of manifestations and ways to recognize God. In contemplating the nature of the universe and mankind, *any genuine knowledge attained represents a form of self-disclosure from God.* Given that God is the source of the universe and all that it contains, as well as the next world, it would not be an exaggeration to say that all true knowledge is *ultimately knowledge of God.* Thus, in the creation and sustenance of the universe, and the design and order displayed therein, God can be known as the Creator, Sustainer and Lord. In the creation and endowment of living beings God is known as the Fashioner and Giver of Life. In the dependence of all creation and the independence of the Creator, God is known as The Necessary Being or Self-Sufficient. In the deeds of human beings and the judgment of choices made, God is known as The Righteous and The Reckoner. Throughout the multitude of signs in the universe and within ourselves, God is ultimately known as The Real and The Truth (see Appendix A for a listing of Divine Attributes according to Islamic theology).

> *In contemplating the nature of the universe and mankind, any genuine knowledge attained represents a form of self-disclosure from God.*

True acceptance of the infinite number of manifestations of God involves more than mere lip service, it also requires sincere submission to Him given that He is the One and Only Ruler over all that is. Claiming some semblance of belief in God while persisting in living as you see fit is not true belief. Without submission, there really is no recognition of the signs and manifestations of the Lord. This theme is taken up further in Chapter 2 in relation to the question of whether we can be "certain" of the existence of God.

Chapter Summary

1. Common Western philosophical arguments for the existence of God, including the Design, First Cause, Kalam Cosmological, Necessary Being, Ontological, Moral, Consciousness Arguments (as well as others not discussed), all provide at the very least, confirmation that the existence of God is not only logically and rationally reasonable, but also highly probable. Furthermore, despite any qualms one may have with a particular argument, when all the arguments are taken as a whole, it significantly increases the justification and validity of belief in God's existence.

2. For those who are skeptical of rational arguments, the experiential argument can be compelling. Detailed methods of experiencing God have been laid out in the teachings of many religions and are available to all sincere seekers of the truth. Although such experiences can be easily dismissed by skeptics, the fact remains that they can be utterly conclusive, convincing and meaningful for those who experience them.

3. Islam teaches that there is only one God who is worthy of worship and who possesses perfection with respect to all attributes described unto Himself. These Attributes have been revealed to mankind through the Qur'an and sayings of Prophet Muhammad (SAW), and are summarized and unified by the Arabic word Allah. Some of these Attributes include Oneness, Life, Power, Knowledge, Will, Love, Mercy and Justice.

4\. It stands to reason that if God is Infinite in the expression of His Attributes, there cannot be more than one God. Multiplicity applies to finite beings, while unity must apply to an Infinitely Supreme Being. There cannot be multiple Infinite, Supreme Beings. Worshipping the One and Only God is for our own good (God is in no need of worship), while worshipping any entity other than God is fruitless since it is ultimately only He who is the Source of all causes and only He who can respond to those in need.

5\. Islam maintains belief in the perfect balance between God's transcendence and immanence. He is Transcendent because He stands infinitely beyond creation in the perfection of His Attributes, and at the same time, He is Immanent because He manifests His Attributes through creation.

6\. Islam teaches that as human beings we have all affirmed the existence of God before we were created in a covenant with Him. There is an innate predisposition within us towards recognizing our Creator. Although we have the potential for disobedience, disbelief is a conscious rejection and denial of our true primordial nature.

7\. There are numerous ways of knowing God. Human beings use their faculties of reason, sense-perception and intuition (associated with our primordial nature) to acquire knowledge, while the sources of this knowledge are basically three-fold:
(a) the surrounding universe
(b) man himself, including both his innate nature, as well as other people and Prophets, both past and present, and
(c) God's Revelations (which for Islam includes not only the Qur'an, but also authentic forms of earlier scriptures) and inspiration.

8\. Some of the Qur'anic passages appealing to our faculties of reason and sense-perception in knowing God were noted in this chapter. However, in order for our faculties of reason and sense-perception to truly recognize God, we must first have a sincere heart and be willing to submit to the Lord.

9. Given that God is the source of the whole universe and our very being and all that is, Islam teaches that all genuine knowledge is ultimately knowledge of God and His Attributes as manifested in the world and within ourselves.

Notes:

1 Based on information in Wolfram van Soden, The Ancient Orient- An Introduction to the Study of the Ancient Near East, Eng. Trans. (Grand Rapids, MI: Wm. B. Eerdmans, 1994).

2 Ether is the element once believed to fill all space above the moon and compose the stars and planets and was once thought as being an all-pervading, mass-less medium through which the propagation of electromagnetic waves occurred.

3 Mana is a supernatural force thought to dwell in certain persons or sacred objects.

4 Qi (pronounced chee) is a Chinese word meaning an invisible vital energy or force that sustains life and pervades the whole universe. In the human body it is believed that it can be controlled to produce healing effects.

5 Prana is a Sanskrit word analogous to the Chinese concept of qi meaning a vital energy or force that sustains life and can also be manipulated in the body to produce healing effects.

6 J.P. Moreland, K. Nielsen, *Does God Exist—The Debate Between Theists and Atheists* (New York: Prometheus Books, 1993), p. 1.

7 R. Swinburne, *The Coherence of Theism* (Oxford: Oxford University Press, 1977), p. 2.

8 See, for example, Paul Davies, *Superforce- The Search for a Grand Unified Theory of Nature* (New York: Simon & Schuster, 1984); John Polkinghorne, Science and Creation (London: SPCK, 1988); Chris Isham, R.J. Russell and N. Murphy, *Quantum Cosmology and the Laws of Nature* (Notre Dame: Notre Dame University Press, 1993); and Frank Tipler, The Physics of Immortality (London: MacMillan, 1995).

9 See Paul Davies, God and the New Physics (New York: Simon & Schuster, 1982).

10 See J. P. Moreland, Yes! A Defense of Christianity, in *Does God Exist- The Debate Between Theists and Atheists* by J.P. Moreland and K. Nielsen (New York: Prometheus Books, 1993), p. 35.

11 Fred Hoyle and N.C. Wickramasinghe, *Evolution from Space* (New York: Simon and Schuster, 1981).

12 Paul Davies, *God and the New Physics* (New York: Simon & Schuster, 1982), p. 189.

13 See Immanuel Kant's Critique of Pure Reason, trans. by N.K. Smith (London: Macmillan, 1933).

14 See David Hume's, *Dialogues Concerning Natural Religion*, ed. N.K. Smith (London and Edinburgh: Nelson, 1947) and *An Enquiry Concerning Human Understanding*, ed. L.A. Selby-Bigge (Oxford: Oxford University Press, 3rd ed., 1975) for eight arguments against the design argument.

15 Michael J. Behe, *Darwin's Black Box- The Biochemical Challenge to Evolution* (New York: Simon & Schuster, 1996).

16 D. Dewar, *The Transformist Illusion* (Murfreesboro, Tennessee, 1957).

17 Keith Ward, *God, Chance and Necessity* (Oxford: Oneworld Publications, 1996).

18 Letter from Charles Darwin to G. Bentham, written at Down, May 22, 1863, The Life and Letters of Charles Darwin, edited by his son, Francis Darwin, vol. 3 (John Murray, 1888) p. 25.

19 See B.B. Mandelbrot, *The Fractal Geometry of Nature* (New York: W.H. Freeman and Co., 1977).

20 Certain philosophers and mystics, especially the Neoplatonists, maintain that all that exists is an

emanation from the primordial Unity, which Plotinus called "the One." Thus, for example, Intelligence emanates from the One, the Soul from Intelligence, and so on. The process of emanation is considered timeless and the One is unaffected and undiminished by it.

21 David Hume, *A Treatise of Human Nature*, ed. L.A. Selby-Bigge, 2nd ed. (Oxford, 1978).

22 Elizabeth Anscombe, *Whatever has a Beginning of Existence* must have a cause- Hume's Argument Exposed, Analysis, 34, 1974 and K. Ward, God, Chance and Necessity (Oxford: Oneworld Publications, 1996), p. 17.

23 Another related argument has been provided by the Muslim thinkers Al-Baqillani, Al-Ghazali and Al-Razi (b. 864). Yasin Ceylan summarizes the argument as follows: "If bodies were eternal they would either be in motion or at rest. It is impossible that they be in motion, for motion means transference of substance from one locus to another; thus, a previous state is always presupposed which is contrary to the notion of eternity. Eternity demands a permanent situation and negates any previous occurrence. The bodies cannot be at rest either. This would amount to the denial of the mobility of the earth, and other heavenly bodies. If they were eternal they should continue motionless forever; but as they are evidently moving any permanent state is out of the question" (Yasin Ceylan, *Theology and Tafsir in the Major Works of Fakhr Al-Din Al-Razi* (Kuala Lumpur: ISTAC, 1996), p. 62).

24 See J. P. Moreland, Atheism and Leaky Buckets: *The Christian Rope Pulls Tighter in Does God Exist- The Debate Between Theists and Atheists* by J.P. Moreland and K. Nielsen (New York: Prometheus Books , 1993), p. 229

25 Ibid, p. 38.

26 Ibid, p. 38.

27 Stephen Hawking, *A Brief History of Time* (New York: Bantam Books, 1998), p. 115-141.

28 J.L. Mackie, *The Miracle of Theism* (Oxford: Oxford University Press, 1982), p. 84.

29 Donald Palmer, *Looking at Philosophy- The Unbearable Heaviness of Philosophy Made Lighter*, 2nd ed., (Mountain View, CA: Mayfield Pub. Co., 1994), p. 108.

30 Ibid, p. 108.

31 See Immanuel Kant, *Critique of Pure Reason*, trans. N.K. Smith (London: MacMillan, 1964).

32 N. Malcolm, *Anselm's Ontological Arguments*, Philosophical Review, p. 69, 1960, reprinted in John Hick (ed.), *The Existence of God* (London and New York, 1964).

33 J.H. Newman, *A Grammar of Assent*, ed. C.F. Harold (London and New York, 1947).

34 Richard Swinburne, *The Existence of God*, rev. ed. (Oxford, 1991), Chap. 9.

35 Keith Ward, *God, Chance and Necessity*, (Oxford: Oneworld Publications, 1996), p. 149.

36 William James, *The Varieties of Religious Experience* (London: Collins, Fontana, 1960).

37 The issue of whether the attributes are identical to or separate from His essence is beyond the scope of this work and is not immediately relevant. Refer to William Chittick, *The Sufi Path of Knowledge- Ibn al-Arabi's Metaphysics of Imagination* (Albany: SUNY Press, 1989) for more information on this issue.

38 Sahih hadith narrated on the authority of Umar Ibn al-Khattab and referenced in *An-Nawawi's*

Forty Hadith, trans. E. Ibrahim and D.J. Davies, 4th ed., (Beirut: The Holy Koran Publishing House, 1979), pp. 28-32.

39 Sahih Hadith narrated on the authority of Abdullah Ibn Abbas and referenced in ibid, pp. 68-70.

40 Deism is generally traced back to the Englishman Edward Hebert (1582-1648) and had the Christian beliefs of a Supreme Being, morality and an afterlife but did not believe in Divine scripture, churches or specific doctrines. Deism is thought to have laid the stage for the "Age of Enlightenment" and questioning of certain Christian beliefs.

41 See Chapter 3, Section 3 for more concerning the Mercy of God. This hadith Qudsi is narrated on the authority of Abu Hurayrah, related by Imam Bukhari, Muslim, An-Nasai and Ibn-Majah as referenced in Ezzedin Ibrahim and D.J. Davies, *Forty Hadith Qudsi*, (Beirut: The Holy Koran Publishing House, 1980), Hadith #1.

42 While some consider the five basic senses as merely supporting our faulty of reason, others distinguish between the two to remind of the difference between empiricism and rationalism

43 This method of acquiring knowledge is described in more detail in Chapter 2, though many atheists and agnostics question whether this is truly a form of knowledge.

44 Hadith narrated in Sahih Bukhari, Jana'iz, 80,92, Tafsir 30:1; Sahih Muslim, Qadar 22-24.

Chapter 2

Is God Compatible with Science and Reason, and Can I be Certain of God's Existence?

> *The rationalism of a frog living at the bottom of a well is to deny the existence of mountains: this is logic of a kind, perhaps, but it has nothing to do with reality.*
>
> Frithjof Schuon, Logic and Transcendence

J.L. Mackie, one of the most celebrated atheists of the 20th century, claimed that "...the central doctrines of theism, literally interpreted, cannot be rationally defended. Even those who have enjoyed what they take to be religious experiences have no good reason to interpret them as they do, as direct contacts with literally divine or supernatural beings, nor can any sort of revelation justify such beliefs."[1] Norwood Hanson has proudly added that "The success of science in developing correct explanations has been solely based on its refusal to take the easy way out and proclaim God as the explanation."[2] Such statements are typical of modern skepticism, disavowal of religion and scientific atheism. Science has become the religion of modern man. Much as Mackie and Hanson would wish to be correct, their statements amount to nothing more than an arrogant denial of Reality.

In this chapter we will seek answers to the questions of, firstly, whether the notion of God is compatible with science and reason, and secondly, the related question of how certain our knowledge and belief in God can be.

In addressing the question of the certainty of God's existence, it is often assumed or taken for granted that "seeing is believing" and that genuine knowledge and "facts" are based on sense-perception. The modern world relies on a "show-me" culture in which the masses are endlessly bombarded with hollow images from television, magazines, the internet and other forms of mass indoctrination. Often accompanying this culture is the notion that empiricism or sense-perception is the only objective and true means to knowledge. However, this notion is, in fact, utterly false as any serious study of epistemology—the science of knowledge and "how we know", would reveal that it encompasses more than just the empiricism of modern science and our five senses. It also encompasses what is known as pure reason or logic, and as most theists and believers would argue, intuition, spiritual experience and Divine revelation. Thus, in order to answer the questions at hand it is first necessary to examine these forms of knowledge in greater detail.

2.1 Sizing Our Senses—The Blindness of Empiricism

Science has been defined to include "the observation, identification, description, experimental investigation, and theoretical explanation of phenomena."[3] Human beings have always engaged in such activity and cannot escape using the faculty of sensory perception to study and explore the world around them. However, the modern age has seen the scientific worldview take on a role far greater than in any other. Movements and ideologies such as scientism, empiricism, materialism and evolutionism have helped promulgate the idea that science represents the only remaining beacon of hope for separating truth from falsehood and advancing the human condition. While it is recognized that modern science has accomplished a great deal through an increased understanding of our world and a material improvement in the quality of life, it must also be realized that there are serious limitations and flaws to ideologies based only on empirical knowledge and the modern scientific method[4], as outlined below:

1. Strict followers of scientism, empiricism and materialism hold that there is nothing real beyond matter and observed phenomena. If this is the case, how can one possibly expect any valuable information to be provided by science and empiricism with respect to the supra-sensory or metaphysical realm? This is analogous to fish claiming that trees do not exist. Restricting the vast fields of physical and social sciences to observed phenomena and the experimental field ensures their stagnation since meaningful conclusions cannot be achieved with respect to that which transcends them, i.e. God, the soul, angels, the after-life, pre-existence, the size of the universe, the emotional and spiritual realms, etc. Furthermore, when science is restricted to sensory and existing phenomena, it cannot conclusively say whether any entity does not exist.

Despite the efforts of certain scientists to reclaim the overall aim of science to be the seeking of Truth and their assertion that science can include meaningful inferences and deductions from the seen to the Unseen, these individuals have been kept on the fringe of the scientific community and their views have been over-ridden by the louder voice of the mainstream secular scientists.

Although science seeks the explanation of phenomena, it clearly falls short of providing an ultimate explanation for all phenomena, as a whole, as to their origin or original cause. Nor can science provide any meaning in a metaphysical sense to such phenomena. The Big Bang theory does not provide any information as to what put the "bang" in the Big Bang, nor does it provide any meaning to such an event. Hence, the First Cause or Prime Mover argument discussed in Chapter 1 was based on logic and reasoning as opposed to scientific methods.

2. Modern scientific "knowledge" is in a state of flux, just as matter is in continuous flux. Plants, animals and human beings are constantly undergoing cycles of birth and death, while all inanimate objects are undergoing transformation and eventual deterioration. Newtonian laws that were considered infallible and "proven" for several centuries have in the 20th century been found to be true in only a limited sense and have been superseded by Einstein's theories. Theories from the early part of the

20th century viewing electrons as tiny balls colliding with each other were revised when it was discovered that electrons can simultaneously behave as both particles and waves. Modern medicine is constantly revising its assumptions as to what constitutes a healthy diet and lifestyle despite conducting endless "scientific studies". How, then, can that which is in a state of flux be considered as an absolute and unalterable fact?

3. Moreover, the scientific method is built on the assumption that past behavior or observed phenomena will always repeat in the same way in the future, but can we take this for granted to be true? Yes, this repeatability usually comes to fruition (by God's power), but not always. How can observed phenomena be posited as absolute facts when they are known to be changing, albeit slowly, and may not necessarily repeat in the future? Stating that "the sun will rise from the east tomorrow" is a statement that is highly likely to come true but cannot be considered an absolutely true statement because it is not absolutely certain that the past will continue to repeat in the future. From a theistic point of view, the sun rising from the east is subject to God's command and can easily be reversed or halted, and in fact, there will come a time when the sun will no longer rise and the world will no longer behave as we know it.

4. Science is not completely objective, neutral and value-free as most people assume it to be. Impartial theories are assumed to be proven by impartial, observed facts, but "some of the pioneers of the experimental method, such as Claude Bernard, have themselves recognized that they could interpret facts only with the help of preconceived ideas, without which they would remain 'brute facts' devoid of all meaning and scientific value."[5] Subjectivity, hidden agendas and intent can and do creep into the scientific method's process of "observation" and especially, interpretation of results.[6] Close examination of, for example, the theories of evolution, and "born homosexuals" will reveal this fact. Multi-national corporations, such as those in the pharmaceutical industry, also fund research that often involves "bogus science" in order to serve their own profiteering interests. Furthermore, the field of quantum physics has conclusively shown that the

"observer" of subatomic particles is not, in fact, neutral, but instead actually affects what is "observed". Differences in methodology by individual scientists have been found to alter the path taken by subatomic particles.

> *Subjectivity, hidden agendas and intent can and do creep into the scientific method's process of "observation" and especially, interpretation of results.*

5. Another limitation of the scientific method is in the assumption that every hypothesis or theory can be proven by observed facts, "whereas in reality the same facts can always be equally well explained by several different theories."[7] Rarely do all potential hypotheses get tested. Here again, hidden agendas and ulterior motives often creep into play. As the previous examples illustrate, alternate theories are not only not tested, but sometimes suppressed in favor of more "popular" ones.

6. Our senses can occasionally deceive us. Unfortunately, seeing is not always believing. It is known that phenomena like optical illusions and mirages can deceive our sight. Rene Descartes (1596-1650), who subjected every belief and substance to what is known as "radical doubt", recognized this fact and even went to the extent of saying that his whole life may be nothing more than a big dream.[8] Thus, from this perspective, we cannot even be 100% certain that objects we observe, such as a flower pot resting on a table, truly exist. Moreover, there is a relativity that accompanies our senses as evidenced by the fact that so many animals, such as dogs or bats, have heightened senses that humans are incapable of perceiving. It is also well known that humans only perceive a very limited portion of the electromagnetic spectrum. Here again, we must remember that just because we cannot hear or see or smell something does not mean it does not exist.

7. Science cannot provide answers to moral and ethical problems, which are particularly rampant in the modern world. This may seem obvious, but there are a substantial number of people whose "blind faith" in science and industrial progress is so extensive that it includes the belief that they will

eventually solve all types of problems facing mankind. This idea of continuous progress based on science has its roots in the Age of Enlightenment and the French Revolution of the 18th century. However, most ethical and moral problems are outside the domain of science and the fact that moral, ethical and social problems have not subsided, and are actually on the rise in this age of industrialization, science and technology is ample evidence that such problems have not been solved.

In critiquing modern science, we are certainly not advocating a complete abandonment of its methods. The findings of science have provided enormous practical value; however, it must also be admitted that such findings have inherent limitations and cannot be considered infallible or absolute truths that transcend doubt.

2.2 God and Science

Having recognized some imperfections of the modern scientific method, we now turn to the related question of the compatibility of God with science. Ultimately, the answer to this question depends upon the extent of belief of the questioner in God and the chosen definition of science. To understand why this is the case, let us first recall how science was earlier defined to include, among other meanings, "the observation, identification, description, experimental investigation, and theoretical explanation of phenomena." For the believer, there is no possibility of conflict since the ultimate explanation of all observed phenomena returns to God as the Creator of the universe. Hence, it is not a question of compatibility, but rather *subservience* of science, and even reason, to God. On the other hand, for the determined atheist or skeptic, it is only the observed phenomena that are emphasized and not the overall explanation or source. As noted in Chapter 1, atheists question why there must be any explanation or beginning at all. For them, God will never be compatible with science or reason since they will always "see" a flaw in any argument or proof presented.

It is, nonetheless, valuable to take a deeper look at why the theistic case for compatibility of science with God is, in fact, well-founded. It is a common criticism of atheists, like Kai Nielsen and Anthony Flew, that the existence of God, which they consider a theoretical, un-definable entity, cannot be indirectly posited just to explain observed effects and phenomena in the universe. Thus, they argue that the concept of God has been proposed as a convenient explanation rather than a sound argument. However, as Stanley Jaki has argued, the modern area of study known as "scientific realism" does, among other things, *postulate theoretical entities to explain effects in the world*.[9] This is a method which bears striking resemblance to that used by theists to explain the existence of God. For example, the term "electron" derives at least part of its meaning from observed effects. Other entities like magnetic fields, gravity, and energy are unobservable, and yet their existence is considered to be a "fact" by the scientific community based on known effects. Nor are these entities "unobservable in practice but observable in principle" as some have claimed. Any sane person also realizes that emotions such as love, anger, joy, sorrow and consciousness which cannot be physically seen, nonetheless exist and are part of our very being. It could be countered that such emotions are by definition, invisible, but then, isn't that also the argument of many theists about God as discussed in Chapter 1?

Thus, when we realize that theoretical entities can be causally posited to explain effects in the world, we realize that modern science does have a role to play in pointing to the existence of God. There is an emerging group of scientists who seek to use scientific methods to "prove" that God's existence is reasonable and logical. Although some theists and believers may consider this effort to be "working backwards" since God's existence is in no need of "scientific proof" given our inherent capabilities to perceive God through spiritual connection and the availability of Divine scriptures, it is still valuable to review some of this literature since science can and should be used to support certain metaphysical truths.

> ... *when we realize that theoretical entities can be causally posited to explain effects in the world, we realize that modern science does have a role to play in pointing to the existence of God.*

In Chapter 1, we noted how a number of scientists have supported the argument for cosmic design by pointing to the many numerical constants that govern natural phenomena. Some of these numerical constants are such that if they were even minutely different the universe would not exist as we know it nor would it even have arisen.

These numerical constants also come into play at each stage needed for the evolution of life on earth. Keith Ward has outlined the first six stages in the evolution of life as the following:

(1) the transformation of superheated energy generated by the Big Bang into simple nuclear particles, which can unite to form stable complexes (such as quarks uniting to form protons, neutrons, and electrons, which form atoms, which, in turn, form molecules),

(2) the formation of self-replicating molecules, like DNA, from complex combinations of chemical elements,

(3) mutations which result in progressively more complex structures and organizations of molecules,

(4) the ability of DNA to produce unique construction codes for development,

(5) the interaction and organization of millions of cells, with identical DNA, to form organisms, and

(6) the formation of the central nervous system including the brain which gives rise to consciousness.[10]

He goes on to eloquently argue that each of these stages is not random, accidental and purposeless as some have claimed, but in fact, evidence "… that it is the postulate of God, with its corollary of objective purpose and value, that can best provide an explanation for why the universe is as it is."

The sixth stage, which involves the development of human consciousness, is crucial since this involves an immaterial state which cannot arise from matter alone. The atheist, Richard Dawkins, has stated that consciousness is "the most profound mystery facing modern biology."[11] There is, in fact, no mystery. Consciousness is a gift that derives from the Universal Consciousness or Mind, which is God's. This argument was discussed previously in Section 1.8.

It is also well-established that science and engineering disciplines are replete with numerical constants and predictive models such as the universal gas constant, speed of light, modulus of elasticity, the Bernoulli equation and Einstein's Theory of Relativity. The very fact that these constants and equations have been used successfully for decades is a clear sign of predictability, consistency and order in the universe that is often taken for granted. After all, something must be "breathing fire" into the equations. In fact, science and engineering would collapse without these fundamental equations and constants.

The field of quantum physics has in recent decades provided strong support for the idea of unity and oneness that pervades the whole universe, in which there is mutual interrelatedness of all things and events, including the experience of such phenomena. These findings were basically initiated by Einstein's revolutionary theories of relativity and of atomic phenomena, which was later to be called quantum theory. Quantum physics showed that subatomic units simultaneously possessed both particle and wave-like properties. Thus, "At the subatomic level, matter does not exist with certainty at different places, but rather shows tendencies to exist, and atomic events do not occur with certainty at definite times and in definite ways, but rather show tendencies to occur."[12] These tendencies are expressed as probabilities and are associated with mathematical quantities which take the form of waves. These probabilities are not probabilities of specific events but probabilities of patterns or interconnections between subatomic units. These patterns of interconnection are so far-reaching that two electrons separated by millions of miles can theoretically affect each other as shown by the Einstein-Podolsky-Rosen experiment.[13]

Furthermore, an unmistakable link has been found between the "observer" and the "observed" such that subatomic phenomena have no meaning by themselves and can only be understood in terms of the interaction between the observed, or more accurately, the participator, and the observed. Differences in the preparation or measurement of subatomic particles result in different properties being observed. The universe is, thus, a participatory universe and as physicist Fritjof Capra has noted, "Quantum theory has abolished the notion of fundamentally separated objects, has introduced the concept of the participator to replace that of the observer, and may even find it necessary to include human consciousness in its description of the world."[14] The underlying unity that pervades the universe makes the case that much stronger for intelligent design on the part of the Master Creator.

Dr. Peter Plichta, a noted scientist, has shown conclusively how a mathematical formula based on prime numbers lies behind many natural phenomena, laws and constants in the universe and explains why the universe could not have arisen by chance.[15] Thus, he argues also that numbers and mathematics were not originated by human invention, but in fact, already reflected throughout the natural world before human existence.

Similarly, the modern study of fractals represents another example of order being discovered where others had only perceived disorder. Many patterns in nature, including everything from the branches of a tree, the winding of a river or coastline, the distribution of galaxy clusters, the branching of blood vessels to even Brownian motion of molecules and particles have been described by fractals or geometric equations that repeat at very small scales to produce amazing shapes and surfaces on a larger scale.[16]

Every advance in science seems to uncover yet another facet of intelligent design and order. As Paul Davies has stated,

> Logically, the universe does not have to be this way. We could conceive of a cosmos where chaos reigns. In place of the orderly and regimented behaviour of matter and energy one would have arbitrary and haphazard activity. Stable structures like atoms or people or stars could not exist. The real world is not this way. It is ordered and complex. Is that not itself an astonishing fact at which to marvel?"[17]

Often when people question the compatibility of God with science there is an implied and related question of whether religion is compatible with science. While it is more straightforward to see how God is completely compatible with science given that He is the source of all phenomena, the relationship of religion with science is more complex due to the existence of numerous religions and the role of human intervention in religious history.

Thus, although science is compatible and subservient to God, science is not necessarily completely compatible with all religions, as evidenced by the bitter struggle between Christianity and science.

In discussing the relationship between religion and science, a number of opposing views can be encountered. On one extreme we find those who believe religion and science to be totally incompatible. Evolutionary naturalism, as propounded by Charles Darwin and Julian Huxley, completely dismisses Biblical authority and theology in favor of science. This idea in conjunction with philosophical naturalism, which holds that matter alone is real, have helped to create the view that we are living in a hostile, meaningless universe and that science alone can improve the human condition.

Some have sought to deflect any conflict by demonstrating that science and religion operate in different realms and that their aims, methods and objects differ. Here it is basically proposed that the aim of religion is to experience God through Divine revelation while science seeks to understand the physical world through the scientific method. Hence, the implication is that any perceived conflict is because of these differences in aims and methods and both scientific and religious findings can be "right" in their own way.

Another view is that of complementarity, which also holds that the aims and methods of science and religion are different, but that their objects are essentially the same. This is similar to the previous view except that the objects being studied, i.e. objects in the universe are the same. This is analogous to the different ways an artist, poet or scientist may view a waterfall. Thus, from this standpoint, the scientist's Big Bang or evolutionary theories could be considered complementary to the creationist view.

The relationship between God and science is discussed further from an Islamic perspective in Section 2.6.

2.3 The Bounds of Reason

Reason refers to the uniquely human capacity for logical, rational and analytic thought. Like sense-perception, no one can escape or deny that reason is a fundamental aspect of human nature. Historically, however, the intellectual movement of rationalism (also known as idealism) considered reason to be more than just a feature of human nature, and instead, considered it to be the primary path to knowledge and truth, as opposed to sensory perception. In philosophical circles, the classic rationalists were Rene Descartes, Baruch Spinoza and Gottfried Leibniz from the 17th-18th centuries, though the case could be made that others like Parmenides, Plato and Hegel were also rationalists. Rationalism as a movement or philosophy holds that reason takes precedence over other ways of acquiring knowledge and extreme rationalists would even consider it to be the unique path to knowledge and certainty.

Common examples of pure reasoning or a priori knowledge are mathematical, logical and definitive truths. Mathematical truths include, for instance, knowledge of $2 + 2 = 4$ or that $3 \times 2 = 6$. Examples of logical truths include knowing that if A is later than B and B is later than C, then A is later than C; or knowing that an object cannot be completely red and completely green at the same time. Definitive truths are based on the definitions of words and phrases, such as knowing that all brides are female or that all lions are animals.

Other more complex and controversial rational truths are thought to include concepts of causation, substance, necessity and infinity, including some of the proofs for the existence of God discussed earlier. For example, the ontological proof is considered to be an exercise in pure reason. While many would consider the concept of God to be fully compatible with reason based on arguments similar to those introduced in Chapter 1, the fact that atheists and agnostics vehemently disagree with such arguments indicates that the fruit of our faculties of reason is not universal.

It is easy to forget, nonetheless, the inherent limitations and imperfections of reason. Forms of reason and logic that rely *only* upon our minds and selves as being authoritative inevitably will end up in some error. Our thought processes are inevitably swayed and colored by our environments, experiences and limitations of time and space. Social, political and economic environments are determinants of our thought patterns, though they are not the sole factors. The imperfection of rationalism is evidenced by the fact that rationalists, both of common and different time periods, have come to vastly different conclusions on the same subjects. You may object that we are incapable of escaping our inherent limitations of space, time and environment. However, it is our view that we can, and this subject is addressed in the next section.

In any case, some examples of the limitations of reason and logic will be helpful in this regard. There are those who claim all metaphysical and supernatural teachings to be false because they are illogical and irrational. However, just because such teachings are perceived to be irrational or unknown to some does not mean that they are unreal. As Frithjof Schuon has noted, "The rationalism of a frog living at the bottom of a well is to deny the existence of mountains: this is logic of a kind, perhaps, but it has nothing to do with reality."[18] The truth is that some things are beyond human comprehension; for instance, God's essence, but this does not mean that God's essence is unreal. The simultaneous transcendence and immanence of God is not immediately logical. The idea from Chinese philosophy that while yin and yang are generally considered opposites, yin also resides within yang and yang within yin, is not necessarily logical. Most mystical traditions within various religions also realize the limitations of reason in the spiritual quest. Transcending that which is material often requires transcending the faculty of reason. This is an integral part of Zen Buddhism, for example, which uses *koans* as exercises to train monks in their spiritual initiation. *Koans* are questions or themes for meditation that cannot be solved by logic or thinking alone.[19] These riddles force one to transcend the limitations with which one has normally categorized experience. For example, what is the sound of a single hand clapping? Another common riddle involves a monk asking Joshu (Chao Chu in Chinese), "Has a dog Buddha-nature or not?" Joshu retorted, "*Mu!* (nothing)".

Furthermore, when a person uses logic to evaluate miraculous events such as Jesus raising someone from the dead, or Moses parting the sea, or Abraham being unscathed by fire, or Muhammad (SAW) traveling from Mecca to Jerusalem and ascending to heaven and returning all in a single night, they will quickly be dismissed as false and inconceivable. However, we know that if we believe in God, all phenomena are subject to His will, and therefore, miracles are eminently plausible. It is in this sense that faith is considered a necessary component in believing in God. However, to stretch this idea to claim that religious faith is "blind", while reason is perfect is to miss the boat altogether. Both faith and reason are necessary tools that enhance each other in our belief in God.

There are still further evidences of the limitations of reason. History is replete with ideas that were considered illogical and downright idiotic at one time, but were later found to be true, such as the idea that communication could occur across the globe in the fraction of a second, or the Einsteinian theory of the inter-conversion of matter and energy. The opposite is also true that certain ideas considered as "facts" at one time were later found to be untrue, such as the already mentioned Newtonian laws and the geocentric view of the universe (where the earth is central and all other planets and stars rotate around it). Explaining the fact that certain otherwise ordinary people possess ESP (extra sensory perception), telepathy and clairvoyance and can predict certain events or know of events in distant locations is also well beyond the pale of logic.

As with sense-perception, recognizing the limitations of reason does not mean the denial of reason. The problem is not with reason itself, but rather, with the denial of other forms of knowledge, as is the case with the rationalist movement, and with those who fail to recognize the limitations of reason.

2.4 Spiritual Certainty Versus Blind Reason

The above discussion makes it apparent that we cannot rely only on our senses and our reason in the quest for Ultimate Truth. Hence, the common criticism of atheists that the existence of God cannot be "proven by universally accepted rational or scientific methods" applies equally well to the findings of science and reason, or for that matter, any statement. If the existence of God cannot be considered an "absolute truth", then nothing can be considered an "absolute truth". The modern war between faith and reason and its implication that belief in God requires "blind faith", whereas reason and science are based on pure fact, is in fact nothing more than another belief and misconception. The findings of modern science and reasoning cannot be considered 'absolute truths'. There is more than a little "blind faith" involved in trusting the sensory and rational faculties. Everyone has some form of faith—whether it be in God, science, reason, wealth or power. There are inherent limitations in relying on our selves as sole authorities for knowledge. The greatest knowledge is in knowing that we cannot know everything. Does this mean we should all give up our search for knowledge, truth and certainty? Are we helpless? Should we become skeptics who claim there is no such thing as objective truth and knowledge?

> *There is more than a little "blind faith" involved in trusting the sensory and rational faculties.*

The answer is clearly no. God has not left us helpless or without access to His Will. Science and reason can and should be used to complement, support and strengthen our understanding of the universe and God's existence; however, there is a more primary source for understanding God and the metaphysical. This knowledge has been provided by God to mankind externally through Divine Revelation, Scripture and the message of the Prophets and internally through the faculties of spiritual intuition and unveiling.

> *Science and reason can and should be used to complement, support and strengthen our understanding of the universe and God's existence; however, there is a more primary source for understanding God and the metaphysical.*

The term "revelation", which has come to take on a number of different modern usages, will be used in this text to refer to direct disclosures and teachings from God in the form of authentic scriptures and the messages conveyed by Prophets. The term, "unveiling" or Divine "inspiration", is also used in this text to represent a form of Divine disclosure, but is intended for chosen servants, and is lesser in degree and rank than that received by Prophets and Messengers of God.

Our senses, reason and intuition help us to realize the existence of God and what He is not, but in order to make any positive statements about God and how to "know Him" we must revert to Divine Revelation. As Dr. Ismail Faruqi has stated, "knowledge of the divine Will is possible by reason, certain by Revelation."[20] In this sense, the primary function of reason is to understand its inherent limitations and realize that we must submit to God for knowledge of God. Divine Revelation is most distinct from reason and science as forms of knowledge in its capacity as a true source of objectivity that transcends our own limitations of space, time and environment. Theological and moral absolutes can only come from the Creator himself. Yes, one can certainly argue over the authenticity of various religions as forms of Divine Revelation (see Chapter 4), but the principle of following Revelation as a source of knowledge and guidance can only be denied if one denies the existence of God. Hence, God's Revelation and unveiling are essential, yet often ignored, forms of knowledge in our quest for certainty and truth. As Dr. Lynn Wilcox states,

> Stop reading for a moment, and focus your attention on something in the room with you. To really see whatever you are looking at, you have to ignore everything else. The same is true for seeking truth. To find truth, one has to be placed in truth, like the fetus within the womb of the mother. We have to do the same thing to receive the vital, precious truth of the Creator. If you wish to find Truth, you, too, must ask. And, you, too, must do as the Prophets have indicated to do.[21]

We will return to further discuss Revelation and unveiling from an Islamic perspective in Section 2.7 and 2.8.

We have offered that certainty of knowledge, or for that matter faith, cannot be provided by science or reason but can only be bestowed by God Himself. This may seem, initially, to be awkward and unfair to some. Eventually, however, one will realize that God has already provided the necessary means to perceive and experience Him through not only various forms of Divine Revelation, but also through one's own inner being and spiritual essence. The truth, reliability and authority of the "external" scriptures and Messengers of God can be recognized by our "internal" faculties of sense-perception, reason and most of all, by our inner spirit. As introduced in Chapter 1, the greatest proof for God is already within us!

We have all heard clichés about body, mind and spirit, but what exactly is this spirit? The spirit cannot be accurately defined by words but basically represents our closest connection to God. It derives from the Divine or Universal Spirit. It is reflected in our ability to know and comprehend Truth as intuition or the intellect (also known as the 6th sense, insight, or gnosis) and in our will or ability to act as our conscience. It is what allows us to say that "God created man in His image."[22] By way of analogy, the human spirit has been likened to what in a plant causes it "irresistibly to turn towards the light"[23] and the migratory instinct in birds.[24] In Islam, the spirit is considered to have been blown into every human being by God from His very own Spirit. Jewish and Christian traditions also consider the human spirit to derive from the Spirit of God. In fact, the word "spirit" derives from the Latin "spiritus" which is associated with blowing and/or breathing. Islam also associates contentment, satisfaction and tranquility with the spirit, not with any material acquisitions. In Hindu philosophy, the very word for spirit, *atman*, also means contentment.

> *It (the spirit) is reflected in our ability to know and comprehend Truth as intuition or the intellect and in our will or ability to act as our conscience.*

In terms of its ability to know, spiritual knowledge is different from our mind's logical knowledge in a number of ways. The spirit's intellection or knowing is by way of remembering and perceiving, not the mind's acquiring and conceiving.[25] Whereas reason is dependent on our senses and subject to the limitations of time and space, spiritual knowledge cuts through phenomena to see things "as they are" and provides a source of true objectivity through its connection to the Divine Spirit. The seat of spiritual knowledge and sincerity is the heart, not the brain. The mind helps us understand the nature of the surrounding world, while the spirit helps us understand the nature of our selves. The spirit's truths are self evident, whereas the mind constantly needs logical proofs.

The spirit is also very different from our physical body. It is invisible and in no need of food, drink, exercise, sensual or carnal pleasures– for its nourishment is the remembrance of God. Our physical bodies are temporary, while the spirit never dies. The physical body is our worldly clothing, but the spirit is our essence.

Why, then, is it that if God has disclosed His revelation, unveiling and the self-evident truths of the spirit, so many people continue to deny and question God? First of all, acceptance of revelation as being authoritative normally requires belief in God as a prerequisite. Secondly, the power of the spirit is *potential* and therefore, we have the *choice* to leave it untapped or to uncover it from the rust that often envelops it. The spirit and the "self" or "ego" are engaged in a continuous battle for control of the heart. The fact is that most people are so occupied in feeding their selfish desires through the pursuit of "material happiness", "carnal pleasures" and enjoying life, that they have forgotten their spiritual essence. God does not place veils between us and have– it is we who do. The biggest veil between our selves and God is our own ego. If we persist in recognizing only our minds as being authoritative, and not God or His scripture or Prophets, how can we expect to achieve any real knowledge of the supra-sensory world? The Truth can be tortuous to the skeptic when it contradicts his or her existing beliefs and lifestyle. Knowledge must be combined with submission and practice to achieve certainty. Knowledge without action, obedience or submission is hollow. After all, Satan is more knowledgeable than any philosopher or scholar and yet has been damned by God because of his arrogance and failure to submit. The more sincerely we approach God, the more we actualize our spiritual potential, and the greater certainty we can achieve. The greater arrogance we have, the further we fall from Truth. This is the real reason why various philosophers, agnostics, atheists, pundits, thinkers and even some adherents of various religions will always squabble over petty details, arguments and counterarguments and remain immersed in doubt.

> *The biggest veil between our selves and God is our own ego.*

As for those who insist that they cannot acknowledge God until they physically see Him, they must first realize that God is inherently immaterial and invisible to the naked eye, and secondly, that seeing is not necessary for believing or knowing: for true knowledge and certainty can only be bestowed upon the heart by God Himself. That which is material cannot behold vision of that which is immaterial. Recall the famous story of Prophet Moses' encounter with God on Mount Sinai—despite being a Prophet, he was unable to bear the vision of God for He cannot be seen in His essence. A sliver of God's glory was enough to decimate Mount Sinai and drop Moses (AS) to his knees.

Should we assume then, looking at the opposite end of the spectrum, that all "believers" in God possess certainty of knowledge and faith and have fully recognized their spiritual potential? Not quite. The fact is that certainty of belief and knowledge is not merely a question of something we either have or don't have, for it involves a *process*. There is an infinite continuum of degrees of knowledge and faith within and between people. Knowledge and faith are also dynamic with respect to time in that everyone experiences periods of both greater and lesser certainty. It is only the Prophets and Messengers of God who possessed complete certainty and who could, as Prophet Abraham did, leap into the fire with no doubt that God will protect. Prophets and Messengers rely, not on the scientific method or on ratiocination, but on direct teaching, inspiration and disclosure from God, which enable them to fully realize the potential within, i.e. that of the endless spirit. Nonetheless, certainty is still approachable for everyday mortals like ourselves with the condition that we fully submit to God and His Messengers and Revelation, which will, in turn, enable us to fully realize our spiritual potential.

Let us now take a deeper look at the question of certainty from an Islamic perspective by starting with a discussion of knowledge itself.

2.5 Islam and Knowledge

The Qur'anic use of the term, *'ilm*, or what is commonly translated as knowledge, can be said to include knowledge of God as disclosed by Himself, knowledge of the next world, and knowledge of the present world and all that it contains as it relates to that for which it was created. Given that God is the source of the cosmos and the next world, it would not be an exaggeration to say that *all genuine knowledge is ultimately knowledge of God*. Stated differently, all genuine knowledge is self-disclosure from God or as Syed Al-Attas has noted, "knowledge… is the arrival of meaning in the soul; and with reference to the soul as being its active recipient and interpreter, knowledge is the arrival of the soul at meaning."[26] Thus, worldly knowledge concerning stock prices, soccer scores, movie stars and the like is not part of *'ilm* but is considered mere information.

The ability to acquire true knowledge or 'ilm is one of the greatest gifts of God to mankind, which should not be surprising given that "Allah created man in His own image"[27] and that "Our Lord embraces all things in knowledge."[28]

Recall that Allah appeals to mankind to reflect, think, contemplate and understand over 125 times in the Qur'an and stresses the importance of knowledge repeatedly:

> …Verily those (truly) are in awe of Allah among His servants who have knowledge. (35:27)

> Are they equal, those who know and those who know not? (39:9)

The first verse indicates the close relationship between knowledge and God-consciousness or awareness. Implicit in this verse is the idea that knowledge which does not lead to God-consciousness is not really knowledge. This is why Prophet Muhammad (SAW) also said, *"Verily the knowledgeable are the inheritors of the Prophets."*[29] One of his most common and cherished supplications was the Qur'anic verse, *"My Lord, increase me in knowledge"* (20:114).

He also emphasized the importance of knowledge in numerous other narrations, such as, *"Seek knowledge even if you must go to China"*[30], and "The search for knowledge is incumbent upon every Muslim (male or female)".[31]

Recall also the Qur'anic verse cited in Chapter 1 regarding the signs of God:

We will show them Our signs upon the horizons and in themselves, until it is clear to them that He is the Real. Is it not enough that your Lord does witness all things? (41:53).

It could be said that the "signs upon the horizons" roughly correspond to sense-based knowledge or science, while the signs "in themselves" refer to our inherent rational and spiritual abilities. How, then, do we begin to know in the real sense of the word? As introduced in Chapter 1, Islamic epistemology includes knowledge acquired by our senses and intellectual and intuitive faculties. Properly used, these faculties are able to recognize the knowledge and wisdom contained in Divine scriptures and Messengers' teachings. Let us take a closer look at these forms of knowledge.

2.6 Islam, Reason and Science

Earlier we noted the importance of knowledge in developing God-consciousness. The Islamic perspective on science as a form of knowledge is characterized by an inextricable connection to God as its source. Modern science, which stops short of connecting phenomena to their ultimate source, is therefore an incomplete explanation of phenomena. There can be no possibility of conflict between God and science, since it is actually science that is subservient to God's commands. Similarly, there is no conflict per se between Islam and science. Islamic history never encountered the bitter struggle with science that was characteristic of Christian history.[32] To the contrary, Islamic teachings fostered and encouraged the spirit of scientific endeavor. In Islamic epistemology, both sense-perception and reason are acknowledged as forms of knowledge that are to be fully utilized. However, their roles lie in supporting and strengthening preexistent metaphysical truths and, hence, are considered below Divine Revelation and unveiling in the hierarchy of knowledge. In other words, they are necessary but insufficient conditions for certainty of belief.

There is a great deal of information in the Qur'an that appeals to our faculties of reason, reflection and understanding, as well as information that could be considered as part of the modern natural sciences. Let us briefly examine each of these in turn.

Firstly, when we speak of reason, we have in mind the Arabic word *'aql*. In the Qur'an, this term does not appear as a noun, but in various verbal forms, such as *ta'qilun or na'qilu,* a total of 49 times. When we include other related words such as reflection, understanding and contemplation *(fakkara, faqiha, dabbara),* these terms appear over 125 times.

The 'aql is similar to but not identical with what is nowadays understood as the rational faculty or intellect. This difference is manifested in the Qur'an by considering the facts that it, firstly, considers those who reject Allah's signs to be among those who do not use their *'aql* (despite their ability to think) and secondly, considers the seat of reason to be the heart and not the brain. A few passages from the Qur'an illustrate the use of the term *'aql* as follows:

> Do you enjoin right conduct upon the people and forget (to practise it) yourselves, and yet you study the Scripture? *Will you not, then, use your intellect"* (2:44)

> Thus does Allah make clear His signs to you in order that *you may use your intellect.* (2:242)

> The parable of those who reject faith is as if one were to shout like a goatherd, to things that listen to nothing but calls and cries—*deaf, dumb and blind, they do not use their intellect (la ya'qilun).* (2:171)

> Have they, then, never journeyed about the earth, letting their hearts *gain wisdom (qulubun yaqiluna)* and causing their ears to hear? Yet, verily it is not their eyes that have become blind—but blind have become the hearts that are in their breasts. (22:46)

> *Tell men to reflect with care* and see what things the heaven and the earth contain. (10:101)

Recall also the arguments for God's existence from the Qur'an referenced in Chapter 1 such as those supporting the arguments from Design, First Cause and Necessary Being. Hundreds of arguments in the Qur'an are posed as questions that urge the use of our rational faculty.

Besides being appealed to repeatedly in the Qur'an, reason also plays an important role in Islamic law or jurisprudence. In Sunni law, *qiyas* or what is translated as "analogical deduction" is the fourth source of law after the Qur'an, Sunna (Way) of Prophet Muhammad (SAW), and *ijma'* or juristic consensus. In Shiite law, reason or the 'aql is considered the fourth source of law and plays an even greater role in jurisprudence than in Sunni law.

Next, when we study the appeals to our basic senses in the Qur'an, we find a broad spectrum covering everything from the creation of the universe to astronomy, the earth's atmosphere, the water cycle, the animal kingdom, the plant kingdom, human reproduction and embryology. The extent of agreement between the Qur'anic statements and current scientific knowledge is such that even modern scientists are surprised by their accuracy. As Dr. Maurice Bucaille states in *The Bible, The Quran and Science:*

> A crucial fact is that the Qur'an, while inviting us to cultivate science, itself contains many observations on natural phenomena and includes explanatory details which are seen to be in total agreement with modern scientific data. There is no equal to this in the Judeo-Christian revelation. These scientific considerations, which are very specific to the Qur'an, surprised me at first. Up until then, I had not thought it possible for one to find so many statements in a text compiled more than thirteen centuries ago referring to extremely diverse subjects and all of them totally in keeping with modern scientific knowledge.[33]

A good example of this agreement lies in the area of embryology. In fact, several medical doctors have converted to Islam based on the detailed descriptions of embryology found in the Qur'an, some of which have only recently been confirmed by science and which no human being could possibly have foreseen over 1400 years ago.[34]

Another example relates to astronomy. Just two of the verses mentioned in this regard are:

> Do the unbelievers not see that the heavens and the earth were joined together before We separated them, and that We brought all living things into existence from water? Why do they still not believe in God? (21:30)

> Then God tuned to the creation of the heavens, when they were but a smoky substance. (41:11)

Although scientists have a number of theories as to the emergence of the solar system, most of them agree that the heavens and earth were originally joined together as a single entity and later separated from each other and that all planets were originally composed of a mass of gas.

Although a thorough study of the Qur'an as it relates to science and the natural world has been presented elsewhere by numerous authors[35], it is important to realize that the Qur'an is replete with appeals to our senses and intellects to reflect on the design and order in the universe. The most frequently cited signs of God in the Qur'an derive from the majestic, natural universe (as introduced in Chapter 1).

The chief commonality encountered in these and similar passages is the appeal to reflect upon the knowledge acquired by our senses and to realize its connection to God's Attributes, such as His Omnipotence, Munificence and Beauty and thereby strengthen our faith in God. Admiration for what is acquired by our senses and reason without the connection to God is just as hollow as praising a beautiful sculpture without praising the sculptor. The Qur'an sternly warns us not to focus only on that which is external and empirical: "They know well the externalities of the worldly life, but of the End of things they are heedless" (30:7).

Historically, this is why great Muslim scientists like Ibn Sina, Ibn Rushd and Al-Biruni were not specialists in a single field such as biology or mathematics, but were well-rounded scholars of not only various fields of science but also the religious, philosophical and social sciences. Modern restriction of knowledge, such as that of the domain of the mind to psychologists and psychiatrists while restricting knowledge of the body to medical doctors, denies the strong connection between the mind and body. Knowledge cannot strictly be compartmentalized into independent branches of study for they are all interdependent and holistically dependent upon the Ultimate Designer.

2.7 The Qur'an and Prophethood

It was noted earlier that knowledge can be acquired by our basic senses and our mind but that Divine Revelation and Prophethood represent the primary source of knowledge of God. For a Muslim, it is obligatory to believe in the original, uncorrupted forms of all Divine Scriptures that were revealed to various Prophets throughout the course of history, including among others, the Psalms of David (AS), the Torah to Moses (AS), the Gospel to Jesus (AS) and, of course, the Qur'an to Muhammad (SAW). Positive statements about God can only come from God Himself, which are communicated to mankind primarily through Divine Scriptures and the Prophets. The intellectual endeavors and discourses of philosophers, thinkers and scientists, however impressive they may seem to some, are no substitute for God's revelation.

> *Positive statements about God can only come from God Himself, which are communicated to mankind primarily through Divine Scriptures and Prophets.*

Muslims believe that God's final message has been conveyed through the holy scripture of the Qur'an as revealed to the last Messenger, Prophet Muhammad (SAW). The Qur'an was revealed piecemeal over the course of twenty-three years to Prophet Muhammad (SAW) through the Archangel Gabriel (refer to Chapter 4 for more on the unique preservation of Islamic sources). Unlike the Bible, the Qur'an is considered by Muslims to be the direct, spoken word of God and is meant not only to be read and understood, but also to be recited. Though the Qur'an contains a great deal of information on various areas such as theology, behavior, morality, society, history, governance, the natural world and more, it is ultimately a book of *guidance*. The purpose of the Qur'an has been stated within the Qur'an itself in verses like,

> This is The Book—in it is sure guidance, without doubt, to those who fear Allah" (2:2)

And thus have We, by Our command sent inspiration to you—you knew not before what was Revelation, and what was Faith, but we have made the Qur'an a light wherewith We guide such of Our servants as We will, and verily do You guide to the Straight Path. (42:52)

The guidance of Divine revelation, thus, stems from two resons:
(1) the frailty, ignorance and forgetfulness of man, and
(2) the Divine Will to guide His creation out of His Mercy and Love.

This guidance and light is comprehensive with respect to both knowledge and action and is intended for both life in this world as well as salvation in the next world as noted in other parts of the Qur'an.[36]

The sayings and way of Prophet Muhammad (SAW) represent the second source of guidance after the Qur'an in Islam. Countless sayings and actions of the Prophet (SAW) were recorded in meticulous detail during his lifetime by close companions, and have been readily available to believers for over 1400 years. While the Qur'an serves as a written and recited source of guidance, Prophet Muhammad (SAW) provides a living example to humanity of how the teachings of the Qur'an should be enacted in our daily lives. As his wife, Aisha (RA), narrated, "surely his character was the Qur'an".[37] He, like all the genuine Prophets of God, is considered to be free from any sin and perfect in his communication of God's message.[38] As the Qur'an says, "He who obeys the Messenger, obeys Allah..." (4:80).

The purpose of sending Prophet Muhammad (SAW) has been clarified in the Qur'an:

O Prophet! Surely We have sent you as a witness, a bearer of glad tidings, a warner, and a summoner to Allah by His permission and as a lamp that gives light. (33:45-46).

The Qur'an also confirms the monotheistic teachings of prior Messengers of God:

The same religion has He established for you as that which He enjoined on Noah—that which We have sent by inspiration to you—and that which We enjoined on Abraham, Moses, and Jesus: namely, that you should remain steadfast in religion, and make no divisions therein... (42:13)

Not a Messenger did We send before you (Muhammad, SAW) without this inspiration sent by Us to him: that there is no God but I—therefore worship and serve Me. (21:25)

With respect to Prophets in general, the Qur'an also states,
We surely sent Our Messengers with clear proofs and revealed on them the Book and the criterion (to judge right and wrong) so that people may establish justice... (57:25).

Thus, the purpose of prophethood can be said to be twofold:
(1) to summon people to obey and return to Allah, and
(2) to establish justice in society. These objectives pertain to both the individual and to society, and to both this world and the next. Salvation is not the expressed objective of the Prophets—for this is ultimately in the hands of Allah.

Having introduced the role of the Qur'an and Prophet Muhammad (SAW), how does this relate to the question of compatibility of God with reason and science? The very fact that God has chosen to bless mankind with such forms of Revelation indicates that our own senses and reasoning are insufficient with respect to knowledge and guidance. *Reason and sense-perception are necessary but not sufficient.* Earlier we noted that our own God-given faculties can and should be used to realize and strengthen our belief in His existence, but that any positive statements about God must come from God Himself. Thus, Muslims are called upon to submit to God for knowledge of God and the obedience or worship that this entails. At the same time, Muslims realize that given that Allah is infinite while His creatures are finite, we can never fully comprehend God in His essence. This, however, does not mean that we should not seek the knowledge and guidance of God.

Because Divine Revelation stands at the apex of the hierarchy of knowledge, the message provided by the Qur'an and His Prophet Muhammad (SAW) is the ultimate criteria for resolving any dispute, as noted in the following verses,

> O you who believe! Obey Allah and obey the Messenger, and those charged with authority among you. If you differ in anything among yourselves, refer it to Allah and His Messenger if you do believe in Allah and the Last Day: that is best and most suitable for final determination. (4:59)

> Yet there is among men such as one disputes about Allah without knowledge, without guidance, and without a Book of Enlightenment. (22:8)

> *Because Divine Revelation stands at the apex of the hierarchy of knowledge, the message provided by the Qur'an and His Prophet Muhammad (SAW) is the ultimate criteria for resolving any dispute...*

2.8 Unveiling and Inspiration

Another avenue by which we can obtain knowledge of God is through Divine unveiling or inspiration, or what is known as *kashf* and *ilham* in Arabic. This is a form of Divine disclosure of knowledge which is of a lesser degree than the revelation received by the Prophets and Messengers.

The means of bestowing such knowledge is not like the transfer of knowledge between human beings:

> It is not fitting for a man that Allah should speak to him except by inspiration or from behind a veil, or by the sending of a Messenger to reveal with Allah's permission what Allah wills—for He is Most High, Most Wise. (42:51)

Exactly how this knowledge is bestowed cannot be described by words and is something to be experienced by the beneficiary of such knowledge. Many express the unveiling of knowledge by God to select individuals as "experiential knowledge". Regardless of the semantics, the important point is to recognize the validity and principle of experience. Earlier in Chapter 1, certain means of experiencing God were discussed, including the path of knowledge.

There is ample evidence in the Qur'an to support the fact that believers in God can be bestowed with direct knowledge from God, including knowledge of the unseen, with His permission. Consider, for example, the account of Khidr (AS) in Chapter 18, *Surah Al-Kahf*. Here, Khidr reveals to Moses (AS) certain elements of the unseen and Divine purpose through various incidents that occur before them. The fact that Khidr's knowledge was bestowed by God Himself is attested to in the Qur'an as follows:

> So they found one of Our servants, on whom We had bestowed Mercy from Ourselves and *whom We had taught knowledge from Our own presence.* Moses said to him, 'May I follow thee on the footing that you teach me something of the *higher truth which you have been taught?'* (18:65-66)

Other historical examples include the famous accounts of the Prophet's companion, Abu Bakr (RA) who was inspired with the knowledge of his baby's sex before its birth and that of 'Umar, who miraculously perceived the coming of a Persian army while delivering a Friday sermon from the pulpit. About 'Umar, Prophet Muhammad (SAW) said, " He is of those who are spoken to (i.e. inspired)". While God is The Knower of The Unseen, He can reveal elements of the Unseen to those whom He wills as noted in the Qur'an,

> (He is) the Knower of the Unseen, and discloses not His unseen to anyone save a messenger whom he approves—for him he places protectors before and behind. (72:26-27)

> They cannot comprehend anything out of what He knows save what He wills. (2:255)

It is also interesting to note that the Arabic word, *wahy*, which is commonly translated as "revelation" is not only reserved for human beings. *Wahy* in the Qur'an refers to knowledge or faith imparted to a living creature by God. All living creatures, including those from the plant and animal kingdom, can receive revelation, though in varying levels and degrees. Allah (SWT) states in the Qur'an,

> "And thy Lord revealed to the bee to build its cells in hills, on trees, and in men's habitations" (16:68)

and speaks of *wahy* to the earth on the Day of Resurrection (99:5). *Wahy* is also mentioned in reference to the mother of Prophet Moses (AS), Asiya, when she was instructed by God to place her child in a river (see 20:38, 28:7). The highest form of revelation, though, is reserved for the Prophets.

Other verses point to the relationship between God's bestowal of knowledge and the general service and piety of His servants:

> And serve your Lord until there come unto you the certainty. (15:99)
>
> Be God-conscious and God will teach you. (2:282)

These verses demonstrate the important relationship between submission and knowledge bestowed by God. Each is incomplete without the other. This relationship is further amplified in the following narration, which emphasizes the beautiful immanence of the Lord. According to Prophet Muhammad, peace and blessings be upon him, Allah has said:

> He who is hostile to a friend of Mine I declare war against. My slave approaches Me with nothing more beloved to Me than what I have made obligatory for him, and My slave keeps drawing nearer to Me with voluntary works until I love him. And when I love Him, I am his hearing with which he hears, his sight with which he sees, his hand with which he seizes, and his foot with which he walks. If He asks Me, I will surely give to him, and if he seeks refuge in Me, I will surely protect him.[39]

This reiterates the concept introduced in Section 2.4 where submission to and worship of God was noted to be a critical factor in the quest for certainty.

2.9 The Heart of Certainty

Following Divine Scripture and Messengers requires us to submit to them as authorities, and not *ourselves*. This requirement may seem obvious in theory, but can be difficult in practice. Submission to God seems restrictive to many, but, in fact, there is *freedom in submission*. One of the reasons why submission to God can be difficult is that recognizing the validity of Revelation as a means of knowledge and guidance requires us to think with not just our minds, but also our hearts. According to a tradition of Prophet Muhammad (SAW), "It should be known that there is a lump of flesh in the body of man on which depends his being good or bad. When this piece of flesh is healthy, man remains spiritually healthy; when it is not healthy, man goes astray- and that lump of flesh is the man's heart."[40] He (SAW) also stated that Allah has said, "My heavens and My earth encompass Me not, but the heart of my gentle, faithful, and meek servant does encompass Me."[41] Reason seeks to delimit and define God, whereas the heart is able to perceive God as being free from all limitations.

> *Reason seeks to delimit and define God, whereas the heart is able to perceive God as being free from all limitations.*

The Arabic word, *qalb*, which is translated as the heart, is used over 130 times in the Qur'an in various contexts (not to mention other words closely meaning 'heart' such as *lubb* and *fuad*). In its Qur'anic usage, the heart or qalb is primarily associated with:
(1) knowledge,
(2) faith (iman),
(3) tranquility and
(4) the spirit.

At the opposite end of the spectrum, disbelief and denial (*kufr* in Arabic) are also associated with a disease in the heart, not necessarily in the mind. Let us briefly examine some Qur'anic evidence relating to the heart.

Knowledge:

We previously discussed how true knowledge (i.e. knowledge of God) and reasoning is associated with the heart, not the mind. The Arabic word *'aql* is commonly translated as "reason" or "intellect" and is mentioned forty-nine times in its various forms in the Qur'an. Allah (SWT) associates 'aql or reasoning and intellection with the heart in the following verses:

> Have they, then, never journeyed about the earth, letting their *hearts gain wisdom (qulubun yaqiluna)* and causing their ears to hear? Yet, verily it is not their eyes that have become blind—but blind have become the hearts that are in their breasts. (22:46)

> Verily in this is a reminder for any that has a heart or who gives ear and earnestly witnesses the truth. (50:37)

Faith and Tranquility:

For those who choose the path of faith in their Lord, God has decreed the bestowal of tranquility and satisfaction in their hearts to strengthen their faith and guide them, as noted below. Here again, there is a clear implication that certainty can only be bestowed by God Himself to those who are sincere and have faith in Him:

> It is He who has sent down *tranquility into the hearts of the believers, that they may add faith to their faith*- for to Allah belong the forces of the heavens and the earth and Allah is full of Knowledge and Wisdom. (48:4)

> No kind of calamity can occur except by the leave of Allah: and *if anyone believes in Allah, He guides his heart,* for Allah knows all things. (64:11)

> The unbelievers say: 'Why is not a sign sent down to him from his Lord?' Say, 'Truly Allah leaves to stray whom He will, but He guides to Himself those who turn to Him in penitence- those who believe, and whose hearts find satisfaction in the remembrance of Allah: *for without doubt, in the remembrance of Allah do hearts find satisfaction. (13:27-28)*

> Allah's Good Pleasure was on the believers when they swore fealty to you (Muhammad, SAW) under the tree- *He knew what was in their hearts and He sent down tranquility to them* and He rewarded them with a speedy victory. (48:18)

Spirit:

In addition to the *'aql* or intellect, the spirit is associated with the heart, though it is invisible and immaterial. Recall that the spirit (or "soul" according to some) represents our closest connection to God and derives from the Divine spirit:

> Behold your Lord said to the angels, 'I am about to create man from sounding clay from mud molded into shape. When I have fashioned him (in due proportion) and *breathed into him My Spirit (ruhi)*, fall ye down in obeisance unto him. (15:28-29).

> Verily this is a Revelation from the Lord of the Worlds. With it came down the *Spirit (ruh) of Faith and Truth to your heart* that you may admonish... (26:192-194)

The term, *ruh,* as used in the Qur'an is not only an entity that has already been breathed into our very beings, but can also be sent by the command of Allah to any of His servants. This spirit is not to be confused with the Christian concept of the Holy Spirit which is contrasted with the Father and Son of the Trinity. This spirit can serve a number of purposes, such as strengthening our faith, reminding of our duty unto God, and reminding of the Hereafter as noted in verses such as,

> He does send down His angels with the Spirit (of inspiration) of His command to such of His servants as He pleases (saying), "Warn (man) that there is no god but I–so perform your duty unto Me. (16:2)

> Raised high above ranks, He is the Lord of the Throne, by His command does He send the Spirit (of inspiration) to any of His servants He pleases, that it may warn of the Day of Mutual Meeting. (40:15)

Disbelief and Denial:

A "disease" of the heart is also associated with disbelief, denial, deviation and hypocrisy as noted in a number of passages:

> ...Woe to those whose *hearts are hardened against celebrating the praises of Allah! They are manifestly wandering in error!* (39:22)

> Oh Our Lord! *Let not our hearts deviate now after You have guided us,* but grant us Mercy from Your Own Presence, for You are the grantor of bounties without measure. (3:8)

> Of the people there are some who say: 'We believe in Allah and the Last Day"; but they do not really believe. Fain would they deceive Allah and those who believe, but they only deceive themselves, and realize it not! *In their hearts is a disease, and Allah has increased their disease; and grievous is the penalty they incur because they are false to themselves.* (2:8-10)

> Lo! *The hypocrites say, and those in whose hearts is a disease:* 'These people-their religion has misled them.' But if any trust in Allah, behold! Allah is Most Exalted in Might and Wise. (8:49)

The "disease" in the heart spoken of stems from "being false to themselves" or insincerity, failure to submit to the Lord and a conscious denial of the infinite signs of God. The root of this disease is the "lower self" or ego which tends toward rejection of any authority other than its own. Thus, the Qur'an states:

> But when Our signs came to them, that should have opened their eyes, they said: 'This is sorcery manifest!' And t*hey rejected those signs in iniquity and arrogance, though their souls were convinced thereof*—so see what was the end of those who acted corruptly! (27:13-14)

> *The root of this disease (of the heart) is the "lower self" or ego, which tends toward rejection of any authority other than its own.*

Herein lies the secret of why seemingly intelligent people try to deny the existence of God. Almost everyone possesses the faculties of reason and sense-perception, but not everyone possesses a sincere heart that is willing to submit to the Lord alone. It is by our own conscious decision that the heart can be ruled by either the lower self or our spiritual essence. The faith of so-called believers that is based solely upon their own reason, and not the heart or spirit, is more susceptible to doubt because of its dependence on rational methods, whereas faith based on both reason and a sincere heart is unwavering because it is bestowed and strengthened by God Himself.

In a famous narration of Prophet Muhammad (SAW), three fundamental principles or stages are identified with respect to religion or the path to God. These are islam, or submission, *iman* or *faith*, and ihsan or virtue and excellence. He stated that islam refers to the five pillars of religion, i.e. the testimony of faith *(shahadah)*, daily prayers *(salat)*, fasting *(sawm)*, alms-giving *(zakat)* and the pilgrimage to Mecca (hajj). *Iman* or faith includes the essential creed of faith in Allah, His angels, His Books, His Messengers, the Day of Judgment, and predestination. Finally, *ihsan*, or virtue is summarized by his saying, "It is to adore God as if you were to see Him, for if you see Him not, then verily He sees you." The first stage involves a conscious outward decision to submit to and obey the Will of God, while the second involves a grace that enters the heart enabling a deeper, more inward, recognition of the Truth of God's signs. The final stage indicates a total commitment, both outwardly and inwardly, such that there is constant awareness and recognition of God in *all that one does*. At this point, the heart is like a pure, well-polished mirror that reflects the Divine and one can truly be considered the vicegerent of God on earth as described in the Qur'an.[42]

Relatedly, the Qur'an speaks of three stages of certainty. These are *'ilm al-yaqin* or knowledge of certainty, *'ayn al-yaqin* or source of certainty, and *haqq al-yaqin* or truth of certainty. Scholars and commentators of the Qur'an have related these stages to the analogy of knowledge of a fire, sight of a fire and touching a fire. The final stage transcends any error in judgment or sight and is realization of "absolute truth". Interestingly, the Qur'an only uses the term *haqq al-yaqin* in two instances: one in relation to the Message or Revelation of God and the other in descriptions of the Hereafter.

It is the Messengers and Prophets of God who have attained the highest degree of certainty, or in Islamic terms the stages of *ihsan* and *haqq al-yaqin*. Nonetheless, "ordinary" believers in God can undoubtedly attain a level of certainty that makes them worthy of the title, "vicegerent of God on earth". God would not have called on man to become His vicegerent if he was incapable. In answering the original question of certainty posed at the beginning of the chapter, it should firstly be remembered that achieving certainty involves a process and is not a singular event in time, and secondly, that certainty of the existence of God is undoubtedly possible with the condition that one has a sincere heart which is willing to submit to and believe in God.

> *God would not have called on man to become His vicegerent if he was incapable.*

God responds to His eager servants by bestowing and strengthening faith in their hearts to the point that certainty can be experienced in the course of their lives.

Chapter Summary

1. Both findings based on the modern scientific method and conclusions reached solely by reason have a number of inherent limitations and cannot be considered "absolute truths".

2. The believer has good reason to believe in the complete compatibility of God with science and reason. The realms of science and reason are subservient to God. Whether from the point of view of science or reason, the best overall explanation for all that exists in the universe lies in the concept of God. On the other hand, for the determined and arrogant skeptic, God will never be compatible with science or reason regardless of any proofs or arguments offered.

3. While the faculties of reason and sense-perception can and should be used to strengthen our understanding of God, human beings also possess an intuitive faculty that is associated with the spirit and the heart. This spirit represents our closest connection to God and derives from the Pure Spirit of God.

4. The faculties of reason, sense-perception and spiritual intuition are capable of recognizing the Truth and authority of Divine Revelation as manifested in holy scriptures and the message of Prophets. Divine Revelation stands at the peak of the hierarchy of forms of knowledge.

5. In Islam, truth and knowledge of God can only come from God Himself. The signs of God have been disclosed externally through the creation of the universe and the message provided by Divine scriptures and Messengers; and disclosed internally through the creation of man and his unique faculties of reason and spiritual intuition.

6. The Qur'an and message of Prophet Muhammad (SAW) present numerous appeals to recognize the signs of God based on our faculties of reason and sense-perception. Islam fostered and encouraged the pursuit of scientific knowledge and never encountered the bitter struggle that Christianity faced with science.

7. Human reason is necessary for attaining certainty of the existence of God but is not sufficient- for certainty also requires a sincere heart which is willing to submit to the Divine Will and Revelation and has faith in Him alone. Only then can God bestow certainty upon the heart.

8. Islam traces disbelief to a "disease" of the heart, not necessarily a disease of thought process or sense-perception. A struggle is constantly waged between the spirit and the "lower self" for possession of the heart. Disbelief stems from a conscious decision to allow the lower self's control of the heart and to deny the signs of God.

Notes:

1 J.L. Mackie, *The Miracle of Theism—Arguments for and Against the Existence of God* (New York: Oxford University Press, 1982), p. 199.
2 Norwood Hanson, *What I Do Not Believe* (Dordrecht: D. Reidel, 1971), p. 310.
3 *The American Heritage College Dictionary* (Boston: Houghton Mifflin Co., 3rd ed., 1993).
4 The scientific method basically includes the steps of observation and accumulation of data, formation of a hypothesis or theory, experimentation and additional data collection, interpretation of results and conclusions.
5 Rene Guenon, *The Crisis of the Modern World*, trans. Marco Pallis and Richard Nicholson, (Ghent, New York: Sophia Perrenis et Unversalis, 4th ed., 1996), p. 68.
6 See Paul Feyerband, *Against Method* (London: Verso, 1984), p. 339.
7 Rene Guenon, *The Crisis of the Modern World*, p. 68.
8 Rene Descartes, *Meditations on the First Philosophy*, trans. John Cottingham (Cambridge, 1986).
9 Stanley Jaki, *The Road of Science and the Ways to God* (Chicago: University of Chicago Press, 1978), pp. 80-95, 246-262, 314-331.
10 Keith Ward, God, *Chance & Necessity* (Oxford: Oneworld Publications, 1996), pp. 105-166.
11 Richard Dawkins, *The Selfish Gene* (London: Granada Publishing, 1978), p. 63.
12 Fritjof Capra, *The Tao of Physics* (New York: Bantam Books, 2nd ed., 1984), p. 56.
13 Paul Davies, *Superforce–The Search for a Grand Unified Theory of Nature* (New York: Simon & Schuster, 1984), pp. 43-45.
14 ibid, p. 129
15 Peter Plichta, *God's Secret Formula* (Boston: Element Books, 1998).
16 See B.B. Mandelbrot, *The Fractal Geometry of Nature* (New York: W.H. Freeman and Co., 1977).
17 Paul Davies, *Superforce- The Search for a Grand Unified Theory of Nature* (New York: Simon and Schuster, 1985), p. 223.
18 Frithjof Schuon, *Logic and Transcendence* (New York: Harper & Row, 1975), p. 42.
19 For an extensive discussion of the significance of koans and the related Zen Buddhist philosophy, see Toshihiko Izutsu, Toward a Philosophy of Zen Buddhism, reprint, (Boulder, CO: Prajna Press, 1982).
20 Ismail Raji Al-Faruqi, *Tawhid: Its Relevance for Thought and Life* (Kuala Lumpur: I.I.F.S.O., 1983), p. 7
21 Lynn Wilcox, *Sufism and Psychology* (Chicago: Abjad Book Designers and Builders, 1995), p. 187.
22 Hadith or saying of Prophet Muhammad (SAW) narrated in Bukhari, Isti'dhan 1; Muslim Birr, 115, Janna 28; Ahmad II 244, 251, 315, 323, 434, 463, 519.
23 Frithjof Schuon, Gnosis: *Divine Wisdom,* Trans. G.E.H. Palmer (London: Perennial Books, 1990).
24 J.S. Cutsinger, *Advice to the Serious Seeker– Meditations on the Teaching of Frithjof Schuon* (Albany: State University of New York Press, 1997), p. 29.

25 The Greek philosopher, Plato, considered all knowledge to be recollection and not acquisition.
26 Syed Muhammad Naquib Al-Attas, *Prolegomena to the Metaphysics of Islam* (Kuala Lumpur: ISTAC, 1995), p. 133.
27 Hadith or saying of Prophet Muhammad (SAW) narrated in Bukhari, Isti'dhan 1; Muslim Birr, 115, Janna 28; Ahmad II 244, 251, 315, 323, 434, 463, 519.
28 Qur'an 7:89.
29 Hadith narrated in *Sahih Bukhari*, 'Ilm 10; Abu Dawud, Ilm 1; Ibn Maja, Muqadddima 17.
30 Narrated by Anas, recorded in Al-Bayhaqi's Shu'ab Al-Iman and Ibn 'Abd Al-Barr's Jami' Bayan Al'Ilm
31 Narrated by Ibn Majah
32 See Karen Armstrong, *A History of God:* The 4000-Year Quest of Judaism, Christianity, and Islam (New York: Knopf Inc., 1993) and Maurice Bucaille, The Bible, The Qur'an and Science, trans, A.D. Pannell, M. Bucaille (Indianapolis: North American Trust Publication, 1979).
33 Maurice Bucaille, *The Bible The Qur'an and Science,* trans, A.D. Pannell and M. Bucaille (Indianapolis: North American Trust Publication, 1979).
34 See Keith Moore, A Scientist's Interpretation of References to Embryology in the Qur'an, *Journal of the Islamic Medical Association of US and Canada* 18:15, 1986.
35 See Suleiman Qush, *The Scientific Discoveries in Correlation to the Glorious Qur'an* (Manila: Islamic Dawah Council of the Philippines, 1988); S. H. Nasr, Islamic Science—An Illustrated Study (Kent, U.K.: World of Islam Festival Publishing Co., 1976).
36 See Qur'an 2:185 and 96:4-5.
37 Hadith narrated in *Sahih Muslim*, Musafirin, 139.
38 See Qur'an, Surah Al-Najm, 53:1-11.
39 Hadith narrated by Imam Nawawi.
40 Hadith Qudsi narrated by Bukhari in Ezzeddin Ibrahim and Denys Johnson-Davies, *Forty Hadith Qudsi*, (Beirut: The Holy Quran Publishing House, 1980), Hadith #25.
41 Narrated in Sahih Bukhari
42 Cited by Imam Abu Hamid Al-Ghazali in *Ihya Ulum Al-Din* (Cairo: Matba'at Al-Amirat Al-Sharafiyya, 1908-1909), III 1.5, III, p. 12.
43 Refer to verses 2:30 and 38:26 where God describes man as His vicegerent on earth.

Chapter 3

Why Does God Allow Evil and Suffering?

*Behold, your Lord said to the angels, 'I will create
a vicegerent on earth.' They said, 'Will you
place therein one who will make mischief and shed blood—while we
do celebrate Thy praises
and glorify Thy Holy Name?' He said,
'I know what you know not.'*

Qur'an 2:30

In the words of Fyodor Dostoyevsky's Ivan, "Imagine that you are creating a fabric of human destiny with the object of making men happy in the end, giving them peace and rest at last, but that it was essential and inevitable to torture to death only one tiny creature—that little child beating its breast with its fist, for instance—and to found that edifice on its unavenged tears, would you consent to bet the architect on those conditions? Tell me, and tell me the truth."[1]

Such a statement exemplifies the utter debasement of the modern mind when it comes to understanding the relationship between God and evil. The so-called problem of evil is the most common argument that skeptics throughout history have clung to in claiming that the existence of God is either unlikely or completely false. Simply stated, it argues that if there really were a perfectly good, all-knowing, all-powerful God, then there would be no evil and suffering in the world. Hence, it is claimed that the common concept of God is irreconcilable with evil and suffering. In this chapter, we will expose the fallacies of this view and Dostoyevsky's objection in explaining why there is no contradiction between either "evil" and God or suffering and God. This is not an issue to be avoided or skirted, as some believers and even religious scholars attempt to do. Rather, it is our view that theodicies, or explanations of why there is evil and suffering in the world, actually serve to strengthen faith in God through a greater understanding of the immutable laws that govern the universe, the role of mankind, and the purpose of creation.

In answering this question we will present an Islamic perspective while understanding that throughout history, Muslims have expressed numerous views on the subject. While there are surely differences among these views, a number of commonalities also exist based on the primary source of the Qur'an. In this chapter, it is the Qur'an that will be most relied upon in addressing these questions. Both similarities and stark differences will also be encountered with "classical" Christian, Jewish and other religious theodicies.

Inevitably, any attempt to explain why there is evil and suffering in the world may seem harsh or callous to some, but assuredly, there is no ill intent on our part to be insensitive to any who have been afflicted. On the contrary, every genuine religion considers it praiseworthy, rewarding and an essential part of one's faith to work to alleviate suffering and struggle against evil. In the Islamic view, part of the very purpose of creation is to enjoin good and prevent evil to the best of our abilities. Moreover, to claim that suffering and affliction are metaphysically necessary is not to say in any way that they are justified or praiseworthy.

3.1 What are Evil and Suffering?

Evil has been defined in *Webster's Dictionary*[32]. to include, among other things, that which is immoral, sinful, wicked, mischievous, repulsive, due to bad character, and causes injury, harm, trouble, pain, misfortune and/or suffering.[2]. "Suffering" is a term that describes the feeling, bearing, and undergoing of pain, punishment, injury, loss or damage. Suffering is usually, but not always, associated with the consequences or results of evil. "Affliction" is a broad term that will also be used at times in this text because it can refer to both a state of undergoing suffering, as well as a cause of suffering.

Despite the presence of such dictionary definitions of evil and suffering, it should not be assumed that such definitions are without ambiguity. Evil and suffering, for example, contain an element of relativity and subjectivity (though this is not to say that there are no moral absolutes from a religious perspective). What is evil for one person may be good for another. For example, killing and destruction in the course of a war would obviously be felt as evil by its victims, but considered necessary and even good by the aggressors. On a more mundane level, the slaughtering of a cow to enable gluttons to enjoy its steak is obviously a joyous occasion for all but the cow. Evil and suffering are also relative with respect to time since there can be short-term evil or suffering for the purpose of a longer term benefit, or the opposite case of short-term joy with long-term suffering. For instance, a doctor's injecting a vaccine in a patient causes short-term pain and suffering but overall relief and well-being in the long-run. Snorting cocaine can provide a short-term "high" but spells long-term disaster. Thus, some regard "good" and "evil" to be merely subjective assessments of whether or not we consider something beneficial or not.

Furthermore, from a metaphysical standpoint, everything other than God must ultimately be considered imperfect, and in a certain sense, "evil". There is only one being that is Perfectly Good and that being is God. If evil is understood to include imperfection, then everything other than God cannot but be evil. To say that God should not have created beings who can err or sin is to say that God should not have created human beings. Some have gone further by equating evil with non-being or non-existence. Thus, if God is considered Pure Being and evil as non-Being, then a good man can be said to be more "real" or display greater Being than a "bad" man. In this sense, some have characterized evil as a lack of goodness, rather than a positive quality in itself.

3.2 The View of Logic

Before further examining the question of evil from a theistic or Islamic perspective, let us first approach it from a purely logical point of view.

Earlier, the problem was stated as an apparent conflict between two statements:

(1) God is an Infinitely Good, Infinitely Powerful Being, and
(2) Evil exists in the world.

Upon closer examination of these statements, however, it will be seen that there is absolutely no conflict from a logical standpoint. In fact, the idea that evil and suffering present an unanswerable challenge to believers is a myth that has been widely propagated by skeptics.

Firstly, if it can be shown that an Infinitely Good Being may allow some form of what we call "evil" for the purpose of achieving a greater good, then there is no logical contradiction. It is not at all logically necessary that an Infinitely Good and Powerful God must prevent every imaginable kind of evil, for it could be that He may allow some form of evil and suffering for the higher order good that can emerge.

> ...*if it can be shown that an Infinitely Good Being may allow some form of what we call "evil" for the purpose of achieving a greater good, then there is no logical contradiction.*

Secondly, the nature of omnipotence, or infinite power, is often misunderstood. Omnipotence encompasses not only unlimited power to act but also unlimited power to determine *what powers to act things or creations should have* (see Section 3.6). The prominent atheist, J.L. Mackie, has called these powers first—and second-order omnipotence. There is no contradiction between an omnipotent God and the granting of limited free will or power to choose to human beings. Human beings are free in the sense that God *does not choose* to control their choosing, not that He *cannot* control their choosing. Even Mackie admits that "a god might have both first—and second-order omnipotence, so long as he did not exercise his second-order power in such a way as to limit his first-order power."[3]

> *Human beings are free in the sense that God does not choose to control their choosing, not that He cannot control their choosing.*

Furthermore, the omnipotence of God does not include the power to do what is logically impossible. Thus, as Richard Swinburne states, God cannot "make the universe exist and not exist at the same time, make 2 + 2 to equal 5, make a shape square and round at the same time, or change the past."[4] Such statements do not limit the power of God in any way, for they do not make any sense and are logically contradictory. This implies that if God has created free beings with the ability to choose between right and wrong, then it is logically impossible to expect the absence of wrongful choices. Thus, it is the absence of disobedience and evil which would actually be in contradiction with the presence of free human beings.

Overall, then, there is no logical contradiction in the so-called "problem of evil". Philosophers have also confessed as much. In Stump and Murray's, *Philosophy of Religion: The Big Questions,* we have the following admission:

> The logical problem of evil has been severely criticized in recent years and is regarded in the contemporary literature on the subject as largely discredited. In brief, the problem with this argument is that it assumes something false. Specifically, it assumes that a good being would prevent every evil it can under any circumstances... Thus, at best, the logical problem of evil shows us that if God exists, the only evil that exists is evil for which there is some good reason.[5]

To satisfy the reader, however, it does remain to be shown what good reason there could be for God allowing some form of evil and suffering. This concept will be examined extensively in this chapter, while also addressing the important question of the source of evil (man, God or Satan?), as well as the question of free will versus pre-determinism.

Any serious theistic analysis of why there is evil must begin by analyzing the question in light of the overall purpose of creation.

3.3 The Purpose of Mankind in Relation to Evil

The Islamic perspective on the purpose of creation is very clear and unequivocal, though it finds expression in a number of equally valid levels. God has stated the purpose of bestowing the gift of existence in the Qur'an as follows:

> I have created jinns and mankind only that they may serve Me. (51:56)

The servanthood referred to is something which is intended for the benefit of man, not the Creator, for He is beyond any needs.[6] Serving God means submitting to His Will. God has created the world with laws that govern not only the natural world, but also the social order of mankind. When man attempts to transgress the boundaries of these laws, he is met with what he perceives as evil, pain, suffering and affliction. Hence, God wills that our will conform with His will for our own benefit and to avoid evil, pain and suffering (see Section 3.4).

The purpose of creating mankind, when contrasted with other forms of creation, extends beyond servanthood and obedience, however. The person that truly fulfills his or her purpose is the one who becomes God's "vicegerent on earth". All of creation worships and glorifies God[7], but it is only man who can be the vicegerent or representative of God. As the Qur'an states,

> Behold, your Lord said to the angels, 'I will create a vicegerent on earth'...(2:30)

The person that truly fulfills his or her purpose is the one who becomes God's "vicegerent on earth".

Man alone is capable of knowing Reality of his own accord, thereby transcending his own earthly and contingent nature. When man realizes his spiritual essence, he has the potential to stand at the apex of creation; when he focuses only on his corporeal, worldly aspect, he can drop to the lowest of low.[8] The immense trust bestowed upon man to be His vicegerent could not be borne by any other creature:

> We offered the Trust to the heavens and the earth and the mountains, but they drew back from bearing it and feared to do so. It is man who bore it… (33:72)

Another way to envision the purpose of creation is in terms of a reflection of Divine Attributes. As noted earlier, " God created man according to His form."[9] The Qur'an also states, "He taught Adam the names, all of them…" (2:31), with " the names" referring to the Divine Names or Attributes, from which all things in engendered existence come into being. Hence, from this angle, the purpose of creation can be said to reflect Divinity and Being to the best of our abilities. In other words, by serving and obeying God we become His vicegerent on earth, and thereby reflect Divinity and partake in Being.

One of the great gifts bestowed upon human beings that distinguishes them from the rest of creation is that of free will. Free will is the ability to voluntarily choose the course of one's actions, whether towards the good or bad, the acceptance or rejection of God's commandments. According to the Qur'an, "Surely We have shown him the way — he may be grateful or ungrateful" (76:3).

Disobedience is a choice that can be enacted but with dire consequences. Evil stems from choosing to disobey God, as will be discussed in more detail in Section 3.6. The angels were aware of this and, thus, it is said in the Qur'an,

> Behold, your Lord said to the angels, 'I will create a vicegerent on earth.' They said, 'Will you place therein one who will make mischief therein and shed blood- while we do celebrate Thy praises and glorify Thy Holy Name?' He said, 'I know what you know not.' (2:30)

Here, God does not deny the statement of the angels, but reminds them of His Infinite Knowledge. Given that God is All-Powerful and that the purpose of creation is to obey Him, why didn't He create everyone without the possibility of any disobedience or evil? The answer has already been alluded to in that, if this were the case, the world would be absent of any free agents and would be full of, in effect, robots or automatons. In other words, if there were no possibility of evil, there would be no human beings and there might only be plants, animals and rocks. It can, therefore, be said that God has mindfully chosen to create a world that includes the possibility of free will, knowing that this necessitates the possibility of evil.

Thus, in order to begin to answer the question of evil we must answer the question of why we have been granted free will. Knowing that man would "make mischief therein and shed blood", God nonetheless asked all the angels to bow before Adam.[10] As Mawlana Jalaluddin Rumi beautifully asked, "How could God's Justice and Gentleness allow a rose to prostrate itself before a thorn?"[11] The fact that God asked the angels, who are perfect and infallible in their obedience to God, to bow to Adam indicates the exalted status of human beings above angels in the overall hierarchy of creation.[12]

Free will is one of the secrets behind this exalted status. There are at least two fundamental reasons in understanding why we have been granted free will. Firstly, it can be reasoned that "achieved virtue" is superior to "conferred virtue". Judging from the bowing of the angels before Adam, it can be inferred that it is more beloved in the eyes of God that a being willfully chooses to obey God over disobedience, as compared to obeying God with no choice in the matter. This is analogous to parents who gain greater pleasure and satisfaction when their offspring choose to obey them based on their own reflection and judgment, as opposed to obeying them simply because they are forced into doing so. This concept is confirmed by Prophet Muhammad (SAW) as he has said, "On the Day of resurrection, nothing will be greater than the children of Adam. Someone said, 'O Messenger of God! Not even the angels? He replied, 'Not even the angels. They are compelled like the sun and moon.'"[13] Man does by choice what the rest of creation has no choice over. It is the process of this struggle to use our abilities of reflection, reasoning and intuition to choose good over evil that warrants the love and reward from God. For all the ups and downs of life, the pain and joys, the struggles and the achievements, it is only the demented who would want to relinquish the gift of being human to be a rock, tree or goat.

Man does by choice what the rest of creation has no choice over.

Secondly, if man is truly created in God's image and his purpose includes the striving to reflect Divine attributes in his own character and life, then some form of free will must be an attribute of his very nature. God chose to give us a small taste of freedom and power that derives from His Divine Will and Power. After all, it is only man whose spirit has been "blown" into from the Divine Spirit. It is only man who has been taught "the Names" by God, and it is only man who has been said by Prophet Muhammad (SAW) to be created in God's image, and not animals, plants or planets (though all creation contains the signature of the Creator).

> *God chose to give us a small taste of freedom and power that derives from His Divine Will and Power.*

The relationship between free will and evil is taken up further in Section 3.6. In the meantime, let us take a deeper look at the role of affliction in the life of man.

3.4 Lessons of Affliction

All of us have experienced or seen at least some form of evil and suffering in the world.

There is no doubt that wicked and vile acts of murder, rape, assault, crime, fraud, and deception abound to the extent that they are almost taken for granted. There are also "natural" events or catastrophes such as earthquakes, floods, tornadoes and accidents that undoubtedly take their toll on the lives of many and can represent some of the most difficult times we will ever face on this earth. Whether in our control or out of control, we experience these events as suffering, pain, hardship, misfortune and injustice. God Himself confirms in the Qur'an that "Verily We have created man in the embrace of hardship" (90:4).

Regardless of whether we consider the root of such suffering to be man, Satan or even God as some claim (see Section 3.5), suffering results in a number of distinct effects. Some of these effects are perceived as negative and some positive. While skeptics focus on the negative and claim that evil and suffering are simply an ugly fact of life and that complete justice is impossible, the believer or theist can see the bigger picture and provide an overall explanation for the role of such affliction.

Although we cannot possibly penetrate the ultimate depths of all phenomena by accessing the complex web of precise causes of events and their intertwined relationships, God has given us the ability to act wisely using our faculties of reason and intuition and to recognize the authority of His commandments and laws. To a limited extent, God has given us the ability to "see through" events and "read between the lines" in order to understand possible purposes and meanings behind them. The passage of time is a creation of God that prevents everything from happening at once. Yet, if it were possible to view our whole lives all at once, as if in a single movie, we would realize the plot behind every scene and the wisdom behind every perception of chaos. While the natural tendency is to focus only on the negative aspects, let us expand on some of the positives that can emerge from what we perceive as affliction.

> ...*if it were possible to view our whole lives all at once, as if in a single movie, we would realize the plot behind every scene and the wisdom behind every perception of chaos.*

1. Affliction can serve to redirect the course of our actions back to "The Straight Path" of God. God has created the world with precise laws that govern not only the natural world, but also the social and moral order of man. In other words, the principle of causality applies to all of the natural, social and moral realms. When we cross the boundaries of these laws, we experience the consequences. If someone desires to jump off a cliff, gravity will not suddenly cease to prevent him from falling. Similarly, when someone chooses to act out of greed, arrogance, hatred or the like, suffering or retaliation will prevail, whether it is immediate, later on in life, or after death, and *whether we like it or not*. Such are the laws that have been decreed by God for our own sake. As Fadhlalla Haeri has said, "God does not sit with a telescope saying: 'Now I am going to let this leaf fall.' Nor equally does He say:

'I am going to afflict that fellow, he deserves it.' God is beyond time. You and I are in time."[14]

The Qur'an states very clearly that "The Divine norm is immutable and unchanging" (33:62).

God's laws have been laid out in the message of the Divine scriptures and Prophets, though they can also be partially known empirically with the passage of time. The limited freedom we have been granted is intended to allow us to "discover", of our own accord, the boundaries of this very freedom and the boundaries of the world we are part of. We are programmed to undergo affliction and punishment whenever we cross these boundaries. There are a number of examples in the Qur'an that demonstrate the consequences of willful disobedience:

> Whoever does the smallest good deed shall experience the result of it, and whoever does the slightest evil deed shall experience the result of it. (99:7-8)

> Nor was your Lord the one to destroy a population until He had sent to its center a Messenger, rehearsing to them Our signs: nor do We destroy a population except when its members become oppressive. (28:59)

> As for Thamud, We showed them the right way, but they chose error above guidance, so there overtook them the scourge of an abasing chastisement for what they earned. (41:17)

> If the people of the towns had but believed and acted with piety, We should indeed have opened out to them all heavenly and earthly blessings, but since they rejected the truth, We punished them for their misdeeds. (7:96)

No one normally desires to undergo repeated affliction and punishment. Punishment and suffering often lead us to question our actions and return us to the obedience of God. Nor should such punishment be equated or confused with the evil perpetrated by man. God does not punish just for the sake of punishing, but as a consequence of our own deeds. It is the failure to recognize the consequences of our actions, the misconception that it is "we who are in charge", and the forgetting of the sovereignty of the Lord that cause us to err. As Shaykh Haeri states, "It is within God's wish that man will transgress in order that he might discover the meaning of transgression and remember that God has created him with the capacity of suffering the consequences of transgression."[15] It is the true servants of God who recognize the boundaries within which we operate, and willfully choose to stay within those very boundaries. Only then does the overall condition of a people change:

> "Because Allah will never change the Grace which He has bestowed upon a people until they change what is within themselves..." (8:53).

The Qur'an also exposes those who only believe when it is in their interests to do so and lose their faith upon the slightest tribulation:

> There are among men some who obey Allah, as it were, on the verge: if good befalls them, they are well content therewith; but, if a trial comes to them, they turn on their faces losing both this world and the Hereafter—that is a clear loss for all to see! (22:11)

There are also specific instances where the Divine Order is in effect, but which we tend to perceive as "cruel" or "unjust" or simply fail to understand. Thus, sometimes what we perceive as "bad" is actually "good" and what is perceived as "good" can actually be "bad". The encounter between Moses (AS) and Khidr[16] (AS) described in the Qur'an in Surah Kahf (verses 60-82), exemplifies this Divine teaching. The teachings begin with an incident where Khidr (AS) cuts a hole in a boat, seemingly without reason, belonging to some honest workers or traders; the second incident involves the killing of a young man who Moses (AS) perceives to be innocent; and the third tells of some inhabitants of a town who refuse to offer any food or hospitality to Khidr (AS) and Moses (AS), and yet Khidr (AS) helps the townsfolk by rebuilding and erecting a certain wall that was on the verge of collapse.

Moses (AS) expresses his failure to understand Khidr's actions, after which Khidr (AS) proceeds to explain the Divine purpose behind each action he was instructed to carry out. The first action was performed because there was an oppressive king who was unjustly seizing boats in the area where the men were wishing to go towards. The simple act of making the boat unseaworthy saved it from seizure. The second act of murder was carried out, not because Khidr disliked him, but because the young man was a constant source of obstinate rebellion and ingratitude towards his pious parents and God desired to "give them in exchange a son better in purity of conduct and closer in affection."[17] The last act of rebuilding the wall for their inhospitable hosts was intended to benefit two righteous youths who were orphans. Had the wall fallen, the other townsfolk would have looted the treasure that was buried beneath the wall by the pious father of the orphans. He had hidden it with the intent that his children would inherit the treasure when they had grown up. Thus, these incidents are related in the Qur'an to explain the Divine Order and purpose that permeates "behind the scenes" and "such is the interpretation of that which you were unable to hold patience."[18]

Nor are such examples merely "stories from the past" that are inapplicable to the present day. God's sovereignty and control are manifested in daily happenings across the world whether we realize it or not. The famous rock star of the 1960's and 70's, Cat Stevens, now known as Yusuf Islam, described a key incident before his conversion to Islam as follows: "After a year of financial success and high living, I became very ill. I contracted T.B. (tuberculosis) and had to be hospitalized. It was then that I started to think; what is going to happen to me? Am I just a body? Is my goal in life merely to satisfy this body? *I realized this calamity was a blessing given to me by God* and a chance to open my eyes, to learn 'Why I am here, Why I am in bed.' I started looking for some of the answers." Such was the role of the severe illness in precipitating various metaphysical thought processes and seeking purpose in life.

Surely, most readers will also be able to recall incidents in their own lives or the lives of others that demonstrate the long-term corrective benefit that is often hidden in short-term affliction. As Imam Ja'far As-Sadiq has noted, "It is God Almighty Who is the source of reliance and toward Whom men look with hope when all doors are closed."[19] Some form of good or overall purpose eventually emerges from every incident of suffering, whether we realize it or not, as indicated in the following verse:

> So, verily, with every difficulty there is relief. Verily, with every difficulty there is relief. (94:5-6)

This leads us to another benefit that can emerge from affliction.

2. *Affliction serves to test our faith and build strength of character.* It is often taken for granted that the virtues of patience, forbearance, empathy, kindness, benevolence, heroism, maturity and piety cannot be realized without experiencing some form of hardship, suffering or misfortune. As Helen Keller stated, "Although the world is full of suffering, it is full also of the overcoming of it." The true value of affliction can only be realized by pondering its absence. How can those who only experience joy after joy and bliss upon bliss be considered among those of genuine faith and elevated character? How can those who have never experienced affliction empathize with those who have suffered? Part of this testing of faith and character by affliction involves the reminding of our dependence on God. However independent we may think we are, it is only God who is completely independent. The Qur'an assures us that we will be tested:

> Do men think that they will be left alone on saying, 'We believe', and that they will not be tested? (29:2)

> Did you think that you would enter Heaven without Allah testing those of you who struggled (in His cause) and remained steadfast? (3:142)

> We shall test you with fear, hunger, the loss of wealth and possessions, death, and the loss of the fruits of your toil. Give glad tidings to those who patiently persevere and who say when afflicted with calamity and pain, 'We are from God and to Him we return on our path to perfection,'—that it is they who receive kindness and mercy from their Lord together with their suffering, and they it is who are truly guided. (2:155-157)

> *How can those who only experience joy after joy and bliss upon bliss be considered among those of genuine faith and elevated character?*

Thus, it is certain that everyone, whether among the most pious or most sinful, will be tested with various trials and tribulations. It is not just the wicked and sinful who will be afflicted as some presume. The test refers to whether we will pass by submitting to and enduring His will or fail by losing all faith and not acknowledging the Divine purpose and wisdom behind all that occurs. For those who patiently endure and persevere through such affliction, there is an immense reward from God that awaits them:

> ... submit then your wills to Him and *give the good news to those* who humble themselves—to those whose hearts when Allah is mentioned are filled with fear, *who show patient perseverance over their afflictions,* are steadfast with prayer, and spend (in charity) out of what We have bestowed upon them. (22:35)

> For Muslim men and women—for believing men and women, for devout men and women, for true men and women, *for men and women who are patient and steadfast,* for men and women who humble themselves, for men and women who give in charity, for men and women who fast, for men and women who guard their chastity, and for men and women who engage much in Allah's praise—*for them has Allah prepared forgiveness and immense reward.* (33:35)

> ... and Allah loves those who are patient and steadfast. (3:146)

For all the pain and suffering that ordinary people go through, it is actually the Prophets and Messengers of God who have endured the most affliction. Prophet Muhammad (SAW), for example, faced a multitude of setbacks in his life that would have devastated any ordinary mortal. His father died before his birth, his mother died at age six, his first wife Khadija died before him, all but one of his children died before him, not to mention the years of persecution and oppression at the hands of the Meccan pagans and polytheists, to name but a few tests. In one particular incident in the year 619 (C.E.), the Prophet (SAW) went alone on a trip to the town of Ta'if to propagate the message of God to the tribe of Banu Thaqif. He was met with such a rude rejection by the chieftains and townsfolk that upon returning, he was jeered, harassed and pelted with stones to the point that he bled from numerous wounds. Rather than give up, lose faith, and seek revenge, he reaffirmed his unwavering faith in Allah and prayed for His help and protection. Allah so loved his supplication that He immediately sent an angel to his aid. The angel informed the Prophet (SAW) that he could cause the mountains surrounding Ta'if to collide with each other and crush all its inhabitants as punishment if he so desired, but the Prophet was to do nothing of the sort, as he instead, prayed for them as follows: "Even if these people do not accept Islam, I do hope from Allah that there will be persons from among their progeny who would worship Allah and serve His cause."[20] Such is the magnanimity of his character that he not only patiently endured ridicule and injury from all sides, but also prayed for the betterment of the very people who inflicted his wounds.

> *For all the pain and suffering that ordinary people go through, it is actually the Prophets and Messengers of God who have endured the most affliction.*

The well-known case of the immense faith of Abraham (AS) and his son also serves as a lesson that stands for all times. As told in the Qur'an (37:99–111), Prophet Abraham (AS) sees in a vision that he is commanded by God to sacrifice his only son at the time, Ishmael (AS)21. Both of them submit their wills to God and at the moment of the sacrifice, God substitutes a ram in place of Ishmael (AS) out of His Mercy. Both Abraham and Ishmael (AS) clearly passed the test by demonstrating their extraordinary faith, patience and perseverance in a way that is unimaginable to most and which remains an extraordinary example for mankind to this day.[22] The extent of the afflictions and trials endured by the Prophets and Messengers of God is such that no ordinary person can complain of having suffered or been tested more than them.

After the passing of Prophet Muhammad (SAW), the most famous affliction for Muslims involved the martyrdom of his grandson, Imam Husayn. Imam Husayn was invested with extraordinary piety and charisma, and vociferously denounced the tyranny and oppression of the Umayyad pretender, Yazid. Rather than capitulate to the dictates of the corrupt Yazid, he fearlessly faced the attack of his immense military forces at the field of Karbala (in present-day Iraq). Grossly outnumbered, Imam Husayn nevertheless stood his ground on matter of principle and thus, was eventually brutally cut down along with most of his family and followers, including his infant son. He is easily the most revered martyr in Islamic history. Despite the gruesome scene at Karbala, Imam Husayn realized the immense importance of standing by Islamic principles to set an example for all ages. We have witnessed the reverence for standing by Divine principles to this day, as exemplified in the brave resistances against oppression of the peoples of Afghanistan, Chechnya, Kashmir, Lebanon and Palestine. As Mawlana Muhammad Ali Jawhar once eloquently said, "With every Karbala, Islam is granted life anew."

Besides the elevated character that can emerge from affliction, God has revealed yet another secret in the way that He deals with creation. This secret is based on the differing needs of people as the following *hadith qudsi* indicates:

> And there are amongst My believing bondsmen those whose belief will not be improved except by poverty and if I enrich them it will be ruined. And there are amongst My believing bondsmen those whose belief will not be improved except by enriching them and if I impoverish them it will be ruined. And there are amongst My believing bondsmen those whose belief will not be improved except by sickness and if I made their bodies healthy it would have corrupted them. And there are amongst My believing bondsmen those whose belief will not be improved except by good health and if I give them sickness it will cause them corruption. And I organize their affairs by My knowledge of what is in their hearts for I am the All-Knowing.[23]

Given that God is All-Knowing and we are not, there will inevitably arise circumstances which we may perceive to be "evil" or "bad", yet are actually beneficial, and vice-versa, as determined by God. Take the example of wealth.

While many assume wealth to be proportional to happiness and are preoccupied with the rat-race to achieve "the next million", it often happens that such large sums of wealth become a source of misery rather than happiness. The exorbitantly rich are often subject to problems of high stress, lack of family cohesiveness, deterioration of social relationships, and lack of inner peace. Islam, thus, emphasizes the need to "purify"[24] one's wealth by generously giving to those in need. Without responsible handling of the gifts bestowed by God, such gifts can become the source of affliction, rather than joy. After all, it is God who is the source of our wealth, not ourselves.

The Qur'an also makes this principle clear using another example, that of fighting for a just cause:

> "Fighting is sometimes prescribed upon you, and you dislike it. But it is possible that you dislike a thing which is good for you, and that you love a thing which is bad for you—but Allah knows and you know not." (2:216)

Thus, such forms of affliction should not be viewed only as misfortune or pointless suffering, but instead, as opportunities to strengthen our faith and character and realize our dependence on God. Only then will we realize that the experience of hardship is ultimately nothing but mercy from our Lord. This leads us to another benefit that can emerge from affliction.

3. Affliction is often a necessary means to experience its opposite feelings of joy and achievement. This idea is based on the law of opposites. God has created the world based on an opposition or duality between, for example, good and bad, joy and sorrow, health and sickness, wealth and poverty, knowledge and ignorance, justice and injustice, and life and death. As the Qur'an states,

> And of everything We have created pairs... (51:49)

> So, verily, with every difficulty there is relief. Verily, with every difficulty there is relief. (94:5-6)

It is very difficult to imagine joy without affliction. How can one appreciate health without sickness? In fact, it can be argued that the knowledge and experience of one characteristic is incomplete without knowledge and experience of its opposite. Ancient Taoist philosophy summarizes this opposition in nature in terms of "yin" and "yang".[25] Each part is necessary to understand the unity of the whole. We have been created to experience these opposites, and in doing so, veer towards that which leads us to the path of felicity in this life and the next.

The law of opposites is so imbedded in our nature that many of us even prefer and desire to experience some form of affliction along our path to joy and achievement. Any mountain climber will admit of no elation in reaching a mountain summit without arduous effort, struggle and pitfalls along the way. No sports team wants to be freely granted a championship without vigorous training and the challenges thrown at them by the opposition. No corporate executive wants to be granted the title of chief executive officer without the ability to experience the ups and downs of "climbing the ladder" and proving one's qualifications. The fact is that human beings often thrive on challenges which knowingly encompass trials, tribulations, pain, and suffering.

> *The fact is that human beings often thrive on challenges which knowingly encompass trials, tribulations, pain, and suffering.*

The source of the overall law of opposition lies in the very nature of God. As discussed in Chapter 1, the Arabic word for God, Allah, represents the unification and summary of all Divine attributes. These attributes include opposites, such as the First and the Last, the Manifest and the Non-manifest, the Giver of Life and the Giver of Death, the Forgiver and the Avenger, the Abaser and the Exalter, and so on. Another way to perceive the Divine attributes is in terms of the unification of transcendent and immanent qualities. Abu Said Al-Kharraz was once asked, "Through what have you known God?" He answered, "through the fact that He brings opposites together." Then he recited the following verse: "He is the First and the Last, the Manifest and the Non-manifest" (57:3).[26]

As man is created "upon His image"[27], it is reasonable to expect that he too must reflect this opposition within his nature. The spiritual path is based on this "assuming the character traits of God", *at-takhalluq bi akhlaq* Allah[28], in the proper balance. Manifesting the attributes of transcendence, such as the Magnificent *(Al-Mutakabbir)*, the Overwhelming *(Al-Qahhar)* or the All-High *(Al-'Ali)* without manifesting the attributes of mercy will result in arrogance. Excessive justice without generosity can result in tyranny, while excessive forgiveness without justice can lead to inequity. Transcendence for man can, in one sense, refer to the transcendence of his spiritual essence beyond his earthly presence, while immanence can reflect his material closeness to the world.

Thus, we see that there is a metaphysical necessity to the existence of opposites, including good and evil, since there is Divine purpose in the experiencing of them.

Overall, from the previous discussion we have noted that the affliction of human beings can be seen in either a negative or positive light, depending on our reaction to it. For those who do not reflect and choose only to focus on the negative, affliction and suffering can seem endless and pointless. For those who reflect and realize the purpose of creation and patiently persevere, affliction and suffering stem from the Mercy and Justice of God and are actually intended to benefit us both in this life and the next. The greater purpose of creating human beings with free will to consciously recognize our relationship to the Creator is indeed a worthwhile goal. In simple terms, conforming of the human will to the Divine Will results in the dissolution of the very concept of suffering. It is related by Imam Ja'far As-Sadiq that the Prophet (SAW) once laughed so that his teeth showed, and he said,

> Do you not ask me what causes me to laugh? They said: 'Yes, O Prophet of Allah.' He said, 'I am surprised with the Muslim, for there can be no decree that Allah makes upon him without a good end to his affairs.'[29]

> *...conforming of the human will to the Divine Will results in the dissolution of the very concept of suffering.*

3.5 With Justice for All

The concept of justice involves what is fair, equitable and rightly due to each individual. We noted earlier that in all events there is, indeed, a greater purpose "working behind the scenes" designed to help us progress along the spiritual axis back to God, whether we realize it or not. Ultimately, there is complete justice for all. No man-made laws, constitutions, supreme courts or justice systems can provide such justice– it is only God who can do so. Man-made justice is but a shadow of Divine Justice. Thus, the Qur'an says, "Is not Allah the best of all Judges?" (95:8).

God, nonetheless, commands us to strive to establish and spread justice in the world to the best of our abilities and loves those who do so:

> *Verily Allah commands justice, the doing of good, and liberality to kith and kin, and He forbids all shameful deeds, injustice and rebellion.* He instructs you that you may receive admonition. (16:90)

> O you who believe! *Be upright for Allah as witnesses to justice and let not the hatred of others incite you to act unjustly. Be just—that is nearer to piety* and be mindful of Allah, for surely Allah is well-aware of all that you do. (5:8)

> … *Surely Allah loves those who are just.* (49:9)

We previously noted the significance of the fact that God is not subject to time while we are "in" time. As human beings, we inevitably tend to judge the notions of justice and injustice, and good and evil, against the constraints of time. The longer the time scale that is considered, the greater the justice and good that is deciphered. The more the role of man is viewed against the backdrop of the continuum of our initial "existence" in the Mind of God, our earthly existence, and our life in the Hereafter, the more the question of evil, suffering and injustice melts away. The more one progresses from the material to the spiritual, the more one partakes of the timelessness of existence. The following hadith beautifully illustrates this concept:

Anas Ibn Malik narrates that the messenger of Allah (SAW) said: "On the Day of Judgment, the most fortunate of the people of the world meant for hell will be brought forward and exposed for an instant to the Fire. Then it shall be asked of him, 'O son of Adam! Did you see any good at all, did you experience any ease at all (while alive)? He will reply, 'I swear O Lord, No' (I did not). The most unfortunate of the people of the world meant for Paradise will be brought forward and exposed for an instant to the Garden. Then it shall be asked of him, 'O son of Adam! Did you see any misfortune at all, did you experience any hardship at all (while alive)? He will reply, 'No O Lord, I swear I did not experience any misfortune at all and I saw no hardship at all'.[30]

> *The more the role of man is viewed against the backdrop of the continuum of our initial "existence" in the Mind of God, our earthly existence, and our life in the Hereafter, the more the question of evil, suffering and injustice melts away. The more one progresses from the material to the spiritual, the more one partakes of the timelessness of existence.*

This striking passage vividly illustrates the element of relativity that inevitably accompanies our perceptions of both joy and suffering. Any experience of "good" and "bad" in this life pales in comparison to that which will be experienced in the Hereafter. This concept should not be surprising when we consider that our earthly life is but a fleeting moment in comparison to the eternal life to come. As the Prophet (SAW) stated, "Be in the world as though you were a stranger or a wayfarer."[31] This fact must always be remembered when considering any evil or suffering that we experience: "Nay, you prefer the life of this world; but the Hereafter is better and more enduring" (87:16-17).

Understanding the role of the Hereafter is paramount to understanding the existence of evil and suffering and is another reason why atheists and agnostics fail to comprehend such issues. While elements of justice are surely manifested in this world, complete and final justice will not be established until all souls are resurrected in the final court of the Day of Judgment. There are two key implications of this Divine justice in the Hereafter that relate to our earthly existence. First of all, it provides one of the meanings, motivations and incentives behind moral striving. Why should one work toward moral perfection if there isn't going to be justice anyway? Secondly, temporary suffering and pain are not pointless if there is a greater purpose working to help us in this life and/or a greater reward that awaits us in the afterlife.

But what about the objections of skeptics that even if there is, generally, a greater purpose at work, are there not instances of "gratuitous evil" or incidents of suffering that simply cannot be explained or justified? In this regard, one of the most commonly cited examples, as demonstrated by the narrative from The *Brothers Karamazov* at the opening of this chapter, is that of the suffering of innocent children or the death of babies that defies justification. As stated at the outset of the chapter, there is no effort on our part to minimize or deny the suffering that can ensue from such events. We must never accept such suffering without combating it to the best of our abilities. However, here too, our judgments are often based on short-sightedness and our own immediate desires.

Two types of suffering of children can be considered: one due to human moral evil and the other due to so-called "natural causes". The first case, which is by far the most common, is a result of free choices made in opposition to the Divine will (see Section 3.6). A simple example is the economic sanctions imposed on a people for political ends that can result in large-scale starvation and disease among children. The disobedience and evil wrought by man cannot be confused with the overall purpose desired by God for him. Here, the overall purpose of creation, inclusive of the granting of free will, must be weighed against the necessary disobedience that this entails.

What about the "natural" death of innocent children that cannot be directly associated with the acts of man? Death, which is considered the ultimate evil or finality by atheists is considered nothing of the sort by Muslims, or for that matter Christians or Jews. There is nothing inherently wrong with death, for it only represents a transition from the ephemeral life of this earth to the eternal life of the Hereafter. Moreover, in Islam, all children who pass away before puberty are considered to be immediate inhabitants of Paradise. A number of sayings of Prophet Muhammad (SAW) indicate that parents who patiently endure the loss of their children are also granted Paradise and will be able to meet their children there. There are a number of cases where parents who have lost a child or children, have also revealed a heightened sensitivity to the suffering of others and been prompted to action to relieve the suffering of others, such as adopting orphans. Who are we to judge the potential meanings behind events?

> ...in Islam, all children who pass away before puberty are considered to be immediate inhabitants of Paradise ... parents who patiently endure the loss of their children are also granted Paradise and will be able to meet their children there.

Another frequently-cited example of perceived injustice lies in the questioning of differences between people. Undoubtedly, there are inherent differences among people, such as in their place of origin, skin color, body type, eyes, beauty, etc. There are also material and economic differences that evolve over the course of our lives. Some are rich, some are poor; some are famous, some are inconspicuous; some are kings, and some are paupers. As Shaykh Haeri states,

> If we imagine the world to be a giant cooking pot in which we are all being cooked at varying speeds, according to our individual states, we will discover that each one of us is given certain limitations, freedoms and possibilities for action suitable to our specific situation. A king has a country at his command, while a blind man, without legs, has as his horizon a circle with a two foot radius around him. Ultimately, if they progress spiritually, they will make the same discovery. The king will find out that nothing in this world will satisfy him and that true satisfaction can only come from inner knowledge, as will the blind man.[32]

Thus, here again perceptions of injustice disappear when viewed against the purpose of creation. We have been created not merely to recognize our differences, but also to realize our greatest commonality—the ability to discover and submit to God. All else pales in comparison to this feature. The

Qur'an states that Allah judges between people based only upon one ultimate, all-encompassing criterion—that of *taqwa*, or what has been translated as God-consciousness or piety:

> O mankind! We created you from a single pair of a male and a female, and made you into nations and tribes, that you may know each other. *Verily, the most honored of you in the sight of Allah is the most pious of you...* (49:13)
>
> *We have been created not merely to recognize our differences, but also to realize our greatest commonality – the ability to discover and submit to God.*

It is also essential to remember that imbedded within God's Justice is His Mercy, and imbedded within His Mercy is His Justice. God does not sit back and throw someone into hell for having one greater bad deed than good deed as some envision. Prophet Muhammad (SAW) stated in a famous saying that Allah has said, "My Mercy prevails over My Wrath."[33] Although a full discussion of the forgiveness and mercy of God is beyond the scope of this work, the relevant point to consider here is its relation to His Justice.

A number of atheists and agnostics have questioned why God has made it so "difficult" for us to obey Him and why we do not have a greater propensity towards good. Regardless of whether we consider man to have a greater tendency to good or evil, God is fully aware of the frailty and limitations with which He has created man. Just as God was fully aware that Adam would disobey Him, He also gave him the opportunity to seek forgiveness, and completely forgave him.[34] Although the Divine Will challenges man to enjoin good and shun evil, Divine Mercy and Forgiveness tilts the balance in favor of man as long as we choose to seek forgiveness:

> ...Unless he repents, believes and works righteous deeds, *for Allah will change the evil of such persons into good,* and Allah is Most Forgiving, Most Merciful. (25:70)

> That is the command of Allah, which He has sent down to you: and *unto everyone who is conscious of God will He pardon his bad deeds, and will enlarge his reward.* (65:5)

> If any does good, the reward to him is *better* than His deed; but if any does evil, the doers of evil are only punished (to the extent) of their deeds. (28:84)

> *Although the Divine Will challenges man to enjoin good and shun evil, Divine Mercy and Forgiveness tilts the balance in favor of man...*

The following *hadith qudsi* narrated by the Prophet is also indicative of the magnitude of God's forgiveness. In it, he says that Allah (SWT) Almighty has said,

O son of Adam, so long as you call upon Me and ask of Me, I shall forgive you for what you have done and I shall not mind. O son of Adam, were your sins to reach the clouds of the sky and were you to ask forgiveness of Me, I would forgive you. O son of Adam, were you to come to Me with sins nearly as great as the earth and were you then to face Me, ascribing no partner to Me, I would bring you forgiveness nearly as great as it.[35]

In another *hadith qudsi*, Allah (SWT) says the following:

> There shall come out of hell-fire he who has said, 'there is no god but Allah' and who has in his heart goodness weighing a barley-corn; then there shall come out of hell-fire he who has said, 'there is no god but Allah' and who has in his heart goodness weighing a grain of wheat; then there shall come out of hell-fire he who has said, 'there is no god but Allah' and who has in his heart goodness weighing an atom.[36]

Thus, the forgiveness of God is so immense that no one can claim that God will hold us accountable for something beyond our capability. This is reiterated in another verse: "On no soul does Allah place a burden greater than it can bear..." (2:286).

What could possibly be better or more merciful than God bestowing the gift of free will, showing us what is good and evil, and forgiving us even if we err, as long as we are sincere in seeking forgiveness from Him? It is, as the saying goes, "like having the cake and eating it too."

> *What could possibly be better or more merciful than God bestowing the gift of free will, showing us what is good and evil, and forgiving us even if we err, as long as we are sincere in seeking forgiveness from Him?*

Hence, the original objection of skeptics questioning why people do not have a greater tendency towards good is severely misplaced. Once again, their failing to understand evil and suffering is often rooted in arrogance, just as arrogance is often the source of denying the existence of God. As long as people persist in thinking they can use their own minds to judge and understand every single occurrence independent of God, such arguments will abound. Only when it is admitted that human knowledge is limited and Divine Knowledge is unlimited can there be any progress in our understanding.

3.6 Are My Actions Free or Determined?

In any discussion of evil and suffering the question of the source of actions, and therefore evil, inevitably arises. Skeptics charge that if God is truly All-Powerful and the source of all that is, then He is the source of our actions, and the source of evil- in effect, God has "determined" our evil. Proponents of free will consider man's disobedience to be the source of evil. Some follow a different route altogether and propose Satan to be the being that stands in opposition to God and is responsible for all evil. The Zoroastrians, for example, considered Ahriman to be the origin of evil and an equal rival to the origin of all good, Yazdan. What are we to make of all this confusion?

In beginning to answer this question from an Islamic point of view, it must first be realized that Islamic history has not been unanimous on this issue, though one will certainly find commonalities expressed therein. Before explaining the predominant Islamic view of this subject, let us briefly summarize some of the arguments of the proponents of each side of the issue.[37]

Determinism and Omnipotence

Some of the Qur'anic evidence used by the school of thought that emphasizes the determinism of man's actions and omnipotence of God is as follows:

> ...If some good befalls them, they say, 'This is from Allah.' But if evil, they say, 'This is from thee (O Prophet).' Say, all is from Allah.... (37:96)

> ...You (God) exalt who you please and You abase who you please, in Your hand is all good. Verily you have power over all things. (3:26)

> God controls whatever exists in the heavens and on the earth, and He has power over all things. (5:120)

> Nothing in the heavens or on earth can weaken God, for He is all-knowing and all-powerful. (35:44)

The extreme determinists claim that man's freedom is simply an illusion since it is actually God who is both One and All-Powerful and cannot have any partner, including man, in His Attributes. Part of this claim is the denial that matter can produce any secondary effects or have causation, as they consider all phenomena to be the direct, unmediated effect of God. Thus, the acts of human beings are said to be performed, but not created, by man. The obvious concern of the determinists is to uphold the supremacy of the Divine Will and Power without compromising it by admitting that man has some freedom and power in the matter. The main issue with this stance is the potential compromising of Divine Justice since man cannot be held accountable for his actions if he does not really cause them. The other problematic implication is that God is responsible for not only all good but all evil that occurs.

Free Will

Proponents of free will argue that to deny the free will of man is to deny the overall thrust of the whole Qur'an which repeatedly enjoins man toward virtue and the "Straight Path". The whole meaning of reward and punishment, and thereby justice, vanishes if mankind is not responsible for their actions. A few verses used from the Qur'an in this context are:

> Certainly you are accountable for what you do. (16:93)
>
> We have shown man the path of truth and the path of falsehood; he may choose either the path of guidance and offer the thanks, or choose the path of ingratitude. (76:3)
>
> Whoever does the smallest good deed shall experience the result of it, and whoever does the slightest evil deed shall experience the result of it. (99:7-8)
>
> Whoever works righteousness, man or woman, and has faith, surely to him we will give a new life, a life that is good and pure, and We will bestow on such their reward according to the best of their actions. (16:97)

While there is no denying the truth of these verses, extreme supporters of free will misinterpret them to hold that man enjoys completely independent freedom in choosing the direction of acts as well as in the enacting of them. Their concern is to maintain the sanctity of Divine Justice and the meaningfulness of reward and punishment, Heaven and Hell. However, in holding to the *complete* independence of man, they have compromised the omnipotence and supreme will of God.

The Middle Road

The Islamic view of the problem that is strongest maintains an intermediate position between the two extremes. Man is neither a helpless creature who is determined by fate or destiny to be good or bad, nor is he completely independent and free to do whatever he wills and whenever he wills. Although this intermediate view may seem convenient to some, it is not without solid grounding from the standpoint of reason as well as the view of the Qur'an and sayings of Prophet Muhammad (SAW). The blessed Prophet (SAW) has said, "He who alleges that Allah, the Exalted, orders evil and indecency has lied upon Allah and he who alleges that goodness and evil are beyond Allah's will has excluded Allah from His power. He who alleges that disobediences are devoid of the power of Allah has lied upon Allah and he who has lied upon Allah, Allah will make him enter the fire."[38]

How can such an intermediate position be maintained? It is first of the utmost importance to realize that the granting of free will to mankind does not compromise the omnipotence or will of God in any way. Omnipotence encompasses not only unlimited power to act, but also *unlimited power to determine what powers to act forms of creation should have*. Human beings are free in the sense that God does not choose to control their choosing, not that He *cannot* control their choosing—nor does this limit His power in any way.

Secondly, the power of choice granted to human beings is clearly a limited power. We do not have the choice to stop breathing, blinking, eating, sleeping, excreting or the like, nor should such acts be taken for granted, "…for if Allah willed, He could take away their hearing and seeing—for Allah has power over all things" (2:20). Nor do we have absolute power over other human beings or societal and environmental factors. Nor do we have any complete control over our birth or death. God can "pull the plug" or alter our circumstances at any time *He wills to do so*. This concept is reflected in the profound verse,

> But you shall not will except as Allah wills—The Cherisher of the Worlds. (81:29)

This verse is not deterministic in the sense that it means that human will is always equivalent to God's will; rather, it means that our will is limited and subservient to God's will.

Earlier, there were two fundamental reasons introduced in understanding why God has "chosen not to control our choosing". The first reason is because God has considered it superior to obey when given the choice versus no choice in the matter. This is the superiority of "achieved virtue" over "conferred virtue" discussed earlier. It is for this reason that man has been granted the highest status among all creation. Man, after all, does by choice what the rest of creation has no choice over. Secondly, given that "God created man in His own image"[39], He desired to give us a small taste of freedom and power that derives from His own Will and Power.

Having said that, it can now be understood why there is no contradiction between the verses of the Qur'an cited above under the headings of free will and determinism. The verses indicating the supreme transcendence of God's power, will, and knowledge do not conflict with the verses pointing to the granting of limited free will. It is not without reason that the Qur'an clearly points to the perfection of His attributes as well as the consequences of good and bad choices, and the concept of reward and punishment on several hundred occasions. God cannot judge man for his actions without man being morally responsible for these actions, nor does this compromise God's omnipotence in any way. Thus, it is said that:

> Whatever evil visits you is from yourself. (4:79)
>
> Evil as an example are people who reject Our signs and wrong their own souls. (7:177)
>
> Verily Allah will never deal unjustly with people; it is rather people who wrong their own souls. (10:44)
>
> Allah commands men to act with justice and virtue and enjoins upon them generosity to kinsfolk. He forbids them evil deeds, injustice and rebellion: He instructs you so that you may accept His advice. (16:90)

It is in this sense that human beings are responsible for the evil they perpetrate. We all make choices for which we are responsible. In Islam there is no concept of redemption of sins or blood atonement by another being or son of God, as in Christianity.

What about parts of the Qur'an often cited by Orientalists as evidence that the God of the Islam is harsh, capricious and fatalistic as He arbitrarily guides and misguides people, such as those stating that God has "set a seal on their hearts and on their hearing and on their eyes…" (2:7) or that "…We will make the path to misery easy for them…" (92:10)? Here again, such critics misinterpret individual passages of the Qur'an without understanding the overall message, for such passages are always mentioned in the context of a conscious rejection and denial of God that *originates in the choice of man*. Habitual denial and disobedience of God create a state of mind that turns a blind eye towards the otherwise manifest signs of God. Only after choosing disobedience, however, is one met with the corresponding consequences from God.

Prophet Muhammad (SAW) in fact, anticipated the wicked lie of those who attribute sin and evil to God by saying, "An age will come for the people of my community when they will commit sin and inequity, and in order to justify their corruption and pollution, they will say, 'God's fate and destiny decreed that we act thus.' If you encounter such people, tell them I disown them."[40] The Qur'an has also exposed the fallacies of their arguments as in the following:

> 'We found our forefathers doing this and God has commanded us to do it.' Tell them, O Prophet, *'God never commands men to commit foul deeds, but you attribute to God every sinful and erroneous act you commit in your ignorance.'* (7:28)

> What! When a misfortune befell you, and you had certainly afflicted (the unbelievers) with twice as much, you begin to say, 'Whence is this?' *Say: it is from yourselves;* surely, Allah has power over all things." (3:165)

> Those who assign partners to God say that their worship of idols and other deeds derive from God's will; had God not willed it, they and their forefathers would not have become polytheists, and they would not practise the deeds of the Age of Ignorance. *Those who went astray in previous times also spoke such nonsense, denying the heavenly teachings and attributing their misguidance to God but they suffered the punishment for their lies and slander. Say to them, O Prophet, 'Do you have a decisive proof for what you say? If you do not, your excuses are nothing but the result of erroneous ideas and fantasies; you speak vainly and lyingly'* (6:148)

> Whatever good happens to you is from Allah; but whatever evil happens to you is from your own soul... (4:79).

Moral evil is considered to occur solely as a result of human disobedience and the misuse of the gift of free will. Free will is part of what characterizes us as human beings and necessitates the concept of reward and punishment. After all, animals and plants are not rewarded or punished because they have no choice in the matter. For human beings, however, there must be consequences for both good and bad choices. Only then can there be complete justice.

What about those who claim that God's eternal knowledge of acts pre-determines the direction of our acts? This is another common argument of those who try in vain to attribute their own wrongdoings to God. Here it is claimed by some that God's eternal fore-knowledge of all actions makes them necessary and, therefore, eliminates freedom. Jean-Paul Sartre, an existentialist philosopher, summarized the erroneous idea as follows: "Because I believe in freedom, I cannot believe in God, because if I believe in God, I will have to accept the concept of fate, and if I accept fate, I will have to renounce my freedom. Since I am attached to freedom, I do not believe in God."[41]

There are at least two essential points to emphasize in addressing the question of pre-determinism. Firstly, as introduced earlier, it is incorrect to assume that God is "in" or subject to time. There is no past or future for God—only an eternal present. God is eternally The Necessary Being and is, hence, external to the constraints of time. Time is, after all, another creation of God. Thus, the notion of pre-determinism or pre-destination is meaningless with respect to God.

> ....it is incorrect to assume that God is "in" or subject to time.

Secondly, just because God has eternal knowledge of our decisions, this does not mean that He causes our decisions to go a certain direction. Foreknowledge does not equal causation. For example, my prior knowledge that the sun is going to rise tomorrow does not mean that I will cause it to do so. Thus, the belief in the decree and destiny of God cannot be interpreted to mean that God is the cause of sin and error.

Foreknowledge does not equal causation.

In conclusion, the overall affair of man lies between the two extremes of those who, on one hand, claim that everything is from God, including evil deeds, and on the other hand, claim that human beings are independent and free to do whatever they will. The limited freedom bestowed upon man does not detract from the Omnipotence and Omniscience of God in any way. Thus, Imam Ja'far As-Sadiq has said, "Neither compulsion nor delegation, but a station between the two stations."[42] The Qur'an also beautifully summarizes this intermediary position in the verse: "You did not throw when you threw but it was Allah who threw, that he might test the believers by a gracious trial from Him" (8:17).

This verse was addressed to Prophet Muhammad (SAW) in relation to the Battle of Badr which was the first major battle between the new Muslim community and the polytheists of Mecca. The verse contains an affirmation of the throwing placed between two negations. As Shaykh Ibn Al-Arabi has stated, "…if the servant negates the throwing from Him, he will be correct, and if he affirms it in Him, he will be correct. There only remains which of the two correct views is better for the servant, though both are good."[43]

3.7 What is the Role of Satan?

Having studied why evil cannot be attributed to God, the question of the role of Satan remains. Some have chosen to avoid the attribution of evil to man or God by attributing it to Satan. Western mythology is replete with images that portray Satan as the opposing power to God who is responsible for all evil and governs hell-fire. There are no such erroneous ideas from an Islamic perspective, though the existence of Satan is acknowledged. In any case, two questions will briefly be addressed in this section:

(1) is Satan the cause of all evil?, and
(2) why does God allow Satan to exist and not destroy him?

In regard to the disobedience of Satan, the Qur'an says:

> Behold We said to the angels, 'Bow down to Adam', they bowed down except Iblis[44] (Satan). He was one of the Jinns[45] and he broke the command of his Lord... (18:50)

Satan also explains his refusal to prostrate as follows:

> I am better than he—You did create me from fire, and him from clay. He (Allah) said: Get thee down from this—it is not for you to be arrogant here—get out, for you are of the meanest of creatures. (7:12-13)

Another passage describes the classic Islamic account of what transpired thereafter:

> Allah said: 'Then get out from here—for you are rejected, accursed. And the curse shall be upon you till the Day of Judgment.' He (Satan) said: 'O my Lord! Give me then respite till the day the dead are raised.' Allah said: 'Respite is granted to you till the Day of the Time appointed.' He (Satan) said, 'O my Lord because you have put me in the wrong, I will make wrong fair-seeming to them on the earth, and I will put them all in the wrong—except Your servants among them, sincere and purified.' Allah said: 'This (way of My sincere servants) is indeed a way that leads straight to Me. For over My servants no authority shall you have, except such as put themselves in the wrong and follow you. And verily, Hell is the promised abode for them all!' (15:33-43)

These passages provide a number of points relevant to the questions at hand. Firstly, it is made clear that Satan does not have any authority over us except to the extent that we allow him to. Thus, any errors committed ultimately revert back to ourselves and Satan cannot be blamed. It is true that Satan does work to entice, tempt and prod us toward evil,[46] but it is equally true that we have the ability to accept or reject him. In a certain sense, Satan personifies the inherent ability within human beings to disobey. The Qur'an re-emphasizes the fact that it is we who are ultimately to blame for any mistakes:

And Satan will say, …I had no authority over you except to call you, but you listened to me; so do not blame me, but blame yourselves' (14:22)

For over My servants no authority shall you have, except those who put themselves in the wrong and follow you. (15:42)

It is true that Satan does work to entice, tempt and prod us toward evil, but it is equally true that we have the ability to accept or reject him.

Nor, for that matter, can we blame anybody else, whether it is other human beings or societal influences:

O you who believe, hold firm to your faith, because the misguidance of others can never compel you to fall into misguidance. (5:108)

The second point of interest is the question of why Satan has been granted respite by God until the Day of Judgment. This question is really another form of the question of why God allows evil. Thus, here too a "greater purpose" can be seen to emerge when we analyze the role of Satan. On the one hand, Satan is an anathema to mankind because of his sinister role in encouraging evil, yet from the other, he can be considered a great blessing. Why? Various scholars, mystics and 'people of unveiling' have realized that in the process of struggling to overcome Satan, human beings *actualize* their potential to become the best of all creation. By overcoming the enticements of Satan, we earn and achieve the elevated status bestowed upon us by God. It is one thing to obey God by compulsion, as in the case of angels, and quite another to obey God in spite of the whispers of Satan to the contrary. The best of mountain climbers are those who have overcome the most obstacles and hardships. Obviously, one who conquers Mount Everest is superior to one who jogs over a mound. Those who struggle and strive are the ones loved by God:

Those who believe and suffer exile and strive in Allah's cause with their goods and their persons, have the highest rank in the sight of Allah—they are the people who will achieve salvation. (9:20)

Say, 'If you do love Allah, then follow Me; Allah will love you and forgive your sins, for Allah is Most Forgiving, Most Merciful. (3:31)

By overcoming the enticements of Satan, we earn and achieve the elevated status bestowed upon us by God.

Defeating Satan and resisting his temptations allows us to ascend the spiritual ladder by a number of different means, as described in Section 3.4. In this sense, Satan is just another test or affliction that we must overcome and conquer. Thus, overcoming Satan's temptations enables us to strengthen faith, build character, and earn the reward and blessings of God.

Even the contrary scenario of following Satan enables us to eventually see and experience the dire consequences of disobeying God and serves to redirect the course of our actions back to the path of God. Satan serves as a manifest example to mankind of what not to be. Arrogance and pride are the roots of his disobedience.[47] As noted in Chapter 2, the arrogance of the ego is the greatest veil between ourselves and God. Desperation and despair are other characteristics demonstrated by Satan as he asks God for respite to try to entice human beings toward evil. Thus, God's banishing of Satan from heaven and condemning him to eternal Hell provides a stern warning to mankind to heed the serious consequences of disobedience.

Overall, we realize yet another way how God is serving a greater purpose to mankind by granting respite to Satan, as is the case with affliction and suffering.

Chapter Summary

1. The so-called problem of evil questions why there is evil and suffering in the world if there truly exists a God who is perfectly good, omnipotent (all-powerful) and omniscient (all-knowing). From a logical point of view, however, there is no contradiction if it can be shown that God may allow short-term "evil" and "suffering" for the purpose of achieving a greater good. Regardless of which side is taken on this issue, arguing that there is a greater purpose at work cannot be disproved.

2. Moral evil is considered in Islam to be a result of disobedience and misuse of the gift of free will. Nonetheless, God has mindfully created us with the possibility of disobedience and evil in order to fulfill the purpose of creation, which is the willful obedience of God, whereby we can become God's vicegerents on earth and fulfill the potential for good that is within.

3. To understand why there is evil we must also understand why we have been blessed with free will. Firstly, "achieved virtue" is superior to "conferred virtue" because it is more beloved in God's eyes that someone willingly choose to obey God instead of being forced to obey Him (as with angels, animal and plants). Secondly, because God has created man according to His image, He has chosen to give us limited freedom and power that derive from His own Will and Power.

4. Skeptics claim that if God is truly omnipotent and the cause of all causes, then He should be considered the cause of all evil. Islam maintains an intermediate position with respect to this issue. Man is neither a helpless creature who is compelled by God to be good or bad, nor is he completely independent and free to do whatsoever he wills. Overall, the Qur'an points to the fact that God cannot judge man for his faith and actions with justice without him being responsible for these, nor does this compromise the Omnipotence or causation of God in any way.

5. The granting of free will by God does not compromise His Omnipotence because it includes the power to confer limited power to certain forms of creation. Human beings are only free in the sense that God does not choose to control their choosing, not that He cannot control their choosing. Nor can anyone claim that the eternal knowledge or pre-determinism of God causes us to commit evil. Divine fore-knowledge of our decisions and actions does not equal causation. Furthermore, God is not "in time" or subject to time constraints since time is just another relative creation of Him.

6. While the negatives associated with evil and suffering are commonly focused on, there are also positives that can emerge from what we perceive as affliction. Affliction can serve to:
(a) direct the course of our actions back to a path of obedience to God,
(b) test our faith and build strength of character, and
(c) be a necessary means to experiencing its opposite feelings of joy and achievement.

7. Regardless of the level of suffering or evil experienced, God ensures and promises there is eventually complete and perfect justice for all. No man-made justice system can pretend to provide such justice. The longer the time scale that is considered, the greater the justice and good that can be deciphered, especially when considering the ephemerality of earthly existence in relation to the eternality of the

Hereafter.

8. Inherent differences between people in origin, race, skin color, body type, beauty, etc. as well as economic, material and social class differences are not signs of injustice on God's part. According to the Qur'an, the only criterion that God uses to judge between people is taqwa, or God-consciousness and piety.

9. Skeptics question why man does not have a greater tendency towards good. Firstly, it cannot be shown that man actually has a greater tendency towards evil than good, and secondly, even if this were the case, the overriding Mercy and Forgiveness of God tilt the balance in favor of man.

10. Satan cannot be blamed for our own disobedience and evil. The Qur'an teaches that while Satan encourages, entices and tempts toward evil, it is ultimately only ourselves that can be blamed.

11. Skeptics question why God allows Satan to operate and entice human beings. This question is similar to the question of why God allows evil. While Satan is an enemy to mankind, he is at the same time also a blessing. This is because in the process of struggling to overcome Satan, human beings actualize their potential to become the "best of creation". By overcoming the temptations of Satan, we earn and achieve the elevated status bestowed upon human beings by God. In this sense, Satan is only another test or affliction to be overcome by man.

Notes:

1 Dostoyevsky, Fyodor, *The Brothers Karamazov*, trans. Constance Garnett, ed. Ralph Matlaw (W.W. Norton & Company, Inc, 1976), p. 226.

2 *The Living Webster-* Encyclopedic Dictionary of the English Language (Chicago: The English Language Institute of America, Inc., 1975).

3 J.L. Mackie, *The Miracle of Theism- Arguments for and Against the Existence of God* (Oxford: Oxford University Press, 1982), p. 160.

4 Swinburne, Richard, *Is There a God?* (Oxford: Oxford University Press, 1996), p. 7.

5 E. Stump and M.J. Murray, eds., *Philosophy of Religion: The Big Questions* (Malden, Massachussetts: Blackwell Publishers, 1999), p. 153.

6 See Qur'an, 35:15- "O Men, it is you who stand in need of Allah. As for Allah, He is above all need, worthy of praise."

7 See Qur'an, 57:1- "Everything in the heavens and the earth glorifies God…"

8 See Qur'an 95:4-6- "We have indeed created man in the best of moulds. Then do we abase him to the lowest of the low- except those who believe and do righteous deeds, for they shall have a reward unfailing."

9 Hadith or saying of Prophet Muhammad (SAW) narrated in Bukhari, Isti'dhan 1; Muslim Birr, 115; Janna 28; Ahmad II 244, 251, 315, 323, 434, 463, 519.

10 See Qur'an 18:50

11 Jalaluddin Rumi, *Mathnawi*, ed. R.A. Nicholson, book 2, v. 332 (London: Luzac, 1925-45).

12 Islam also considers another form of creation, called Jinn in the Qur'an, to possess free will but they are not considered to have the potential of man to be vicegerent of God on earth.

13 Hadith cited in Sachiko Murata, *The Angels, in Islamic Spirituality*, ed. S.H. Nasr, (New York: The Crossroad Publishing Co., 1987), p. 340.

14 Fadhlalla Haeri, *Decree and Destiny- The Freedom of No Choice* (Longmead, U.K.: Element Books, 1991), p. 83.

15 Ibid., p. 51.

16 Khidr is a Messenger of God who has been described in the Qur'an, 18:65, as having been bestowed Mercy and Knowledge directly from God.

17 See Qur'an 18:81.

18 See Qur'an 18:82

19 Quoted in Sayyid Mujtaba Musavi Lari, *God and His Attributes: Lessons on Islamic Doctrine*, trans. Hamid Algar (Potomac, MD: Islamic Education Center, 1989), p. 24.

20 Muhammad Zakariyya Kandhalvi, *Stories of Sahabah*, trans. Abdul Rashid Arshad (West Yorkshire, UK: Anjuman-e-Islahul Muslimeen, 1994), p. 15.

21 Unlike the Jewish-Christian version in the Old Testament, the Qur'an maintains that it was Ishmael, not Isaac, who was to be sacrificed. In fact, the Qur'anic argument is supported by the Book of Genesis. In it, Ishmael is said to be born fourteen years before Isaac (see Gen. 21:5 and 16:16) and yet, in Gen. 22:2 Abraham is asked to sacrifice his only son. The only son can, thus, be

none other than Ishmael.

22 The Qur'an is full of stories of the trials and tribulations of numerous Prophets, including for example, Joseph (12:4 – 101), Moses (7:103 – 137), and Job (38:41 – 44).

23 Fadhlalla Haeri, *Decree and Destiny- The Freedom of No Choice* (Longmead, U.K.: Element Books, 1991), p. 34-35.

24 The Arabic word for spending in charity, *zakat*, comes from the root word *zaka*, which means to purify and to increase or grow.

25 See Giovanni·Maciocia, *The Foundations of Chinese Medicine*, (New York, Churchill Livingstone, 1989), p. 1-14.

26 William Chittick, *The Sufi Path of Knowledge- Ibn al-Arabi's Metaphysics of Imagination* (Albany: State University of New York Press, 1989), p.67.

27 Hadith of Prophet Muhammad (SAW) narrated in Bukhari, Isti'dhan 1; Muslim Birr, 115, Janna 28; Ahmad II 244, 251, 315, 323, 434, 463, 519.

28 Term used by Shaykh Ibn al-Arabi. See William Chittick, *The Sufi Path of Knowledge- Ibn al-Arabi's Metaphysics of Imagination*, Albany, State University of New York Press, 1989, p.22.

29 Hadith narrated by Imam Ja'far As-Sadiq in Fadhlalla Haeri, *Decree and Destiny- The Freedom of No Choice* (Longmead, U.K.: Element Books, 1991), p. 66.

30 Related in Al-Naysaburi, Abul- Husayn, Sahih Muslim, 8 vols. in 4, 8:135, Beirut: Manshurat Dar Al-Afaq Al-Jadida, n.d., reprint of the 1334 Istanbul edition.

31 Related by Ibn 'Umar in Sahih al-Bukhari.

32 Fadhlalla Haeri, *Decree and Destiny- The Freedom of No Choice* (Longmead, U.K.: Element Books, 1991), p. 118.

33 Hadith Qudsi on the authority of Abu Hurayrah, related by Imam Bukhari, Muslim, An-Nasai and Ibn-Majah as referenced in Ezzedin Ibrahim and D.J. Davies, Forty Hadith Qudsi, (Beirut: The Holy Koran Publishing House, 1980), Hadith #1.

34 See Qur'an 2:37: "Then Adam received words from His Lord, who forgave him. He is indeed the All-Forgiving, the Merciful."

35 Hadith Qudsi on the authority of Anas bin Malik, related by Imam Tirmidhi and Ahmad Ibn Hanbal as referenced in Ezzedin Ibrahim and D.J. Davies, Forty Hadith Qudsi, (Beirut: The Holy Koran Publishing House, 1980), Hadith #34.

36 Hadith Qudsi on the authority of Anas bin Malik, related by Imam Bukhari.

37 See Majid Fakhry's *A History of Islamic Philosophy* (London and New York: Columbia University Press, 1983) for a complete discussion of the various sides of the issue, including the position of the Ash'arites, Mu'tazilies, Shiites and Maturidis.

38 Hadith narrated by Imam Ja'far As-Sadiq

39 Hadith or saying of Prophet Muhammad (SAW) narrated in Bukhari, Isti'dhan 1; Muslim Birr, 115, Janna 28; Ahmad II 244, 251, 315, 323, 434, 463, 519.

40 Hadith related by Sayyid Mujtaba Musavi Lari in *God and His Attributes: Lessons on Islamic Doctrine*, trans. Hamid Algar (Potomac, Maryland: Islamic Education Center, 1989), p. 193.

41 See ibid. p. 193

42 Fadhlalla Haeri, *Decree & Destiny- The Freedom of No Choice* (Longmead, U.K.: Element Books, 1991), p. 44.

43 Shaykh Ibn Al-Arabi quote from William Chittick, *The Sufi Path of Knowledge: Ibn al-Arabi's Metaphysics of Imagination* (Albany: State University of New York Press, 1989), p. 211.

44 The Qur'an refers to Iblis as the actual name of Satan, with Satan referring to a system of evil and not necessarily a single person.

45 Satan, or more accurately, Iblis, is a "jinn", who is a creature created from fire and who has also been bestowed with limited free will. In Islam, Satan is not considered a "fallen angel" as in some Christian and Jewish traditions.

46 See also the Quran, 7:20, where Satan is described as "whispering suggestions" to Adam and Eve.

47 See Qur'an 2:34 and 7:13 for references to the arrogance and pride of Satan.

| Chapter 4
How Can We Understand Religious Diversity?

> *Say: 'We believe in Allah and in what has been revealed to us and what was revealed to Abraham, Ishmael, Isaac, Jacob and the Tribes, and in the Books given to Moses, Jesus and the Prophets from their Lord—We make no distinction between one another among them and to Allah do we bow our will.'*
>
> Qur'an 3:84

Among the more perplexing questions that confront the skeptic who gazes upon the immense variety of religious faiths and their contrasting and contradictory claims is the nature of religious diversity. If there is indeed only one supreme God, why is it that there are a multitude of differing faiths, including the intolerance and sometimes violent clashes between them? Even if one were devoted to God, toward which faith should one turn? At one end, one is confronted by the exclusivist claims of Christianity of vicarious sacrifice of the god-man Jesus in expiation and atonement for the sins of an ontologically evil humanity as sole condition for salvation, while at the other, we find the even greater exclusivist claims of a nomocentric Judaism with God being the sole possession of the Israelites. In contrast with the so-called monotheistic Judaeo-Christian tradition of the West, we encounter the Eastern traditions of Hinduism and Buddhism. Hinduism defies characterization as a single faith and embodies a panoply of teachings, doctrines and rituals ranging from the crudely polytheistic cult and caste system of the masses to the metaphysical monism of a tiny elite. Buddhism is widely characterized as a non-theistic faith, inasmuch as it does not speak of a personal God and Creator and takes as its point of departure, the bare fact of human suffering whose transcending it sets as its supreme goal.

As for Islam, it has all too often been caricatured by the media as an intolerant, militant Arab faith, spread by the sword,[1] too simplistic to satisfy the modern mind, yet presenting a dire threat to Western political hegemony. Thus, this cartoon-like portrayal casts the Muslim as both midget and superman. It will be the goal of this chapter to present a more realistic picture of Islam and its views on religious diversity. In confronting this issue, three central questions will be addressed:

(1) how does one approach and account for such religious diversity?

(2) how does Islam view other religions?, and

(3) what are the distinguishing principles of Islam.

4.1 Approaches to Religious Diversity

There are basically four kinds of approaches to the question at hand. John Hick has called the first three: the exclusivist, pluralist, and inclusivist stances.[2] The first emphasizes the differences between religions, the second the commonalities, and the third represents an intermediary position. The fourth position, which we term the skeptical stance, considers all religions, and for that matter, even God, to be mere human inventions, all *devoid of truth*. Most of those who consider all religions to be false also reject the concept of God. In this case, the reader is urged to refer back to the first three chapters where it is shown that, at the very least, a strong case for the existence of God can be presented based on logical, scientific and experiential premises. Part of the belief in God entails belief in His Supreme Attributes, which include those of Mercy, Love, and Guidance. In manifesting these Attributes, God has not left His creation helpless. Without guidance there is no justice in God calling us to account for ourselves on the Day of Judgment. Thus, part of the belief in God involves a belief that He has provided His creation with guidance and access to the Truth, regardless of whether that is to be found in one or many ways.

In any case, in Hick's classification of the theistic approaches, the exclusivist position claims that the teachings of a particular religion are the sole means of attaining salvation and truth. Other religions may share certain teachings but they are ultimately on the wrong path and only one religion can be exclusively true. The revelation of God is considered to be found in only one religion. If it were otherwise, then it is claimed there would be no sound reason for following a particular religion. Exclusivists tend to support their claims based on theological, philosophical, historical or experiential proofs.

The medieval Jewish philosopher, Juda Halevi (1085 – 1141 C.E.), presented a historical argument as evidence for the superiority of the Jewish faith. In it, he stressed the fact that God miraculously saved and preserved Moses (AS) and his followers from the torture of the Pharaoh as the primary evidence supporting the notion that God favored the Jews as His "chosen people".[3]

Christian doctrine is largely considered to be exclusivist, though a minority of Christians has tried to indicate otherwise. The Catholic Church and its numerous Ecumenical Councils have long maintained that the salvation of humanity depends on accepting the blood sacrifice of Jesus, the presumed Son of God. The twenty-first Ecumenical Council, also known as Vatican II, went as far as stating: "All must be converted to Christ as He is made known by the Church's preaching."[4] Karl Barth, considered one of the most eminent Protestant theologians of the 20th century, also presents an exclusivist doctrine. Barth claims that the revelation of God only occurs through the medium of Jesus Christ. He does not necessarily consider Christianity a superior 'religion', for he considers religion to be a man-made invention; rather the revelation of Jesus Christ is considered to be the one true path to salvation.[5] Similarly, there are followers in every religion, including Islam, who advocate the exclusivist approach.

Of course, critics are quick to point out that such a stance often leads to intolerance and question why God cannot in His infinite Power provide guidance to different peoples in different ways. Moreover, does an exclusivist stance mean that all followers of other faiths are doomed and cannot access the Truth? Even if one were to accept the principle of exclusivism, how is one to decide which religion lays claim to the Truth? What should such criteria be based on?

It is not surprising then that some, especially in this modern era of global communication where there is unsurpassed awareness of other religions, have chosen the pluralist route, which holds that God reveals Himself through many religions and that salvation is not the birthright of any single group. Here it is claimed that there are numerous scriptures, saints and messengers of God, all of which can be 'right' by providing different angles to the same Truth and salvation. A common example used to illustrate this concept is that of the blind men who examined different parts of an elephant's body and came to very disparate conclusions about its nature, all of which were somewhat true, even though the animal, being analogous to God in this case, was a single being. Another example is that of a wheel, in which the many spokes, representing different paths or religions, all point to the center, which is God. Although pluralists acknowledge the differences that exist between religions, they often seem to be more concerned with the practical, moral benefits to society, rather than individual truth claims. Certain Hindu sects and the Perennialist School of Frithjof Schuon are examples of groups that espouse a pluralist approach. The Perennialist School claims there is a "transcendent unity of religions". John Hick has also presented a pluralist philosophy in which it is claimed "that the great religious traditions of the world represent different human perceptions of and response to the same infinite Divine Reality."[6]

Although this approach sounds appealing, here too the pluralist stance must confront certain problems. If all religions are valid, it does not eventually matter what one believes and one is left with doubt on critical questions concerning God, morality and salvation—in other words, another form of agnosticism. Another major question concerns what is to constitute a valid religion or path. Are the worshippers of Satan or idols or secular humanists to be admitted within the fold of Truth? Some have developed sets of criteria for evaluating religions, including for example, internal, logical consistencies and experiential adequacy. However, these criteria are often subjective and even if one were to accept them, then it would contradict the pluralist philosophy by admitting that some religions are "better" or more reflective of the Truth than others. Another problem arises in establishing the form of obedience or worship. Is one to adopt different religious practices into a smorgasbord of worship, or adopt the practices of a single religion, or simply follow one's own limited understanding?

Finally, we have the inclusivist stance which is intermediary in that it affirms that God can and does reveal Himself in a number of different ways, yet it also argues that absolute truth can be found in only one religion. In the former part of the argument, its exponents agree with the pluralists, but in the latter they are more at home with the exclusivists. Thus, they agree that God can manifest Himself to adherents of different religions as He pleases, with their descriptions of such experiences being colored by existing religious, social, cultural and geographic backdrops, but that eventually, the truth claims of a religion have to be assessed as true or false since there is only one Truth.

The Catholic theologian, Karl Rahner, proposed such a position by stating that Christianity is the only religion that provides salvation, but that Jesus' blood atonement can be made available to anyone, even if they do not necessarily know that it is Jesus who has manifested himself and saved them—hence his idea of "anonymous Christians".[7]

Here again, the major question that remains is how to determine which religion contains absolute truth and salvation. Can we use logical or scientific criteria? Although such criteria can 'narrow the field', there are inherent limitations in logical and scientific methods as discussed in Chapter 2. Nor can moral excellence be used as the criterion since morally upright people can be found among people of all faiths. Some have suggested using the degree of spiritual experience, internal consistency or applicability to modern times as the criterion, but here again we inevitably find a great deal of subjectivity. Furthermore, this is to say nothing of the problem of varying interpretations and sects within a religion. So, what are we to make of all this confusion?

It is hoped that some answers will be presented, God-willing, in the next few sections where the unique perspective of Islam on religious diversity is introduced. It is important, however, to keep this backdrop of different approaches in mind to appreciate the magnitude of the issue and the various ends that people have gone to in trying to address it.

4.2 The Primordial Religion: Peaceful Submission

In order to understand where the view of Islam falls in this spectrum, we must begin with an understanding of religion itself. Technically, the Qur'an does not contain any terms meaning religion in the modern sense of a set of rituals and beliefs associated with belief in some deity. Instead, it uses the term, *din*, which is often translated as religion or way of life, but is actually distinct from it. Nor does it ever use this term in the plural form. Syed Al-Attas has clarified the primary significations of the term, *din*, to include:
(1) indebtedness,
(2) submissiveness,
(3) judicious power, and
(4) natural inclination or tendency.[8]

The Qur'an, thus, presents a unique perspective with respect to "religion":

> "So set your face truly to the din being upright, the nature in which Allah has made mankind: there is no change in the work wrought by Allah: that is the true religion, but most among mankind do not understand." (30:30)

Thus, to follow religion is to follow and be faithful to one's very nature. Allah informs us that there is no changing of our innate nature, nor are there multiple religions. But what is this nature? It is the tendency or inclination to submit to and know our Creator, the One and Only God. Man is not confined only to physical and social needs. The nature to submit and recognize God is not absolute in excluding the disobedience of God, but rather is an inclination towards Him. Moreover, the act of submission to God is not restricted to human beings, but includes all of creation:

> "Do they seek other than the religion of Allah?- while all creatures in the heavens and on earth have, willingly or unwillingly, submitted *(aslama)* to His Will, and to Him they shall all be brought back." (3:83)

> *... to follow religion is to follow and be faithful to one's very nature.*

Here, the term *aslama* is used, which is the verbal form of the word *Islam*. *Islam* derives from *silm*, which primarily means peace, but also carries a meaning of submission or surrender. Thus, Islam is most commonly translated as peaceful submission or submission that leads to peace. It is the only major religion that is not named after its founder (Christianity and Buddhism) or a group or race of people (Judaism and Hinduism).

It is only through the submission, which includes connotations of obedience, worship, service, gratitude and love of God, that true peace can be attained both internally and externally. Only human beings have been given a choice in this affair—it is for us to realize that refusal to obey God is to be false to our own nature and in disharmony with the laws of the universe. While surrender and submission may conjure images of a ruthless master with unwilling slaves to some, what is intended is, instead, a form of voluntary self-sacrifice (*Let there be no compulsion in religion* (Qur'an 2:256)) that is part of every revealed religion, where the secret of felicity lies in controlling the desires of the lower self and obeying of the commandments of God. As discussed in Chapter 2, there is profound freedom in submitting to His Will. It is through servanthood that we also indicate our gratitude to the Lord for bestowing the gift of creation. Prophet Muhammad (SAW) was once asked by a companion why he prayed continuously for so long that his feet became swollen while he is sinless and forgiven. He answered, "Should I not be a grateful servant"?[9] Islam, thus, believes that man can aspire to nothing greater than being a servant of the Lord.

With this concept in mind, it is now easy to see why the Qur'an presents a clear message that throughout history, for God there has only been and will only be one eternal, primordial, and revealed religion—that of *Islam*, or peaceful submission to the Will of God. Whether it is Adam, Noah, Solomon, Abraham, Ishmael, Isaac, Moses, David, Joseph, Jesus or Muhammad, they are all part of one great family—that of Muslims, or those who practice Islam. The Unity of God is also reflected in the Unity of Truth. Thus, Allah states:

> Abraham was not a Jew nor a Christian, but he was true in faith and submitted to Allah as a Muslim, and he joined not gods with Allah. (3:67)

> The same religion has He established for you as that which He enjoined on Noah- that which We have sent by inspiration to you-and that which We enjoined on Abraham, Moses, and Jesus: namely, that you should remain steadfast in religion, and make no divisions therein... (42:13)
>
> Not a Messenger did We send before you (Muhammad, SAW) without this inspiration sent by Us to him: that there is no God but I-therefore worship and serve Me. (21:25)
>
> Say: 'We believe in Allah and in what has been revealed to us and what was revealed to Abraham, Ishmael, Isaac, Jacob and the Tribes, and in the Books given to Moses, Jesus and the Prophets from their Lord-We make no distinction between one another among them and to Allah do we bow our will.' (3:84)

Although God's message to mankind of worshipping the Lord by obeying His genuine Scriptures and Messengers has always been clear and consistent, the response from mankind has been anything but clear and consistent. Although there is only one God, being as He is in His essence, there are innumerable gods created by man. Although there is only one religion in the eyes of God, there are countless religions established by man. The history of mankind has been checkered with the erection of hundreds of individual gods and deities. Through the rigor of daily life, man tends to insidiously forget the Lord and digress from the primordial teachings laid out in Divine scriptures and by the Messengers—hence, the Arabic word for human being of *insaan*, meaning one who forgets. Herein lies the reason for the repeated sending of countless Messengers spanning all regions and ages. Man must be reminded of his true nature and redirected to worship the One and Only God, and the proper form of this worship must be prescribed. It is through Mercy, Love and Guidance that God repeatedly sent Messengers to warn their people when they strayed:

> For we assuredly sent among every people a messenger, (with the command) 'Serve Allah and eschew evil'... (16:36)

...And there was never a people without a warner having lived among them. (35:24)

...And to every people there is a guide. (13:7)

Although there is only one God, being as He is in His essence, there are innumerable gods created by man. Although there is only one religion in the eyes of God, there are countless religions established by man.

Thus, no one can claim the excuse that no warner or Messenger was sent to him or her. We are all accountable for following the Divine law laid out by a Messenger. Allah in His Infinite Mercy, has provided guides and guidance for all people. The Qur'an mentions a total of twenty-five prophets by name whom all Muslims must devoutly believe in. The discussion of their message and experiences occupies one of the most important and central themes in it. Prophet Muhammad (SAW) has added in a famous narration that 124,000 Messengers have been sent to mankind throughout history.[10] Not only must Muslims believe in these Prophets, but also in the Scriptures that accompanied some of them, in their original forms, such as the Scrolls of David (AS), the Torah of Moses (AS) and the *Injeel* of Jesus (AS).

Unlike "great" philosophers and scientists, who have always differed in key respects, none of the Messengers differed in their fundamental message of worshipping and following the One Supreme God (although the fundamental principles have never changed, the application of their respective Laws differed in some respects, as appropriate for their people and time). Nor did Muhammad (SAW) ever claim to have brought a new religion to mankind. Islam has never claimed to be a brash, new ideology that suddenly sprung on the scene with the coming of Muhammad (SAW). Rather, Islam is the primordial monotheistic religion (the necessity of Islam as a modern religion will be clarified in Sections 4.4 and 4.5). As the Qur'an clarifies,

Say, 'I am no bringer of new fangled doctrine among the Messengers, nor do I know what will be done with me or with you. I only follow what is revealed to me by inspiration-I am but a warner, open and clear.' (46:9)

Muslims, thus, believe that throughout history, the only religion, or more accurately the only din, acceptable before God is that of the primordial religion, which is principled on sincere submission to the One and Only Supreme God as prescribed by Divine Revelation and Prophethood. Thus, Allah clearly states that:

> Verily the religion *(ad-din)* with Allah is Islam… (3:19)

> If anyone desires a religion other than Islam (peaceful submission to Allah), never will it be accepted of him, and in the Hereafter he will be in the ranks of the losers. (3:85)

What does this mean, then, for the question of religious diversity? It means that Islam presents a unique inclusivist approach where Allah has manifested and will continue to manifest His Revelation and Signs to all people throughout the universe, regardless of what faith they are born into, but that there is indeed a critical criterion for establishing the truth of any religion or way of life.

Every religion must establish what is the source of all its beliefs and practices. Divine Revelation must be the criterion, foundation and source of all teachings and knowledge in true religion. Only when Revelation pervades all teachings and principles will a religion verify its reliance on the One, Supreme God and negate any dependence on the fallible findings of man. There must be complete reliance on God—not the gods we create. The direct Revelation of God is communicated in the form of Divine Scriptures and Messengers. In them, the critical questions of the *object of worship* and the *relationship of creation to this object of worship* must be clearly answered. Although the criterion of Divine Revelation as the basis for religion and worship of One God may at first glance seem simplistic, this is far from the case, as we shall study in more detail in the remainder of the chapter. Objective analysis reveals that Islam is the only religion which, in both theory and practice, advocates the simple and direct worship of One God.

> *Objective analysis reveals that Islam is the only religion which, in both theory and practice, advocates the simple and direct worship of One God.*

Islam acknowledges that God manifests in numerous ways so as to disclose His Attributes, but regards Truth and Guidance as being singular since God has provided only one consistent message with respect to His nature and our relationship to Him. Thus, the Qur'an states: "…Truth stands out clear from error…" (2:256).

The primary sources of all Islamic teachings, i.e., the Qur'an, and the Way (*sunnah*) of Prophet Muhammad (SAW) have clearly communicated that the object of worship is Allah, the One and Only God possessing perfection of all Attributes described unto Himself, while the relationship of creation to Allah is one of submission, which encompasses all aspects of love, obedience, gratitude and worship.

While Islam includes obligatory belief in the prior Messengers and Revelations sent by God, it contends that all other religions, in their current forms, have deviated from or are entirely removed from Divine Revelation as a source and have severely compromised the Unity of God. The primary criticism of Islam against other religions is not in their original forms (as taught by genuine Messengers), but in their historical forms, i.e., the scriptures and doctrines they accepted and developed. Thus, while other religions may have been valid in their own times, they are no longer valid in the present day.

> *The primary criticism of Islam against other religions is not in their original forms (as taught by genuine Messengers), but in their historical forms, i.e., the scriptures and doctrines they accepted and developed.*

While it is true that all religions, including Islam, undergo change and evolution, Islam is unique in that its primary sources have not undergone any change and retain their immutable Divine character (see Sec. 4.5). Thus, despite inevitable differences among Muslims, they may always revert to its primary sources for final guidance. As we shall detail in Sections 4.4 and 4.5, other religions have lost this grounding in pristine Revelation to the extent that they have deviated on fundamental questions of creed. Other religions also stress the importance of obeying God, but there are a number of critical differences that distinguish Islam, as we shall study in Sections 4.4-4.6.

In the meantime, it is important to note that such an inclusivist view is not an attempt at veiled exclusivism—for submission to and worship of one God is the eternal religion and primordial function of all creation. That which is eternal and practiced by all cannot be labeled as sectarian or exclusivist, for it, in fact, transcends all worldly boundaries. Moreover, if Islam were exclusivist, it would not have recognized the validity or the necessity of prior Revelations and Messengers. Before Adam stepped foot on earth, all of creation, whether they be dinosaurs or ducks, trees or twigs, mountains or mounds, all sang the praises of the Lord in submission and will continue to do so (only man has been given a choice in the affair):

> The seven heavens and the earth and all they contain praise God. There is no creature not engaged in praise and magnification of its Lord, but you do not understand their praise…17:44)

At this point, however, there are still a number of questions that remain. What does this mean for the fate of non-Muslims? If Islam is the primordial religion of all Prophets, what was the need for the historical advent of Islam? Why is Islam different from any other religion? Why does God allow such diversity of faiths? We will attempt to address these questions, God willing, in the remainder of the chapter.

4.3 The Key to Salvation

Among the many misconceptions prevalent among non-Muslims is the presumed "lack of tolerance" in Islam for other religions. Even a cursory study of the Qur'an and sayings of Prophet Muhammad (SAW), however, would reveal the truth of the tremendous appreciation and respect of Islam for other faiths and the common threads that exist between them (see also Sec. 4.4). A case, in point, lies in the area of salvation (in the sense of deliverance from Hellfire, not in the Christian sense of deliverance from original sin).

Islam does not present a harsh or arrogant stance when it comes to the salvation of other faiths, as many have tried to portray. Nowhere in the Qur'an or sayings of Prophet Muhammad (SAW) are there any blanket statements condemning all non-Muslims to the depths of hellfire as some imagine. On the contrary, the Qur'an repeatedly returns to the message of the primordial religion, i.e. that of sincere submission to Allah as the key to salvation, not mere lip service professing to be Muslim, Christian, Jew or Hindu or blind imitation of our forefathers. Both faith and works are required for the salvation and Mercy of God, with each being incomplete without the other.[11] Thus, the Qur'an states:

> And they say: 'None shall enter Paradise unless he be a Jew or a Christian.' Those are their vain desires. Say, 'Produce your proof if you are truthful.' Nay-whoever submits his whole self to Allah and is virtuous- he will get his reward with his Lord; on such shall be no fear, nor shall they grieve. (2:112-113)
>
> If any do deeds of righteousness-be they male or female-and have faith, they will enter Heaven, and not the least injustice will be done to them. Who can be better in religion than one who submits his whole self to Allah, does good, and follows the way of Abraham the true in faith? (4:124-125)

...the Qur'an repeatedly returns to the message of the primordial religion, i.e. that of sincere submission to Allah as the key to salvation, not mere lip service professing to be Muslim, Christian, Jew or Hindu or blind imitation of our forefathers.

The Qur'an does not limit itself to mere generalities with respect to salvation, but also conveys specifics concerning the fate of the "People of the Book". The "People of the Book" is an oft-used Qur'anic title of respect that refers to Christians, Jews and other communities that received earlier Revelations or Scriptures. A significant portion of the Qur'an is devoted to discussion of them, including both their criticisms and praises. A balanced portrayal of them is presented where it is said that "not all of them are alike"

(3:113)—some are condemned for knowingly associating partners with God and will face a grievous penalty (see Sec. 4.4), while others are praised for being among the righteous and are specifically said to believe in Allah:

> *And there are certainly among the People of the Book those who believe in Allah, in the revelation to you, and in the revelation to them, bowing in humility to* Allah-they will not sell the signs of Allah for a miserable gain! For them is a reward with their Lord and Allah is swift in account. (3:199)

> Not all of them are alike- of the People of the Book are some that stand for the right; they rehearse the signs of Allah all night long, and they prostrate themselves in adoration. *They believe in Allah and the Last Day; they enjoin what is right and forbid what is wrong; and they hasten in good works- they are in the rank of the righteous. Of the good that they do, nothing will be rejected of them,* for Allah knows well those who do right. (3:113-5)

> Those who believe (in the Qur'an), and those who follow the Jewish (scriptures), and the Christians and the Sabians[12]-a*ny who believe in Allah and the Last Day, and work righteousness, shall have their reward with their Lord: on them shall be no fear, nor shall they grieve.* (2:62)

While some Muslims have incorrectly presumed Islam to be exclusivist based on verses like "Verily the religion (*ad-din*) with Allah is Islam" (3:19), such verses do not conflict with the above passages in any way. "Islam" must be understood in its most comprehensive meaning and one cannot assume that all non-Muslims are bereft of sincere submission to the One and Only God.

Some have interpreted the above passages to allude to those among the People of the Book who eventually converted to Islam. Regardless of whether this is the case or not, an equally valid and more literal interpretation of the above passages includes the fact that there are those who may *profess to be Christians or Jews, and yet believe and submit to Allah,* without necessarily having formally converted to Islam, since there is no reference to conversion in any verse. These people could be called "anonymous Muslims" analogous to Karl Rahner's use of the term "anonymous Christians". Even today, it is not altogether uncommon to encounter Christians, Jews, Hindus or Buddhists, who despite what their official doctrines may proclaim, *in their hearts believe in Allah, and in their actions manifest submission.* Currently, for example, there exists a minority of Unitarian Christians who clearly reject the Divinity of Jesus and the innovation of trinity.

It is no wonder that some Islamic scholars make exceptions with respect to the salvation of certain groups of people. The famous scholar, jurist and Sufi, Imam Ghazali (d. 1111), has referred to the special cases of:

(1) those who have never heard the message of Islam, and
(2) those who have only heard a highly distorted message of Islam.

He noted that the "majority of the Christians of Byzantium and the Turks (meaning a variety of pagan Turkic peoples) in this age shall be encompassed by the Divine Mercy, Allah-willing."[13] While these groups existed at a time when the world of Islam was expanding, most of them had never even heard the name of Muhammad (SAW), much less the message of Islam. The other group consists of those who have heard about Islam, but have only heard a highly distorted picture, having been told, for example, that Muhammad (SAW) is a sorcerer, that Islam is a false religion of the Arabs, or that Islam is a religion of terrorism. It is for God to judge such people and not we.

4.4 The People of the Book

Besides the question of salvation, there are a number of other areas in which the tolerance of Islam can be appreciated. There is no inherent contradiction between the concept of Islamic rule and tolerance, as is widely perceived.

The Qur'an is very clear in setting a standard of tolerance:

> Let there be no compulsion in religion... (2:256)

> Say, 'The Truth is from your Lord': Let him who wants believe in it, and let him who wants reject it... (18:29)

In this age of secularism and skepticism, it is particularly important for members of all faiths to cooperate in reestablishing faith-based societies. With this spirit of tolerance, Muslims are called upon to come to common terms with people of other faiths in establishing the obedience of God:

> Say, 'Oh People of the Book! Come to common terms as between us and you—that we worship none but Allah, that we associate no partners with Him, that we erect not from among ourselves, lords and patrons other than Allah.' If then, they turn back, say, 'Bear witness that we (at least) are Muslims (bowing to Allah's Will).' (3:64)

Such cooperation and tolerance is not merely theoretical, but has been demonstrated in practice as well. Despite the inevitable fact that every religion has its share of intolerant followers, Islamic history has shown a degree of tolerance for other religions that is rarely appreciated. The rule of the first four Caliphs of Islam (632-661)[14], the Muslim rule of Spain spanning seven hundred years, and the Ayyubid Dynasty of Saladin (Salahuddin Al-Ayyubi) from 1171-1259 are but a few examples of extraordinary tolerance demonstrated on a grand scale. To this day, many Jewish historians remember the period under Muslim Spain as the "Golden Age of Spain", having produced some of their finest works of literature, philosophy and learning and some of their most well known scholars and personalities, such as Maimonides, Ibn Pakuda, Ibn Gabirol, Saadya Gaon, and Hasday b. Shaprut.[15] The historian of the Crusades, William of Tyre, acknowledged the military general, Salahuddin, as a truly generous, fair, energetic and ambitious leader who was to be respected for the threat that he posed to the onslaught of the Crusaders.[16] Tolerance for other faiths was so ingrained in Islamic character that previous Muslim societies rendered the separation of Church and State, that is now considered mandatory, unnecessary and irrelevant.

> *Tolerance for other faiths was so ingrained in Islamic character that previous Muslim societies rendered the separation of Church and State, that is now considered mandatory, unnecessary and irrelevant.*

The extensive interaction of the early Muslim communities with the People of the Book also provides numerous lessons. Islamic law, for example, confers to non-Muslims rights of freedom of worship, belief, independent religious and educational institutions as well as full autonomy concerning family law, personal law, marriage and divorce. Freedom in financial, transactional, civil and social matters is also allowed except for that which publicly violates Islamic law. The oft-maligned *jizya*, or tax levied on non-Muslims by an Islamic state, is another example of a legitimate practice portrayed as intolerant and oppressive. Objective scholars understand that non-Muslims living in an Islamic state were offered complete protection against foreign armies despite not having to serve in the military. If any non-Muslims served in the army, the *jizya* was not levied. Moreover, the amount charged as *jizya*, usually around one *dirham* per year, was considerably less than the *zakat*, or charitable tax of 2.5% of savings, that was obligatory upon every Muslim.[17]

Despite the respect Islam holds for other religions, one must also precisely understand certain inherent deficiencies of other modern religions and the underlying basis for the Islamic critique of them. Only then can the unique and extraordinary nature of Islam be appreciated. It is important to remember that the Qur'an does not criticize other faiths on the basis of their Prophets, scriptures, places of worship or forms of worship such as baptisms, davenings, Hanuka and Easter celebrations or the like. Rather, the Qur'an primarily criticizes the People of the Book for *compromising the nature of God, distorting His Message, rejecting the Final Prophet, and failing to submit to and obey Him*. Although a comprehensive discussion of all sections pertaining to the People of the Book are beyond the scope of this work, let us expand upon these main areas of criticism:

(a) *Compromising Monotheism.* This is demonstrated most clearly in the doctrine of trinity among Christians and the taking of Rabbis and Pharisees as demagogues in Judaism. In the case of Christianity, why is God attributed with having begotten a son? Why must one pray to the "Father" through the intercession of the "Son"? How can Jesus (peace be upon him) simultaneously be the infinite, infallible God and the finite, fallible human? It is not surprising that Christians often resort to "Divine Mystery" in attempting to answer such dilemmas. The Qur'an is very clear and uncompromising in its condemnation of such association with God. It is exceedingly limiting of His Majesty and transcendence to consider God as having begotten a son or to delimit Him in human form:

> They say, 'The Most Gracious has begotten a son! Indeed you have put forth a thing most monstrous! As if the skies are ready to burst, the earth to split asunder, and the mountains to fall down in utter ruin, that they should invoke a son for the Most Gracious. It is not consonant with the Majesty of the Most Gracious that He should beget a son. (19:88-92)

> The Jews and the Christians say that Ezra and Jesus were the sons of God. This is what they say with their tongues, following those who were unbelievers before them...They take their rabbis and monks as lords in derogation of Allah... (9:30-31)

> They do blaspheme who say Allah is one of three in a trinity—for there is no god except One God. If they desist not from their words (of blasphemy), verily a grievous penalty will befall the blasphemers among them. (5:73)

Few Christians realize the astounding admission of both Christian and non-Christian historians that the doctrine of trinity and the "official creed" was not even established until the Council of Nicaea (also known as the First Ecumenical Council), held 325 years after Christ! As the historian Thomas Bokenkotter has pointed out,

> *Like its worship, the faith of the Church underwent some development, and, in fact, its chief dogma, belief in the divinity of Jesus Christ, was not defined until the Council of Nicaea in 325. This council was called to settle a controversy over Christ's divinity, which erupted with violent intensity during the reign of Constantine when the presbyter Arius of Alexandria challenged his bishop, Alexander, on the question of God the Son's relation to God the Father"* [italics added].[18]

...the doctrine of trinity and the "official creed" was not even established until the Council of Nicaea (also known as the First Ecumenical Councl!, held 325 years after Christ!

Arius is quoted as having called God "absolute one" and "unbegotten". It is no wonder he was immediately suspended from his duties. The emperor Constantine went a step further by brutally persecuting and even killing off certain "heretical" groups, such as the Arians, Basilidians, Corinthians, Unitarians, and prominent individuals, all of whom professed belief in Jesus but did not consider him God or even that he was crucified on the cross[19]. Modern Christianity is, in fact, based more on the innovations of Paul and the modern Church, than the teachings of Jesus as the Christian author, David Moore and Jewish scholar of the Bible, Hyam Maccoby, have argued at length in *The Christian Conspiracy*[20] *and Paul and the Invention of Christianity.*[21]

The New Testament itself sends mixed signals about the nature of Jesus. While most Christians take it for granted that Jesus is "God-incarnate", there are many verses in the Gospels that clearly express the subordination of Jesus to God[22], refer to Jesus as a Prophet[23], distinguish between Jesus and the Father[24], discuss the praying of Jesus to God[25], ascribe the miracles of Jesus to the Power of God[26], and even question the necessity of bloodshed for forgiveness.[27]

The Christian doctrine of blood atonement for the sins of humanity is yet another aspect of its flawed understanding of God. As Paul had stated, "Without the shedding of blood there is no remission." Augustine went as far as saying that any un-baptized children are doomed to hellfire due to original sin! When it was feared that a fetus may die before birth, it was believed by some Christians that the fetus must be washed with holy water while still in the womb.[28] To demand the shedding of blood of the "Son of God" because as Paul stated, "In Adam all have sinned"[29] is not only illogical, but also an insult to the Mercy and Justice of God. It is a mockery of God's Mercy if man is not forgiven by sincere repentance and reformation by which God directly forgives, but instead requires the death of another. It is a mockery of Divine

Justice to punish all of humanity for the mistake of one person as the Qur'an clearly rejects such notions:

> "That no one who carries a burden bears another's load; that a man receives but only that for which he strives..." (53:38-39).

The peculiar doctrine of blood atonement is, in fact, a remnant of the pagan belief system which considered blood sacrifice necessary to appease the wrath of God. It is not blood that washes away sin, but sincere repentance, reformation and determination to encourage good and forbid evil, which is exactly what Adam did and the reason why he was forgiven.

While the Christian innovation of "trinitarian monotheism" is relatively obvious to the objective observer, the polytheism of the Jews is less blatant, but no less real, if not more pervasive. Besides their perpetual claims to being the "chosen people of God" despite being immoral, "stiff-necked" and "rebellious" according to the Old Testament (Deuteronomy 9:5-7), the Jews further compromised the transcendence of God by claiming, for example, that Jacob confronted God "face to face" as a man and wrestled and nearly defeated him (Genesis 32:24-30), that God "begot" a Jewish King as His son (Psalm 2:7), and that He was the literal father of the children of Israel (Hosea 1:10).

Moreover, Jews admit that their modern form of religion is a "Rabbinic Judaism" based not on the Old Testament or Torah, but primarily on the Talmud, which is a massive collection of Rabbinic writings spanning several centuries that are supposedly commentaries on the Torah. The Babylonian version of the Talmud, which is widely favored over the Palestinian version, is divided into two main parts, the *Mishnah*, which was written at the end of the second century (C.E.), and the *Gemara*, which was composed as late as the sixth century (C.E.). Rabbi Jacob Neusner admits in *Rabbinic Judaism* the extreme importance of the Talmud:

> *"For 'Judaism' is Rabbinic Judaism, and the Talmud of Babylonia is the authoritative statement of the Torah that Judaism embodies.* The Talmud is the prism, receiving, refracting all light. To state the proposition in

academic language: *into that writing all prior canonical writings emerged; to it, all appeal is directed; upon it, all conclusions ultimately rest.* In the language of Torah itself: study of the Torah begins, as a matter of simple, ubiquitous fact, in the Talmud... In all times, places, and writings, other than those rejected as heretical, from then to now, *the Talmud formed the starting point and the ending point, the alpha and the omega of truth;* justify by appeal to the Talmud, rightly read, persuasively interpreted, and you make your point; disprove a proposition by reference to a statement of the Talmud and you demolish a counterpoint" [italics added].[30]

Professor Robert Goldenberg, Professor of Judaic Studies at the State University of New York, also adds:

> "*The Talmud was Torah.* In a paradox that determined the history of Judaism, the Talmud was Oral Torah in written form, and as such it became the clearest statement that the Jew could hear of God's every word...*The Talmud provided the means of determining how God wanted all Jews to live, in all places, at all times... The Talmud revealed God speaking to Israel, and so the Talmud became Israel's way to God.*"[31] [italics added]

The rabbis have relished their absolute authority to the extent of rendering themselves as gods. Detailed study of the Talmud reveals this fact—note passages such as *Berakhot 7a*, where God asks a rabbi for his blessing; in *Abodah Zarah 3b*, where it is pompously claimed that God spends the first three hours of each day studying the Torah; and *Baba Mezia 59b*, where it is claimed that God is debated and He admits defeat by His sons[32]!! In regard to the authority of the rabbis, Rabbi Jacob Neusner admits, "So the rabbis believe that the man truly made in the divine image is the rabbi; he embodies Revelation—both oral and written—and all his actions constitute paradigms that are not merely correct, but holy and heavenly. Rabbis enjoy exceptional grace from heaven."[33] It is no wonder that Michael Hoffman II, a Christian researcher, states: "Judaism's god is the Jewish people themselves as embodied in their rabbis. Judaism is the worship of Jewish blood in the person of the rabbi. The Jewish "race" itself is rendered god by this means."[34]

(b) *Distortion of Divine Scripture.* History testifies that such association of partners with God went hand in hand with the corruption of Divine scripture. Both the Torah / Old Testament of the Jews and the New Testament of the Christians have suffered from scriptural tampering and perverted interpretations by followers who had particular inclinations that often did not match that of the original message nor that of their many co-authors. As the Qur'an states:

> Then woe to those who write The Book with their own hands, and then say, 'This is from Allah' … (2:79)

> There is among them (People of the Book) a section who distort the Book with their tongues: (as they read) you would think it is a part of the Book, but it is no part of the Book; and they say, 'That is from Allah', but it is not from Allah. It is they who tell a lie against Allah and they know it well! It is not possible that a man, to whom is given the Book and Wisdom and the Prophetic Office, should say to people, 'Be my worshippers, rather than Allah's'. On the contrary, (he would say) 'Be worshippers of Him who is truly the Cherisher of all—for you have taught the Book and you have studied it earnestly. (3:78-79)

> Can you entertain the hope that they will believe in you?—seeing that a party among them (the Jews) heard the Word of Allah, and knowingly perverted it after they understood it. (2:75)

In considering the reliability of the four gospels in conveying the teachings of Jesus, a number of facts, acknowledged even by Christian scholars and historians, must be kept in mind: *(a) the teachings of Jesus were not recorded during his lifetime; (b) the gospels are generally thought to be written between 65-115 C.E. with none of the evangelists having met or seen Jesus;* (c) the gospels *were written in Greek, not Aramaic, the language spoken by Jesus (AS)* and *(d) the earliest extant manuscripts of the gospels, the Codex Sinaiticus,*

Codex Vaticanus, Codex Alexandrinus, belong to the fourth and fifth centuries, and contain a number of contradictions between them. This is to say nothing of the interpretations and inclinations of the authors of the gospels, the many contradictions between and within gospels, or the lost gospels, such as the *Gospel of Barnabas*. The Christian scholar, Dr. David Moore, has discussed fifteen gospels that were omitted from current versions of the Canonical Bible and states that "it is believed that some otherwise worthy works were eliminated solely because they were admired by sects which had been declared heretical".[35] As we shall study later, all of these question marks stand in stark contrast to the historical and textual reliability of Islamic teachings.

The distortion and corruption of scripture is not merely a claim of the Qur'an but is attested to by a number of Western authors. Regarding the New Testament, the Episcopal Bishop, John Shelby Spong, has this to say in *Rescuing the Bible from Fundamentalism:*

> ...of the four Gospels, Luke and Mark do not ever claim the authority of being apostles. Neither is listed by any gospel writer among the chosen Twelve. So their material cannot be of the eyewitness variety. *The question must also be raised as to whether we have the actual words of Jesus in any Gospel. Certainly the words of Jesus we have in the New Testament are not in the language that Jesus spoke. How much did the needs of the Christian community at the moment the Gospels were written prove stronger than the historicity of the words themselves? Frequently one quotation of Jesus in one Gospel will not harmonize with another word of Jesus, either in the same Gospel or in a different one* [italics added].[36]

He goes on to challenge the theory of Divine inspiration that was developed to counter the many fallacies encountered in the Bible:

> Clearly these difficulties have been sensed in the past, and the theory of divine inspiration has been developed to counter this threat to inerrancy claims. The divine inspiration theory suggests that the human scribes wrote as they were directed to write by the Holy Spirit. *Whatever disharmony might be discovered to exist in the total text is then blamed on the*

humanity of the scribe, thus leaving intact the inerrancy of the ultimate source of the word of God. It is not a helpful argument, and is not normally employed until the fundamentalist's back is against the wall... Such ideas may be ingenious, but they do not finally hold water [italics added].[37]

The case of the Old Testament - which is usually presumed to have been written by Moses - is even worse as we have the admission from the Biblical scholar, Richard Friedman, that *"At present, however, there is hardly a biblical scholar in the world actively working on the problem who would claim that the Five Books of Moses were written by Moses- or by any one person."*[38] In fact, he goes on to say that research into the authorship of the Bible revealed that there were at least four authors or sets of authors involved:

There was evidence that the Five Books of Moses had been composed by combining four different source documents into one continuous history. For working purposes, the four documents were identified by alphabetic symbols. The document that was associated with the divine name Yahweh/Jehovah was called J. The document that was identified as referring to the deity as God (in Hebrew, Elohim) called E. The third document, by far the largest, included most of the legal sections and concentrated a great deal on matters having to do with priests, and so it was called P - And the source that was found only in the book of Deuteronomy was called D. *The question was how to uncover the history of these four documents- not only who wrote them, but why four different versions of the story were written, what their relationship to each other was, whether any of the authors were aware of the existence of the others' texts, when in history each was produced, how they were preserved and combined, and a host of other questions* [italics added].[39]

David Moore has added that "there is a lot of historical evidence which states that the Old Testament, in its present form, did not exist until some 60 years after the death of Christ". How can any reasonable person trust a document whose authorship is both unknown and multiple and composed hundreds of years after its original Revelation?

(c) *Denial of the Truth.* The denial of Truth becomes evident when it is realized that the coming of Muhammad (SAW) was foretold in both the Old and New Testaments and there were a number of Jews and Christians at the time of Prophet Muhammad (SAW) who realized and knew of his genuine Prophethood. Both the Qur'an and sayings of Prophet Muhammad (SAW) speak of various Jews and Christians who had encountered Muslims and knew the Truth of his message, but refused to obey it due to arrogance and envy that the final Prophet was not "one of them":

> And when there comes to them a Book from Allah, confirming what is with them—although from old they had prayed for victory against those without faith—when there comes to them that which they should have recognized, they refuse to believe in it, but the curse of Allah is on those without faith. Miserable is the price for which they have sold their souls, in that they deny (the revelation) which Allah has sent down, in insolent envy that Allah of His Grace should send it to any of His servants He pleases. (2:89-90)

> Oh People of the Book! Why do you reject the signs of Allah, of which you are (yourselves) witnesses. Oh People of the Book! Why do you clothe Truth with falsehood and conceal the Truth, while you have knowledge. (3:70-71)

> Without doubt it is announced in the Revealed Books of former peoples. Is it not a sign that the learned of the Children of Israel knew it as true? (26:196-197)

Prior to Muhammad's (SAW) birth in 570 C.E., both Christians and Jews had eagerly awaited the coming of a great Prophet. Many authors have discussed at length the prophecies contained in both The Old and New Testaments concerning the awaited one who would be "like unto thee (Moses)" expressed in Deuteronomy 18:18, and the "Paraclete" prophesied by Jesus (John 14:16, 15:26, 16:7), which are, in actuality, prophecies in reference to Muhammad (SAW).[40]

Even as a young child, various Christians and Jews in the Arabian Peninsula knew of his coming greatness. One such account occurs when as a boy, Muhammad (SAW) encountered a Christian monk near Bostra while accompanying his uncle on a trip to Syria. Martin Lings describes the result of the meeting, originally narrated by the historian Ibn Ishaq, as follows: "Bahira had already felt certain, but now he was doubly so, for there, between his shoulders, was the very mark he expected to see, the seal of prophethood even as it was described in his book, in the selfsame place... 'Take thy brother's son back to his country and guard him against the Jews, for by God, if they see him and know of him that which I know, they will contrive evil against him. Great things are in store for this brother's son of thine.'"[41]

Karen Armstrong in *Muhammad. A Biography of the Prophet,* also speaks of a Jewish awaiting of the Prophet: "A rabbi of great piety had actually emigrated to Yathrib (Medina) from Syria. When people asked him why he had left that gentle, fertile country for 'a land of hardship and hunger', he had replied that he had wanted to be in the Hijaz when the 'Prophet' arrived. 'His time has come,' he said to the Jewish tribes of Yathrib, 'and don't let anyone get to him before you, O Jews, for he will be sent to shed blood and to take captive the women and children of those who oppose him. Let not that keep you back from him.'" She goes on to conclude, "The stories of Jewish and Christian expectation reflect the spiritual disease in Arabia at the beginning of the seventh century but they also show the powerful effect that a prophetic hero like Jesus or Muhammad had on his own and later generations: what they achieved was so remarkable and so perfectly attuned to the needs of the day that it seemed foreordained in some mysterious way and to have fulfilled the religious aspirations of the past."[42]

(d) *Disobedience of God's Covenant and Messengers.* The early history of the Children of Israel and Christians was plagued by a disavowal of their covenant with God and a rejection of their Messengers. The covenant included the agreement to obey none other than God and abide by the Divine Law and moral code conveyed by the Messengers. However, the majority of them did not stand by their covenant, to the extent that they slew their Messengers in the process. In return, God's blessing was withheld and they suffered the consequences:

And remember We took a covenant from the Children of Israel to worship none but Allah; treat with kindness your parents and kindred, and orphans and those in need; speak fair to the people; be steadfast in prayer; and practice regular charity. Then did you turn back, except a few among you, and you backslide even now. (2:83)

For those, too, who call themselves Christians, We did take a Covenant, but they forgot a good part of the Message that was sent them: so We estranged them, with enmity and hatred between the one and the other, to the Day of Judgment and soon will Allah show them what it is they have done. (5:14)

We took the Covenant of the Children of Israel and sent them Messengers. Every time there came to them a Messenger with what they themselves desired not—some of them they called imposters, and some they slay. (5:70)

If only the People of the Book had believed and been righteous, We should indeed have blotted out their iniquities and admitted them to the Garden of Bliss. If only they had stood fast by the Law, the Gospel, and all the revelation that was sent to them from their Lord, they would have enjoyed happiness from every side. There is among them a party on the right course, but many of them follow a course that is evil. (5:65-66)[43]

The Christian transgression against the commandments of God consists not only in its "polytheistic monotheism" and rejection of the final Messenger, but also in the severe compromising of Divine moral and ethical standards by maintaining belief in the expiation of sins through the blood of Christ. Modern Christianity has so deeply ingrained the myth of God's Son "dying for our sins" that many of its followers have adopted an attitude of moral laxity and complacency to the detriment of society-at-large. Thus, despite the Christian condemnation of such sins as pre- and extra-marital sex, abortion, homosexuality and substance abuse, these transgressions have become so rampant in Western societies that most either turn a blind eye toward them or wholeheartedly embrace them, instead of abhorring and preventing them as the anathema to society that they are.

The extent of Jewish transgression against the commandments of God is even more striking than the Christian case. The Talmud itself, which has become the primary text of modern Judaism as explained earlier, is replete with passages that are repugnant to common ethics and sensibilities, not to mention in violation of Divine Law. A few examples of the sins sanctioned therein include sexual intercourse with toddlers; stealing, subterfuge and murder of gentiles; and considering disobedience of rabbis worse than disobedience of the Torah. Malevolent insults of Jesus (AS) and Mary (AS) are also to be found in the Talmud, as admitted by authors like the Jewish scholar, Hyam Maccoby[44] and the historian and linguist, Daniel-Rops[45] (though most current editions have predictably been edited to avoid fueling historical tensions between Catholicism and Judaism). The following direct quotations are from "The Babylonian Talmud", and can be verified by any objective seeker: include sexual intercourse with toddlers; stealing, subterfuge and murder of gentiles; disobedience of Rabbis is considered worse than disobedience of the Torah; and the insulting of Jesus as a soothsayer and the Virgin Mary as a harlot![44] The following direct quotations are from "The Babylonian Talmud"[45], and can be verified by any objective seeker:

> *When a grown up man has had intercourse with a little girl it is nothing,* for when the girl is less than this, it is as if one puts the finger into the eye; but when a small boy has intercourse with a grown up woman he makes her as a girl who is injured by a piece of wood... (Ketuboth 11b)

> My son, be more careful in (the observance of) the words of the Scribes than in the words of the Torah, for in the laws of the Torah there are positive and negative precepts; but as to the laws of the Scribes, *whoever transgresses any of the enactments of the Scribes incurs the penalty of death.* (Erubin 21b)

> *Whoever mocks at the words of the Sages is punished with hot excrement.* (Gittin 57a)

For murder, whether of a heathen by a heathen, or of an Israelite by a heathen, punishment is incurred, *but of a heathen by an Israelite, there is no death penalty*...To what can this apply in the case of robbery? Rabbi Alia b. Jacob answered...One heathen from another, or a heathen from an Israelite is forbidden, but an Israelite from a heathen is permitted. (Sanhedrin 57a)

If one finds therein a lost object, then if the majority are Israelites it has to be announced, but if the majority are *heathens it has not to be announced.* (Baba Mezia 24a)

When a suit arises between an Israelite and a heathen, if you can justify the former according to the laws of Israel, justify him and say, 'This is our law'; so also if you can justify him by the laws of the heathens justify him and say, 'This is your law'; *but if this cannot be done we use subterfuges to circumvent him.* (Baba Kamma 113a)

Unfortunately these are but a few examples of the perversions of the Talmud. It is a testament to the propaganda machine of the Jews that such information is not more widely known. The constantly ingrained fear of being labeled "anti-Semitic" or "insensitive to the victims of the Holocaust" instilled in the masses has been instrumental in preventing the dissemination of such dirty truths. Another important factor is the fact that the Talmud is a massive set of commentaries spanning several centuries and comprising at least twenty-one volumes (depending on the edition), which few people, including Jews and gentiles, have the patience to study. Most popular writings regarding the Talmud contain only the choicest of "selections" that have been sanitized for public consumption.

The point of such references is not to denigrate any religion (the presented material has been provided by Christian and Jewish authors and their texts), but to make the reader fully aware of the very serious digressions and deviations that have occurred over the years from the original Revelations of God. It is no wonder that the Qur'an accuses some Jews and Christians of creating divisiveness and sectarianism (*ahzab*) in the primordial religion of

God (13:36, 11:17). In the process, Christians have ended up expounding the polytheistic doctrine of trinity, Jews have slain His Messengers and proclaimed themselves the "chosen people of God" despite owing greater allegiance to their Rabbis; while both parties have besmirched the pristine nature of their Divine revelations and rejected the Final Messenger of God. It is not the secondary differences between the religions pertaining to their respective laws or rituals that are criticized in the Qur'an. The seriousness of digression from Revelation and disobedience of God, however, are such that Muslims also are rebuked in the Qur'an that "Unless you go forth (in the cause of Allah), He will punish you with a grievous penalty and put others in your place..." (9:39).[46] Thus, Muslims are sternly warned that unless their actions reflect a sincere desire to strive in His Path, they too are not worthy adherents of Islam.

4.5 Eastern Religions

The case of Hindus and Buddhists, though not mentioned specifically by name in the Qur'an, is also not immune to the fundamental criticism presented of the Jews and Christians. Although it is safe to assume that the earliest Muslim community did not physically encounter Hindus, Buddhists or members of other religions of the Far East, certain principles from the criticism of Jews and Christians can be applied to them. Nonetheless, based on the Islamic belief that all nations had their share of Messengers, it is reasonable to believe that what we know of as Hinduism, Buddhism, Taoism and Confucianism had their origins with the teachings of Divine messengers, but that over the course of thousands of years, they too digressed from their original forms of monotheism such that they have now devolved into forms or mixtures of polytheism, pantheism, monism and in some cases, even atheism.

Modern Hinduism presents the classic case of a religion that has undergone so much change that it now defies definition and characterization. As Ed Viswanathan, a Hindu scholar, has stated:

As you study Hinduism from one end to the other you will find it to be filled with all kinds of ideas. It has highly spiritualistic Advaita and Raja Yoga on one side and highly materialistic, atheistic, hedonistic Charvaka philosophy, which does not believe in God or the Vedas, on the other side. On one side, idolatry is a part of Hinduism, and on the other, as expressed by the German philosopher Max Muller, 'The religion of the Vedas knows no idols.'[47] The Jahala Upanishad says, 'Images are meant only as aids to meditation for the ignorant.'[48]

Such relativism with respect to belief and practice only leads to confusion and insults the Divine Guidance that has been provided for the benefit of mankind. Moreover, despite such diversity in Hinduism, the overwhelming thrust of modern Hinduism revolves around a confusing disarray of deities that includes human beings, animals, animal-human hybrids, and various entities from the natural world. While Islam recognizes the *signature* of the Creator in all creation, it is very clear in not equating the two.

When we revert to what the Hindus consider holy scriptures, here too there is confusion not only with respect to unknown authorship, but also the many conflicting views expressed therein:

"We have only speculative guesses on the authorship of different Hindu scriptures. Almost all Hindu scriptures are written by anonymous authors. Through all Hindu scriptures one can see the authors deliberately trying to avoid signing their names anywhere."[49]

One such "holy scripture" is the *Manu Shastri* from which the curse of the caste system originated and has now prospered for well over a thousand years. As a result of the caste system, the Brahmins who are the highest class created from the head of the Lord Brahma, have sabotaged all forms of authority in a manner reminiscent of Rabbis in Judaism. A common saying recited by most Brahmins is "The universe is under the power of gods, the gods are under the power of the mantras, the mantras under the power of Brahmins, therefore the Brahmins are gods."[50] Only in recent years has the Indian government banned the caste system, though few would argue that it does not exist in much of Indian society. As the late Dr. Ambedkar, a former "untouchable" member of Parliament explained, the caste system advocates the superiority of the Brahmins and the complete denigration of the lower Shudra and "Untouchable" classes, including their prohibition from education, positions of authority, and acquisition of property as well as disarmament. Thus, Brahmins monopolize not only priestly positions but also prominent positions in government, educational institutions and business.

As with Hinduism, Buddhism must confront a number of problems when attempting to establish its core beliefs and principles. While modern Buddhism has tried to do so, despite the significant differences between the Mahayana and Theravada schools, the major problem remains in the reliability of its sources. When we try to analyze the original teachings of Gautama Buddha, we find that such records do not really exist, as Huston Smith, the world-renowned religious scholar, has noted: "The Buddha's outlook on life is not easy to come by for three reasons: he did not commit his teaching to writing; a century and a half elapsed before the first written records appear; and when they do appear they pour forth in bewildering variety and number."[51] The eminent scholar of Buddhism, Edward Conze, adds that:

> Buddhism is a body of traditions in which few names stand out, and in which fewer dates are precisely known. It is indeed most exasperating when we try to apply our current ideas of historical criticism. Langlois and Seignobos in their textbook of historical method, state that a 'document whose author, date and provenance (source) cannot be determined, is just good for nothing'... Alas that is the case with most of the documents on which we build a history of Buddhism.[52]

He goes on to say that the Buddhism of today is most likely unrepresentative of what Buddha actually taught:

> One thing alone do all these attempts to reconstruct an original Buddhism have in common. They all agree that the Buddha's doctrine was certainly

not what the Buddhists understood it to be. Mrs. Rhys Davids, for instance, purges Buddhism of the doctrine of 'not-self', and of monasticism. To her, some worship of 'The Man' is the original gospel of Buddhism. H.J. Jennings, in cold blood, removes all references to reincarnation from the scriptures, and claims thereby to have restored their original meaning. Dr. P. Dahlke, again, ignores all the magic and mythology with which traditional Buddhism is replete, and reduces the doctrine of the Buddha to a quite reasonable, agnostic theory."[53]

Notwithstanding such historical criticisms, the Buddhist belief with respect to God also stands at odds with the Islamic view. Buddhists are very clear in denying attributes relating to God as a Creator or an omniscient, omnipotent and infinitely Good Being, though there are those who have tried to relate the concept of *nirvana* to certain qualities of what would be considered "God" in the monotheistic sense. K.N. Jayatilleke has explained this widespread Buddhist belief as follows:

Using the word (theism) in the above sense of a Personal Creator God, who is a Supreme being possessed of the characteristics of omniscience, omnipotence and infinite goodness, if we ask the question, 'Does God exist?' there are four possible answers. They are (1) those theists who say 'yes' and affirm God's existence, (2) those atheists who say 'no' and deny God's existence, (3) those skeptics or agnostics who say 'we do not know' or 'we cannot know' and (4) those positivists who say that the question is meaningless since the meaning of the term "God" is not clear. What is the Buddhist answer to this question? Was the Buddha a Theist, an Atheist, an Agnostic or a Positivist? The answer is fairly clear. *Given the above definition of God in its usual interpretation, the Buddha is an atheist and Buddhism in both its Theravada and Mahayana forms is atheism.*[54]

Here again, the point of such criticisms is to bring attention to certain historical and textual criticisms that remind us how removed certain religions are from Divine Revelation and True Monotheism when compared with Islam. In light of these criticisms, it is now time to turn our attention to what Islam has to offer as a complete system and way of life grounded in Divine Revelation.

4.6 The Beauty of Islam

It is rather peculiar that in the very modern societies that are so eager to encourage the use of rational and scientific methods in all wakes of life, such faculties are often quickly dismissed when it comes to evaluating and studying the truth claims of religions. Modern Western societies, in particular, are characterized by an increasing skew towards a deeply ingrained belief in either skepticism or pluralism when it comes to matters of religion. While there are indeed a number of fundamental similarities between all religions, there are also a number of fundamental differences and unique elements in any religion.

In the case of Islam, most Western authors and media outlets have gone to great lengths to falsely portray Muslims as backward, fanatic terrorists who are bent upon destroying the modern world rather than to even remotely understand the teachings of Islam or its commonalities with other faiths. While such misconceptions have been dealt with elsewhere,[55] even a cursory study of Islam would reveal a number of distinguishing features valuable to the plight of modern man, including for example, its teachings with respect to belief in all genuine Prophets and Scriptures, the importance of knowledge and scientific endeavor, implementation of social justice, means of self-purification, establishing an equitable economic system, the role of the family unit, and establishing a moral and ethical society. Nonetheless, for the purposes of this chapter, we will focus on three essential and distinguishing features of Islam. These features, which correspond to the theme of Divine Revelation as the critical criterion for true religion, are the: (1) *Preservation of its Sources*, (2) *Concept of Tawhid or Pure Monotheism*, and (3) *Finality of its Message* (additional distinguishing features relating to Islamic ethics will be discussed in Chapter 5).

Preservation of Sources:

The first distinguishing feature concerns the preservation of the primary sources of Islamic teachings, i.e. the Qur'an and Sunnah, or Way of the Prophet. The immutability and extent of preservation of sources in Islam stands in stark contrast to all other religions, both in the sense of being the most representative of its original Divine guidance, and in the sense of meeting the strictest criteria of historical and textual criticism. No other religion better represents the primordial religion of God. Christianity, Judaism, Hinduism, Buddhism and other revealed religions may contain remnants of the eternal religion but have severely compromised aspects of the nature of God and/or worship, nor do they require belief in all Prophets as discussed earlier.

> *The immutability and extent of preservation of sources in Islam stands in stark contrast to all other religions, both in the sense of being the most representative of its original Divine guidance, and in the sense of meeting the strictest criteria of historical and textual criticism.*

The task of preserving the Qur'an until the end of time has been promised by none other than Allah. Not a single verse, phrase, word or even letter has ever been altered or ever will be. Thus, Allah promises that: "We it is Who have sent down this Qur'an and We it is Who will protect it" (15:9).

The preservation of the Qur'an from any kind of blemish is not simply a belief of blind faith, but is a fact attested to by history and its parallel is unfound in any other religion. For over 1400 years, all Muslims spanning a wide variety of locations and eras have had the same Qur'an as a source of guidance. Historically, Islam has relied on both written documentation and memorization or oral tradition in its preservation. Both methods work to supplement and verify each other. Unlike other religions that lost portions of their scriptures or did not record their particular scriptures until many years after revelation, Prophet Muhammad (SAW) himself oversaw the dictation of Qur'anic passages by certain scribes as they were revealed piecemeal during a twenty-three year period of his life.[56] These verses were recorded on palm leaves, slate-like stones, hide pieces, palm leaves, shoulder blades and the like.

The Prophet (SAW) also inculcated these revelations into the minds of the companions by repeated recitation in the daily prayers.

The quality of the Arabic used in the Qur'an is such that not only was it miraculous and unparalleled when it was revealed, but also remains the finest model of classical language in the field of Arabic literature over 1400 years later. The challenge presented to non-believers in the Qur'an to produce even one chapter comparable to it (2:23), whether in literary quality or spiritual value, remains to be met. Unlike the scriptural languages of Sanskrit, Pali, and Aramaic, the Arabic language remains vibrant and alive among the masses of the Arab world. This has aided another aspect of the extraordinary safeguarding of the Qur'an, which is the fact that history has witnessed millions of people throughout the world who have memorized it, end-to-end, including children as young as five years of age. The memorization of entire scriptures is virtually unheard of, even among the priestly and scholarly elite of other religions, let alone ordinary believers. Numerous efforts by conquering armies, non-Muslims, Orientalist academics, and even deviant Muslim sects to alter or destroy the Qur'an have all failed miserably.

> *The challenge presented to non-believers in the Qur'an to produce even one chapter comparable to it (2:23), whether in literary quality or spiritual value, remains to be met.*

Sir W. Muir has commented that "Except the Qur'an there is no book under the sun which, for the last twelve centuries, has remained with so pure a text."[57] Even the great enemy of Islam, John Noss, who considered the Qur'an to be written by Muhammad (SAW) as a forgery of Jewish and Christian traditions, and considered the spread of Islam to be based on the sword and forced conversion, has said: "It (Islam) has kept one basic scripture, preserved from the first in a state of textural purity such that no variant readings have ever arisen to confuse the commentators."[58]

It is not surprising, then, that many Western scholars and Orientalists studying Islam have veered away from textual purity in their criticisms and, instead, tried to portray the Qur'an not as a direct Revelation from God, but as being written by Muhammad (SAW) and being a forgery of existing Jewish and Christian traditions[59]. Notwithstanding mal-intent, they conveniently ignore the facts that (1) Muhammad (SAW) was never taught the basics of reading and writing, let alone that of Arabic poetry or prose, and (2) the Qur'an contains numerous prophecies verified later by history and (3) the Qur'an contains numerous statements pertaining to the natural order that have only recently been verified by modern science. In answering the lies against Muhammad (SAW), the Qur'an returns to the critical fact that Muhammad (SAW) was unlettered:

> And you did not recite any book before it (the Qur'an), nor did you transcribe one with your right hand, for then would those who utter falsehood have doubted. (29:48)

As for the claim of forgery, the Qur'an is very clear, on the one hand, in stating that Islam is not a new religion, but rather a continuation of the primordial religion whereby similarities with prior Revelations are to be expected, but on the other hand, in distinguishing itself from prior revelations in several key areas. Not only does Islam differ greatly in its understanding of God and our relationship to Him (as detailed in Sections 4.3 and 4.4), but also in the way that the Qur'an describes many prior historical incidents, such as the creation of Adam, the role of Satan, the flood, the Abrahamic sacrifice, the crucifixion of Christ, etc. Why does Islam present different historical accounts and unique principles if it is merely a forgery of earlier traditions? Despite this fact, the Qur'an does not respond to the charges of forgery by dwelling on details, but rather by reiterating that it is Allah who knows the secret of the heavens and the earth and it is He who has sent His Revelation to those eager for guidance:

> And the unbelievers say: 'This is nothing but a lie which he has forged and others have helped him at it.' So indeed have they produced iniquity and uttered a slander. And they say: '(They are) Tales of the ancients which he has caused to be written and they are dictated before him morning and evening.' Say: 'It (the Qur'an) was sent down by Him who knows the secret of the heavens and the earth; verily He is Oft-Forgiving, Most Merciful.' (25:4-6)

As for the second source of Islam, the Sunnah or Way of Prophet Muhammad (SAW), the extent of its preservation too is a feature whose parallel is glaringly absent in all other religions. Unlike the Old and New Testaments of Judaism and Christianity, Islam also maintains a clear separation between the Divine Word and the Prophetic Word, i.e. the Qur'an and the Sunnah. The sayings, actions and behaviors of the Prophet (SAW) were recorded to the minutest detail during his lifetime by a multitude of companions, with at least one thousand companions having narrated at least one saying or hadith. There are tens of thousands of *ahadith* (sayings) that have been authenticated and agreed upon by not only all scholars of Islam, but are also used as historical record by non-Muslim scholars. Although certain forged or false sayings were inevitably attributed to the Prophet (SAW) after his passing, these were known to be so, and the scholars of the science of *hadith* have gone to great lengths and rigorous detail in analyzing complete chains of narrators and checking against other *ahadith* in order to grade levels of authenticity. Islam is unique in being the only religion to classify the sayings of its Prophet according to various levels, such as authentic, sound, weak or fabricated (*sahih, hasan, daeef, mawdu'*).

Can any other religion even remotely come close to possessing tens of thousands of detailed sayings and actions of their Prophet or founder, let alone with complete chains of narration? It is no wonder that the renowned historian, A. Toynbee, declared:

The sources for the study of Islamic History from Muhammad's lifetime onwards, are copious, and many of them are of first-rate value from the historian's point of view. Muhammad's career, unlike Jesus', can be followed point by point—and, in some of its chapters, almost day by day—in the full light of history.[60]

Can any other religion even remotely come close to possessing tens of thousands of detailed sayings and actions of their Prophet or founder, let alone with complete chains of narration?

Tawhid: Pure Monotheism

The second distinguishing feature is the concept of *tawhid* that is central to all Islamic teachings. *Tawhid* is the belief in the unity and centrality of God that must pervade all belief and practice, as introduced in Chapter 1. God is the Absolute Being that possesses perfection of all Attributes described unto Himself through His Scriptures and Messengers. One of these attributes is the Unity of God. All other religions have either severely compromised or opposed this aspect as described at length earlier. Christianity has lent considerable credence to the notion of "blind faith" by maintaining belief in the triune God and salvation through the blood sacrifice of the "Son of God"; Judaism has devolved into an elitist following of rabbis turned demagogues; Buddhism is highly uncertain as to Gautama Buddha's teachings, nor does it even believe in God as a Creator; while Hinduism is a large smorgasbord of beliefs with an array of gods and deities so numerous that one would struggle to list them all. It would, thus, not be an exaggeration to say that Islam is the only religion that emphasizes, in theory and practice, a simple and direct relationship with the One and Only God.

The Islamic *tawhid* is not merely a belief, but a living principle that encompasses all belief, practice and spheres of life. Everything and everyone is from Allah and to Him will all return. Hence, there is an underlying unity that pervades all natural systems and scientific laws of the universe; all knowledge is unified when it ultimately leads to a greater understanding of the Infinitely Knowledgeable (unlike that taught in modern educational institutions); all of mankind is unified in purpose and needs, for which no other religion has had better success than Islam in implementing a global civilization while shattering the barriers of race, color, nation and social status; all economic wealth and natural resources are from Allah, and must therefore be used not just for personal profit and free enterprise, but also in establishing justice and equality; all political power is subservient to the Power of Allah, and thus, all rule must be conducted according to the commandments of Allah; and all daily activities must be performed with the intention to please Allah without any artificial divides between the public and the private, the secular and the profane, or the Church and the State.

Thus, *tawhid* is not merely belief in one God, but also entails submission to Him in all aspects of life. The form of this submission must be prescribed by Revelation. As Syed Muhammad Naquib Al-Attas has profoundly stated,

> It is a mistake to think belief in One God alone is sufficient in true religion, and that such belief guarantees security and salvation. *Iblis* (Satan), who believes in the One True God and knows and acknowledges Him as his Creator, Cherisher and Sustainer, his *rabb*, is nevertheless a misbeliever (*kafir*). Although *Iblis* (Satan) submits to God, yet he submits grudgingly and insolently, and his true *kufr* (disbelief) is due to arrogance, disobedience and rebellion. His is the most notorious example of unwilling submission. Unwilling submission, then, is not the mark of true belief, and a *kafir* (misbeliever) might therefore be also one who, though professing belief in one *God, does not submit in real submission, but prefers instead to submit in his own obstinate way—a way, or manner, or form neither approved nor revealed and commanded by God. Real submission is that which has been perfected by the Holy Prophet as the model for mankind, for that is the manner of submission of all the Prophets and Messengers before him, and the form approved, revealed and commanded by God.* Thus, the fundamental core of true religion, then, is not the belief, but rather, more fundamentally, the submission; for the submission confirms and affirms the belief to be true and genuine.[61] [italics added]

Thus, having some notion of God with some semblance of following him according to one's own limited understanding is not enough. That is why Islam, as a revealed religion, emphasizes following Divine Revelation when it comes to understanding God and the manner of following His commandments-not our own whims and fancies, nor the beliefs of others, nor beliefs deriving from cultural traditions, nor the speculation of philosophers or academics, nor the findings of modern scientists. Without submission to His Will the belief in Him is incomplete.

The Final Message:

Islam is also distinguished by the fact that Muhammad (SAW) and the Divine Law that he shared represent the Final Messenger and Revealed Law, respectively, sent to mankind until the end of the world as we know it.

Earlier we explained that Islam considers every nation to have been blessed with at least one Messenger from God. Who, then, is the Messenger for our times?

Muhammad (SAW) is not only the final Messenger of God but also the only Messenger sent to mankind as a whole. The Qur'an calls him the *"khatam an-nabieen"* or Seal of the Prophets. The Prophet (SAW) himself described the finality of his message as follows: "Prophethood is like a house, the building of which has now been completed. There is room for only one more brick, and I am putting that brick in its place."[62] Despite various pretenders to prophethood, history testifies that there has been no prophet, or religious movement for that matter, after Muhammad (SAW) with any significant global following. God has sealed prophethood just as an envelope or document has been sealed, with no possibility of adding to or deleting from it:

> Muhammad is not the father of any of your men, but he is the Messenger of Allah and the Seal of the Prophets, and Allah has full knowledge of all things. (33:40)

Why, however, has prophethood and Revelation been sealed? Earlier we referred to the primary reason for the sending of Prophets as being to warn and remind people of the necessity of worshipping God in His Unity and Essence and to proclaim how He is to be worshipped. Given the immaculate preservation of the Qur'an and Sunnah and its vast teachings concerning these two aspects, the reason for sending Prophets is no longer present in our times. Those who have knowledge of these sources have the responsibility of propagating this message to those who do not. As the Prophet (SAW) has said, "The knowledgeable are the heirs to the Prophets."[63] While it is true that having the preserved teachings of a Messenger is not identical to having him physically present in our midst, this aspect too is taken into account in Allah's judgment of us.

The universality of Prophet Muhammad's (SAW) message is another aspect that is unique among all Prophets. While other Prophets confined their messages to their respective peoples, Allah Himself confirms the universality of Prophet Muhammad's message: "We have not sent thee (Muhammad) save as a blessing for all mankind" (21:107).

History also confirms that it is only Islam that has been able to provide a truly universal civilization. Not only has Islam spread to every corner of the globe, it does not recognize any notion of the modern nation-state–it only considers one nation, or *Ummah*, that of mankind as a whole, for whom Muhammad is the Messenger. The early Caliphs of Islam, Abu Bakr, 'Umar, 'Uthman and 'Ali, led a vast cross-section of peoples, races and colors united simply in the common desire to follow Allah. Even as recent as the eighteenth century (C.E.), the rule of the Ottoman Caliphate which extended over what is now known as the Balkans, Central Asia and the Middle East, was based on the unifying feature of Islam, not any colonial, imperialist or economic domination. Today, in the melting pot of American society, the only religion that is consistently able to bring together peoples from every corner of the globe in its place of worship is that of Islam.

> *Today, in the melting pot of American society, the only religion that is consistently able to bring together peoples from every corner of the globe in its place of worship is that of Islam.*

The devout Muslim belief in the message of Muhammad (SAW) and all prior Prophets begs another question. If Muslims accept all prior Messengers of God and their Scriptures in their original forms, why is it that other religions do not accept Prophet Muhammad (SAW)? The Qur'an alludes to this question:

> Say, 'We believe in Allah and the revelation given to us, and to Abraham, Ishmael, Isaac, Jacob, and the Tribes, and that given to Moses and Jesus, and that given to all Prophets from their Lord- we make no difference between one another of them, and we bow to Allah as Muslims.' So, if they believe

as you believe, they are indeed on the right path, but if they turn back, it is they who are in schism… (2:136-137)

So, if they (People of the Book) dispute with you (Muhammad, SAW), say, 'I have submitted my whole self to Allah and so have those who follow me.' And say to the People of the Book and to those who are unlearned: 'Do you (also) submit yourselves?' If they do, they are in right guidance, but if they turn back, your duty is to convey the message, and in Allah's sight are all His servants. (3:20)

We must all objectively ask ourselves if any Messenger of God, be he Abraham, Moses, David, Jesus or Muhammad (peace be upon them), were currently present among our midst, would we follow him? All believers should answer in the affirmative. Muslims argue that the situation is, in fact, such that it is as if Muhammad (SAW) is present amongst ourselves, although not in physical form, certainly in the more important form of his precise teachings and actions that have been immaculately preserved to this day. As noted earlier, even non-Muslim scholars have acknowledged the unparalleled extent to which the Islamic sources of knowledge have been preserved; how then can any objective person refuse to heed the message of Allah as conveyed by Muhammad (SAW)?

> *We must all objectively ask ourselves if any Messenger of God, be he Abraham, Moses, David, Jesus or Muhammad (peace be upon them), were currently present among our midst, would we follow him?*

Anyone aware of the message of Muhammad (SAW) is obliged to follow him and cannot claim the excuse that he or she prefers to follow the teachings of a prior Messenger. As explained in Sections 4.4 and 4.5, the precise teachings of prior Messengers are now either missing or incomplete or altered to the point that the Divine origins of other religions are indiscernible. Moreover, the Laws of previous Prophets have been abrogated by that of Islam for many of the reasons described in Sections 4.4 and 4.5. Thus, we have in the Qur'an that:

None of Our revelations as We abrogate or cause to be forgotten, but We substitute something better or similar; know you not that Allah has power over all things? (2:106)

This Qur'an is not such as can be produced by other than Allah: on the contrary it is a confirmation of prior revelations, and a fuller explanation of The Book- wherein there is no doubt—from the Lord of the worlds. (10:37)

While each Prophet had been provided with a respective Law[64], the Law for our times is that provided to Muhammad (SAW). The existence of prior Laws does not indicate a sudden change in the Will of God or an alteration of eternal principles, but rather, that God realizes the nature of different peoples and different eras, and correspondingly has changed certain details of the Laws as appropriate. The crux of the message of the Unity of God and the need to follow Him has always been consistent. The binding nature of the message of Islam for our present times, however, is such that Muhammad (SAW) stated, "Had Moses been alive, even he could have no alternative but to follow me."

4.7 The Wisdom of Religious Diversity

While we have dealt at length with a number of unique facets of Islamic teachings and the importance of Islam as a way of life in our present day, it is nonetheless a fact of our existence that the majority of the world is not formally Muslim. What then could be the Divine Wisdom behind the multitude of religions[65] among our midst?

At the outset, it must be stated that given the earlier presented concept of the primordial religion of Islam being the only acceptable religion in the eyes of God, the question should not be why God has allowed so many religions, but rather, why men have evolved so many religions? Thus, the question of why there is religious diversity is rather similar to the question of why there is disobedience (addressed in Chapter 3)-for the root of deviance from the Straight Path of one eternal religion grows from disobedience and failure to submit.

> *...the question of why there is religious diversity is rather similar to the question of why there is disobedience – for the root of deviance from the Straight Path of one eternal religion grows from disobedience and failure to submit.*

While God has decreed that "everything in the heavens and the earth glorifies God" (57:1, 17:44), He has also, in the case of human beings, prescribed the correct manner that this glorification should take. Rejecting the prescribed glorification and submission entails chastisement.[66] Thus, the first part of answering why God has allowed religious multiplicity requires understanding that God has created us with the possibility of disobedience, and therefore, the possibility of creating numerous false religions. This is similar to understanding the purpose of creation in relation to the question of evil and suffering discussed in Chapter 3.

Another aspect of understanding the Divine Wisdom behind allowing multiple religions relates to the Divine understanding of human nature and the competitive instinct therein, which is alluded to in several passages of the Qur'an:

> ...To each among you have We prescribed a Law and an open way. If Allah had so willed, He would have made you a single people, but (His plan is) to test you in what He has given you; so strive as in a race in all virtues. The goal of all of you is to Allah- it is He who will show you the truth of the matters in which you dispute. (5:48)

> If it had been the Lord's Will, they would all have believed—all who are on earth! Will you then compel mankind against their will to believe!" (10:99)

> "To each is a goal to which Allah turns him; then strive together (as in a race) towards all that is good. Wheresoever you are, Allah will bring you together, for Allah has power over all things. (2:148)

> O you who believe! Persevere in patience and constancy: vie in such perseverance; strengthen each other; and be conscious of Allah so that you may prosper. (3:200)

Such passages indicate that while God acknowledges that people follow different Laws and Paths, His appeal is for us to strive in establishing virtue on earth as well as patience and perseverance. Who better to understand the competitive instinct that lies within us than the Creator Himself? The establishment of virtue and patience at the levels of both individual and society is more important than arguing over contentious issues, for "it is He who will show you the truth of the matters in which you dispute" (5:48). Another aspect alluded to is the fact that what is being asked for is a healthy competitive spirit, not one based on ill-will or malice, for in doing so we are commanded to "strengthen each other and be conscious of Allah so that you may prosper." This concept is borne out in practice, for example, in the cases of charity work conducted by many religious organizations. Such activities only encourage other organizations to partake in the efforts.

Finally, the appeal of Allah to mankind, Muslim and non-Muslim, is to come to common terms in establishing the one primordial religion of submission to God:

> Say, 'Oh People of the Book! Come to common terms as between us and you—that we worship none but Allah, that we associate no partners with Him, that we erect not from among ourselves, lords and patrons other than Allah.' If then, they turn back, say, 'Bear witness that we (at least) are Muslims (bowing to Allah's Will).' (3:64)

In this age of doubt, there can be no greater cause than to join hands in re-establishing faith in God and worship of Him.

Chapter Summary

1 There are basically four kinds of approaches to the question of religious diversity. The exclusivist stance maintains that the teachings of one particular religion are the sole means of attaining salvation and truth. The pluralist view holds that God reveals Himself through a multitude of religions and that truth and salvation cannot be confined to any particular religion. The inclusivist stance is intermediary in that it affirms the many ways in which God can Reveal Himself, but that ultimately there can only be one absolute Truth. Finally, the skeptical position contends that all religions are mere figments of human imagination with no one being capable of acquiring absolute truths.

2 Islam presents a unique position in that it considers God to have revealed only one religion through the course of human history—that of Islam, which means peaceful submission to God (submission being inclusive of the obedience, worship, gratitude, service and love of God). By following such a religion one is faithful to one's innate nature. All the genuine Prophets and Messengers of God, such as Adam, Noah, Solomon, Abraham, Ishmael, Isaac, Moses, David, Jesus and Muhammad (peace be upon them all) are considered part of the greater family of Muslims, or those who practice Islam.

3 Muslims believe that Allah has manifested and will continue to manifest His Signs and Revelation to all peoples but that there is only one Absolute Truth with respect to His nature and our relationship to Him. While Islam includes obligatory belief in all the prior Messengers and Revelations (including the original Bible) sent by God, it contends that all other religions, in their current forms, have deviated from or are entirely removed from Divine Revelation as a source, and have severely compromised the Unity of God. Islam is the only remaining religion that advocates, in theory and practice, the simple and direct worship of One God. Thus, while some religions may have been valid in their own times, they are no longer valid in the present day.

4 With respect to salvation, Islam returns to the message of the primordial religion, i.e. that of sincere submission to Allah as the key to salvation, not mere lip service professing to be Muslim, Christian, Jew or Hindu or blind imitation of forefathers. Nowhere does Islam contain blanket generalizations condemning all non-Muslims to the depths of Hell as some try to portray. Some Muslim scholars also make specific exceptions with respect to the salvation of those who have never heard or have only heard a highly distorted message of Islam—it is for God to judge them and not ourselves.

5 The Qur'an devotes considerable discussion to both the criticism and praise of the "People of the Book", which is a respectful title used to refer to Christians, Jews and other communities that received earlier Scriptures. The Qur'an states that "not all of them are alike"(3:113)—some are condemned for knowingly associating partners with God and will face a grievous penalty, while others are praised for being among the righteous and are specifically said to believe in Allah (see 2:62, 3:199, 3:113-5).

6. Muslims are called upon in the Qur'an to come to common terms with people of other faiths in establishing the obedience of God in society (3:64) while clarifying that there can be no compulsion in religion (2:256). Islamic law also confers to non-Muslims freedom of worship, belief, independent religious and educational institutions, as well as autonomy in maters of family law, personal law, marriage and divorce. Freedom in financial, transactional, civil and social matters is also allowed except for that which publicly violates Islamic law, such as its prohibition on interest and alcohol consumption.

7. The primary areas of criticism of the People of the Book in the Qur'an are in their compromising the nature of God, distorting His Message, rejecting the Final Prophet (Muhammad, SAW), and failing to submit and obey in the manner prescribed by Him. In doing so, they have replaced the Divine character of their original teachings with their own fallible desires and cultural influences.

8. The case of Hinduism, Buddhism and other Eastern religions, though not specifically mentioned by name in the Qur'an is also not immune to the fundamental criticisms of Judaism and Christianity. Although Hinduism and Buddhism may have had their origins in the teachings of Divine Messengers, over the course of thousands of years, they have now devolved into forms or mixtures of polytheism, pantheism, monism and/or atheism. They also face numerous textual inconsistencies within their Scriptures and in the case of Buddhism, its adherents admit that the teachings of its founder, Gautama Buddha were not committed to writing.

9. There are a number of features that distinguish Islam from other religions. For the purposes of this chapter, three features were discussed: the immutability and extent of preservation and of its sources, i.e. the Qur'an and Sunnah, (b) the concept of Tawhid or Pure Monotheism, and (c) the finality of its message as Muhammad (SAW) and the Qur'an represent the final Messenger and Scripture sent by God to mankind.

10

Understanding religious diversity entails understanding why human beings have evolved numerous religions, not why God has allowed numerous religions. Thus, the question of religious diversity is rather similar to the question of why there is disobedience and transgression, which was discussed at length in Chapter 3.

Notes:

1 An example of such propaganda comes from the Christian author, John B. Noss in *Man's Religions*, rev. ed. (New York: Macmillan, 1956), p. 682: "In its early years the religion of Muhammad had a swift and spectacular spread, often to the terrible accompaniment of fire and sword, and so it made an unforgettable impression upon many peoples both East and West. In the first century of its existence it must have appeared to those who stood in the path of its advance like a devouring fire enlarging from its center, which rushed upon them with remorseless and inexorable speed; before they knew what to do, it was upon them."

2 See John Hick, *Philosophy of Religion*, 4th ed., (Englewood Cliffs, NJ: Prentice Hall, 1990).

3 See Judah Halevi, On Non-Jewish Religions, in Philosophy of Religion: The Big Questions, ed. Eleonore Stump and Michael Murray (Malden, MA: Blackwell, 1999), pp. 435-440.

4 L. David Moore, *The Christian Conspiracy- How the Teachings of Christ Have Been Altered By Christians* (Atlanta: Pendulum Plus Press, 1994).

5 See Karl Barth, Church Dogmatics (Edinburgh: T&T Clark, 1975).

6 John Hick, Philosophy of Religion, 4th ed (Englewood Cliffs, NJ: Prentice Hall, 1990), p. 119.

7 Karl Rahner, *Theological Investigations*, Vol. V (New York: Crossroad Publishers, 1966), pp. 115-34

8 For a complete discussion of these aspects, refer to Syed Muhammad Naquib Al-Attas, *Prolegomena to the Metaphysics of Islam: An Exposition of the Fundamental Elements of the Worldview of Islam* (Kuala Lumpur: International Institute of Islamic Thought and Civilization, 1995), pp. 41-89.

9 Narrated in Sahih Muslim, Book 39, No. 67773.

10 Based on hadith narrated in Musnad of Ahmad bin Hanbal, Hadith #21257.

11 Even faith and works still require the Mercy and Grace of God for salvation. Prophet Muhammad (SAW) has said, "None of you will enter Paradise on account of your good deeds alone." The people asked him, "Even you, O Prophet of God?" He replied, "Yes, even me, unless God bestows His favor and mercy on me." (narrated in Sahih Bukhari)

12 Refer to Abdullah Yusuf Ali's commentary on the Qur'an, where he has provided possible explanations for the identity of the Sabians: The Holy Qur'an- Text, Translation and Commentary, rev. ed., (Brentwood, Maryland: Amana Corp., 1989), p. 33.

13 Abu Hamid Muhammad Ibn Muhammad al-Ghazali (d. 505/1111), F*aysal a-tafriqa bayn al-Islam wa'l-zandaqa*, Ed. Riyad Mustafa al-'Abdullah (Damascus/Beirut: Manshurat Dar al-Hikma, 1986), pp. 105-110.

14 The first four Caliphs after the passing of Muhammad (SAW) were Abu Bakr, 'Umar, 'Uthman and Ali (may Allah be pleased with them).

15 See Norman Stillman, *The Jews of Arab Lands- A History and Source Book* (Philadelphia: Jewish Publication Society of America, 1979) and Eliyahu Ashtor, The Jews of Moslem Spain, Vol. I,II, III, trans. Aaron Klein, Jenny Klein(Philadelphia: Jewish Publication Society of America, 1979).

16 Jonathan Bloom, Sheila Blair, *Islam- A Thousand Years of Faith and Power* (New York: TV Books, 2000)

17 Muhammad Abdel Haleem, *Understanding the Quran* (London and New York: IB Tauris), p.77.

18 Thomas Bokenkotter, *A Concise History of the Catholic Church*, rev. ed. (New York: Bantam Doubleday Dell, 1990), 45.

19 See L. David Moore, *The Christian Conspiracy- How the Teachings of Christ Have Been Altered By Christians* (Atlanta: Pendulum Plus Press, 1994); Sulaiman Mufassir, Jesus, A Prophet of Islam (Indianapolis: American Trust Publications, 1980), 8; and Muhammad Ata ur-Rahim, Jesus, A Prophet of Islam (London: MWH London, 1979).

20 L. David Moore, The Christian Conspiracy- How the Teachings of Christ Have Been Altered By Christians (Atlanta: Pendulum Plus Press, 1994).

21 Hyam Maccoby, *The Mythmaker- Paul and the Invention of Christianity* (New York: Barnes and Noble, Inc., 1986).

22 See John 5:30, 8:28-29, 8:39-40, 14:10, 14:28, 14:31, 17:3, Matthew 20:23, 24:36, Mark 10:18

23 See Luke 13:33-34, 7:16, 24:19, John 6:14, 6:40

24 See Matthew 23:8-10

25 See Mark 1:35, 14:32, 15:34, Luke 5:16

26 See John 5:30, 14:31

27 See Psalms 30:515:22-23, Matthew 9:13

28 See L. David Moore, *The Christian Conspiracy- How the Teachings of Christ Have Been Altered By Christians* (Atlanta: Pendulum Plus Press, 1994), p. 159.

29 Ibid, p. 155.

30 Jacob Neusner, *Rabbinic Judaism: Structure and System* (Minneapolis: Augsburg Fortress, 1995), 205.

31 Robert Goldenberg, *Talmud- Back to the Sources: Reading the Classic Jewish Texts* (New York: Simon and Schuster, 1984), 166-7.

32 See Berakhot 7a: "R. Ishmael b. Elisha says: I once entered into the innermost part (of the Sanctuary) to offer incense and saw Akathriel Jah (the crown of God), the Lord of Hosts, seated upon a high and exalted throne. He said to me: 'Ishmael, My son, bless Me!' "; Abodah Zarah 3b: "Rab Juda said in the name of Rab: 'The day consists of twelve hours; during the first three hours the Holy One, blessed be He, is occupying Himself with the Torah…' "; and Baba Mezia 59b: "R. Nathan met Elijah and asked him, What did the Holy One, blessed be He, do in that hour- He laughed (with joy), he replied, saying 'My sons have defeated Me'" in The Babylonian Talmud, trans., comm. by Dr. Isidore Epstein (London: Soncino Press, 1935)

33 Jacob Neusner, *Invitation to the Talmud*, rev. ed. (San Francisco: Harper & Row, 1989), 8-9.

34 Michael A. Hoffman II, *Judaism's Strange Gods* (Coeur d'Alene, Idaho: The Independent History and Research Co., 2000), 32.

35 L. David Moore, *The Christian Conspiracy- How the Teachings of Christ Have Been Altered By Christians* (Atlanta: Pendulum Plus Press, 1994), p. 82.

36 John Shelby Spong, Rescuing the Bible from Fundamentalism (San Francisco: Harper San Francisco Publishers, 1991) 78.
37 Ibid., 79.
38 Richard Elliot Friedman, *Who Wrote the Bible?* (New York: Summit Books, 1987), 28.
39 Ibid, p. 24.
40 See Abdul Haq Vidyarthi, *Mohammad in World Scriptures* (Delhi: Adam Publishers & Distributors, 1990); Abdul Ahad Dawud, *Muhammad in the Bible* (Selangor, Malaysia: Polygraphic Press, 1969); Ahmed Deedat, *What the Bible Says About Muhummed* (Riyadh: Obekan Publishing, 1987).
41 Martin Lings, *Muhammad, His Life Based on the Earliest Sources* (London: George Allen & Unwin and The Islamic Texts Society, 1983), 30.
42 Karen Armstrong, Muhammad, *A Biography of the Prophet* (New York: HarperCollins, 1992), 73-74.
43 See also 2:93, 3:81-82, 4:46-47, 4:153-162.
44 Hyam Maccoby admits, "The Talmud contains a few explicit references to Jesus…These references are certainly not complimentary…The passage in which Jesus' punishment in hell is described also seems to refer to the Christian Jesus. It is a piece of anti-Christian polemic dating from the post-70 CE period…" in Judaism on Trial: Jewish-Christian Disputations in the Middle Ages (E. Brunswick/ London, 1982) ,26-27.
45 Daniel-Rops writes, "All that the rabbis let us know about him (Jesus) is hostile, insulting and malevolent. Sometimes he is referred to (in the Talmud) under the name Balaam the Son of Behor, 'the false prophet', who led Israel astray; sometimes under his real name of Jesus of Nazareth, but always with some insulting qualification, such as the liar, the impostor or bastard." *in Jesus and His Times* (Garden City, NY: Image Books, 1958), 66-67.
46 This verse was revealed in relation to certain Muslims who were reluctant to accompany Prophet Muhammad (SAW) in the expedition of Tabuk (630 C.E.) and contains a warning for Muslims to continue to strive in the path of God or else be replaced with another people.
47 An example of a monotheistic strand within Hinduism is provided by Bhaktivinode Thakura (1834-1914), who stated: "The religions in which there prevail the evils like atheism, skepticism, materialism, no-soulism like epicureanism, pantheism, polytheism and nondistinct monism- should not be regarded as the devotees of God. They should be known as counterreligions, pseudo religions and false religions. There followers are really unfortunate. Jivas (living beings) should be, as far as practicable, protected against those evils. Pure love is the eternal virtue of jivas. Even though the five kinds of difference as said above are noticeable, that religion is true religion in which the attainment of pure love of God is the object aimed at. It is improper to quarrel over extraneous differences. If the aim of a religion is pure love, then all the other circumstances are to be looked upon as proper. The doctrines of atheism, etc., as cited above, are unnatural and antagonistic to love" (cited in Tamal Krishna Goswami, Reason and Belief: Problem Solving in the Philosophy of Religion (Dallas: Pundits Press, 1997), p. 112).

178 GOD, ISLAM, AND THE SKEPTIC MIND

48 Ed Viswanathan, *Am I Hindu?- The Hindu Primer* (Halo Books, 1992), 2-3.
49 Ibid, p. 26.
50 Abbe J.A. Dubois, *Hindu Manners, Customs and Ceremonies*, reprint (Dover Pub., 2002).
51 Huston Smith, *The Illustrated World's Religions* (New York: HarperCollins, 1994), 77.
52 Edward Conze, Buddhism, Its Essence and Development (Oxford: Bruno Cassirer, 1960), 29-30.
53 Ibid, p. 27.
54 K.N. Jayatilleke, *The Message of the Buddha*, ed. *Ninian Smart*, (London: George Allen & Unwin Ltd, 1975), 104-5, 1975.
55 See for example, John Esposito, *What Everyone Needs to Know About Islam* (Oxford: Oxford Univ. Press, 2002)
56 The first complete bound compilation of the Qur'an was ordered by the first Caliph Abu Bakr through the companion Zaid bin Thabit, who was one of many who had memorized the complete Qur'an. Virtually every verse in this first bound copy was supported by numerous copies of written fragments possessed by companions that were provided to Zaid.
57 Sir W. Muir, *Life of Muhammad* (London, 1903)
58 John B. Noss, *Man's Religions*, rev. ed., (New York: Macmillan, 1956), 683.
59 See Richard Bell, *The Origin of Islam in its Christian Environment* (London, 1926); C.C. Torrey, *The Jewish Foundation of Islam* (New York, 1933).
60 A. Toynbee, *A Study of History*, Vol. 12, (Oxford, 1962), 463.
61 Syed Muhammad Naquib Al-Attas, *Prolegomena to the Metaphysics of Islam: An Exposition of the Fundamental Elements of the Worldview of Islam* (Kuala Lumpur: International Institute of Islamic Thought and Civilization, 1995) 54-55.
62 Hadith narrated in Majma' Al-Bayan, Ahzab 40
63 Hadith narrated in Sahih Bukhari, 'Ilm 10; Abu Dawud, Ilm 1; Ibn Maja, Muqadddima 17.
64 See Qur'an 5:48, "To every one (of the Prophets) We have appointed a Law and a Way."
65 It must be remembered that the concept of religion among Muslims only includes those systems which are based on Divine Revelation and Prophethood. Although Muslims believe Islam is the only primordial religion that preserves its basis in Divine Revelation, they nonetheless agree that Christianity and Judaism at least have their origins in Divine Revelation and Prophethood (hence the term, People of the Book), despite what they have may have currently devolved into. It is also reasonable to believe that this is the case for Hinduism and Buddhism, though they are not religions specifically mentioned by Muhammad (SAW). However, any so-called religions or cults that have emerged after Islam are not considered to have any legitimacy other than in the minds of their founders and followers.
66 Here, it is important to distinguish between the "engendering command" and "prescriptive command" of God which Muslim theologians have long realized. See William Chittick, Imaginal Worlds- Ibn al-Arabi and the Problem of Religious Diversity (Albany: SUNY Press, 1994), p. 142: "Through the first command (engendering), God brings all creation into existence: 'His only command when He desires a thing is to say to it 'Be' and it is' (36:82). Through the second

(prescriptive), He sets down the instructions whereby people can achieve felicity. Hence, the prescriptive command entails activities such as prayer, fasting, almsgiving, and the observance of moral constraints." The engendering command cannot be rejected, but the prescriptive command can be disobeyed, whether partially or completely.

|Chapter 5
Does Morality Require God?

It is not righteousness that you turn your faces towards the East or the West; but it is righteousness to believe in Allah and the Last Day, and the Angels, and the Book, and the Messengers; to spend of your substance out of love for Him, for your kin, for orphans, for the needy, for the wayfarer, for those who ask, and for the ransom of slaves; to be steadfast in prayer and practice regular charity, to fulfill the contracts which you have made, and to be firm and patient in pain (or suffering) and adversity, and throughout all periods of panic. Such are the people of truth, such are the God-conscious.

(Qur'an 2:177)

Among the casualties of the scientific worldview is the illusion that humanity is slowly progressing and "evolving" towards a highly advanced state of being – the zenith of "civilization", hitherto unseen, with scientific endeavor and blind skepticism of anything "sacred" leading the way in ridding the world of its ailments. While a Darwinian elite has certainly celebrated extraordinary embellishments in the material quality of life, mankind as a whole has sullenly witnessed a decline in the quality of the human being that is being produced. The pride of those who rejoice in the achievement of modern man is only matched by their indifference to the moral crisis and suffering that plagues humanity as a whole. The 20th century alone has witnessed over 100 million deaths as "collateral damage" of the wars waged for global domination. Almost 3 billion people live on less than $2 per day, while the world's richest 225 people have a combined wealth of over $1 trillion, which is equal to the combined annual income of the world's 2.5 billion poorest.[1] Ten million hectares of ancient forest are destroyed every year, or the equivalent of a football field every two seconds.[2] At the turn of the century, in "the year of the millennium", the United States of America alone witnessed: 2.18 million violent crimes including homicide, rape, robbery and aggravated assault; 1.37 million adult and 203,900 juvenile drug arrests; over 1 million victims of abuse by intimate partners; 879,000 confirmed child victims of sexual, physical and psychological abuse; over 30,000 suicides; and 17.8% of all households being victimized by theft or burglary.[3] The U.S. also contains over 12 million alcoholics with 104 million alcohol users; over 14 million illicit drug users; between 16-25 million people living at or below the federal poverty level; over 2 million people homeless at some point during the year (with at least 444,000 homeless on any night); over 1.9 million prisoners in over-flowing jails and prisons; 46,000 new AIDS cases with over 13,000 deaths annually; and an estimated 22% of the adult population suffering from a diagnosable mental disorder in a given year.[4] The sad and ugly truth is that such grim statistics are only the tip of the iceberg. Regardless of whether one considers moral deficiencies to be the root of such problems, it is undoubtedly a moral problem when one turns a blind eye toward them.

No society, throughout the course of human history, has been without at least some standards for what is considered "right" and "wrong". In fact, it would be difficult to conjure any facet of life that does not have an ethical dimension. Economics, politics, education, family life, socialization, health care, war, peace, science and technology are all imbued and permeated with moral and ethical implications. Prior to the "Age of Enlightenment", the source of such moral and ethical standards for much of the world was primarily religious teachings.

The last two hundred years, however, is roughly the first period in human history where the dominant worldview has advocated the superiority of moral and ethical standards *devoid of God or religious influences.* As noted in the opening chapter, such notions have their roots in seventeenth and eighteenth century Europe, during the so-called age of Enlightenment, where the scientific and technological revolution began to question and supplant the belief system and authority of the Church. Secular ideologies were, nonetheless, predictable reactions to the Catholic Church, with its increasingly authoritarian role in not only religious affairs, but also political and economic, as well as its discrimination against non-Catholic segments of society. The "Free Thought" movement of the nineteenth century in America and Western Europe continued to make it more "acceptable" to reject the dogmatic ways of the Church. Finally in the Age of Science and Information, catalyzed and spread by capitalist globalization, it is not surprising that such a major paradigm shift has occurred.

In this chapter we hope to:

(1) examine popular secular theories of ethics,

(2) examine religious ethics, particularly that of Islam, concerning the dependence of morality on God, and

(3) provide an overview of Islamic principles of morality.

5.1 Is Morality Relative or Absolute?

Morality and ethics are terms that are often used interchangeably. Some distinguish the two terms by defining ethics to be "the philosophical study of morality", including the systematic reasoning behind morality[5], while others designate ethics more narrowly to include "the moral principles of a particular tradition, group, or individual", such as Christian ethics or Aristotle's ethics. In any case, while the field of ethics and morality is vast and has numerous branches, it fundamentally includes the study of what constitutes goodness, right action and responsibility and its motivational factors. Embedded within the question of goodness is the critical question of the ultimate source of goodness, morality and ethics.

To understand whether morality is dependent on God, the question of ethical relativism or subjectivism, which forms one of the central questions of ethics, must first be addressed. No system of ethics, sacred or secular, can be discussed until the challenge of relativism is dealt with, for it undermines the very notion of "meaningful ethics or morality". Modern Western civilization is, in fact, characterized by an "absolutization" of the relative. Ethical relativism denies any objective or absolute moral values that are common to all people and times, and instead promotes the individual as the only source and criterion of moral judgments.[6] The philosophical theory of existentialism, which basically emphasizes the freedom and uniqueness of each individual in a hostile and indifferent world, also promotes a type of relativist and subjective ethics. Thus, any moral value, such as marital fidelity, is considered meaningful only for the holder of such a value, and not necessarily for anyone or everyone else. Proponents of ethical relativism often use cultural variability to support their theory, and argue that culture usually defines morality. The renowned American psychologist, B.F. Skinner, stated that:

> What a given group of people calls good is a fact; it is what members of the group find reinforcing as the result of their genetic endowment and the natural and social contingencies to which they have been exposed. Each culture has its own set of goods, and what is good in one culture may not be good in another. To recognize this is to take the position of "cultural relativism." What is good for the Trobriand Islander is good for the Trobriand Islander, and that is that. Anthropologists have often emphasized relativism as a tolerant alternative to missionary zeal in converting all cultures to a single set of ethical, governmental, religious, or economic values.[7]

Relativists, thus, argue that all moral values, and even values in general, are largely or completely determined by particular circumstances or social environments. They also point to the many differences and controversies that abound in the field of ethics.

While ethical relativism may initially sound appealing, it is mired by serious flaws. Its conclusion that there is no "objective truth" in morality does not follow from its premise that different individuals, cultures and societies have different moral codes. For example, many people and societies, both past and present, have believed that the earth is flat—does this mean that the earth is not spherical (roughly), or that there is no objective truth in the matter? We may disagree about various laws of physics, but that does not mean there are no fixed laws of physics. Just as it is possible to be mistaken in beliefs, it is also possible to be mistaken in moral beliefs or unaware of objective moral truths. We must, therefore, distinguish between our opinions of morality and morality itself.

Another significant problem with relativism is its utter impracticality. While many claim to be ethical relativists, almost none can live accordingly. Do we not hold everyone responsible for their actions, judge actions according to right and wrong, and even try to impose our own values on others? Are there any societies that are without laws, including laws governing the domain of morality and ethics? The very fact that most of us engage in debate over right and wrong also assumes there must be an objective and common morality. There can be no absolute goodness or absolute evil in a relativist society. Nor can there be any meaningful criticism, reform or progress of moral practices in a relativist society.

> *There can be no absolute goodness or absolute evil in a relativist society.*

It is not surprising then, that many people advocate ethical absolutism—which affirms that there are at least some moral values which are independent of individual opinions, and are fixed, objective realities valid for all people and as some argue, all times. Greg Krehbiel summarizes the argument for moral absolutes as follows:

> Let's say you have two people in a room who are examining the fact that every time they jump up in the air, they fall back down. One of them believes that gravity is a universal, real thing. The other believes that the fact that they fall is just a particular—it may or may not apply in another room, or at another time, but for now it certainly applies. These two people could agree that they are likely to fall when they jump. But if we ask them if they will fall tomorrow, or if they would fall in the next room, what answers should we expect from them? The one who believes that gravity is real says that he will fall tomorrow, and the next day, and at any time, and his belief in gravity justifies that claim—it provides warrant for his belief. But the one who believes that falling is a particular wouldn't be able to say that. In order to be consistent with his belief that gravity is a particular,

he'd have to say that he doesn't know if he'd fall tomorrow, or the next day. This is the problem of the atheist. His humanity compels him to make universal moral claims, but his philosophy provides no warrant for them. The one who believes that morality is a real thing has a philosophical justification for his belief that things are right or wrong. The one who believes that morality is just a particular—the way people in this society feel, or something like that—has no justification for applying his belief outside that particular. All he can say is, "such and so people regard this as evil."

This issue provides a powerful argument for the existence of God. As humans, we can't avoid making general, universal moral statements. It's simply a part of who we are. And only theism provides the philosophical warrant for those claims.[8]

5.2 Secular Ethics – Hedonism and Perfectionism

After confronting the issue of relativism and meaningful ethics, one is still faced with an array of ethical systems that try to provide a framework for what constitutes goodness and its motivational factors. In this and the next section we provide an overview of ethical systems that try to avoid any religious derivations, while limiting ourselves to an overview of hedonism, perfectionism and secular humanism for the purposes of this chapter.

According to the theory of hedonism, pleasure (or happiness) is the only intrinsic good in life, and maximizing pleasure is the only criterion for right action.[9] Its most famous exponent in ancient times was the Greek philosopher Epicurus. Although hedonism often conjures images of endless sensual gratification, many philosophers who espoused hedonism had in mind various forms of philosophical and intellectual pleasures. In any case, this view not only includes the assertion that it is morally obligatory to seek pleasure, but also that persons naturally seek pleasure whether they realize it or not. The primary motivation behind all action is the prospect of either present or future pleasure. Hedonists can be further divided into ethical egoists and utilitarians. Ethical egoists measure actions according to the pleasure derived for one's own self, while utilitarianists focus on maximizing pleasure to a group of people or society as a whole.

As one might expect, hedonism faces a number of problems. Hedonism derives from an appeal to human nature or the way people act "in reality"—however, just because people act in a certain way, does this make it "right"? In other words, how can a "should" be derived from an "is"? Furthermore, although people often act with their own pleasure in mind, it is highly questionable as to whether this is the only motivating factor in human nature. In fact, some activities purposely target suffering. Are ascetic monks seeking pleasure in their retreats? Do firefighters seek pleasure as they rush into a burning building? Not only are all actions not motivated by pleasure, but it is also dubious as to whether the best way to achieve pleasure is to seek it. Certain activities, like raising children or going to work can provide immense pleasure without necessarily intending to seek pleasure. Another major problem for hedonism is in the definition of "pleasure" (similar problems occur with Aristotelian notions of "happiness"). Some hedonists argue that pleasure is defined according to the individual or to society. If for the individual, then how does one morally justify selfish pleasure to the detriment of others? What about those who claim to derive pleasure from seemingly immoral acts like killing or stealing? If for society, how does one judge between different types of pleasure? Are spiritual pleasures considered as pleasurable as physical ones? Is the pleasure of intellectual discourse superior to that of eating a chocolate bar or are they equal? Yet another problem concerns the pain and affliction that can follow pleasure. Everyone is aware of the suffering that can follow recreational drug use or overeating. Is one to maximize long-term or short-term pleasure? If advocating the long-term, then what about religious believers who claim they are acting in the interest of eternal pleasure in the afterlife?

Not all forms of ethics assume that we naturally seek a good life—perfectionism is a theory which maintains that goodness is inherently worthy of pursuit. Some of its most famous exponents are the philosopher Plato and more recently, Friedrich Nietzsche. Plato's well known theory of "forms" postulates that goodness is a truth or form that is independent of human beings, but can be discovered by some of them, and when it is discovered, it is followed by them. Constituting goodness or virtue are other forms, such as that of life, truth, justice, happiness, pleasure, knowledge, virtue, friendship, beauty and harmony. Thus, for example, while paintings and sculptures, flowers and peacocks are all considered beautiful entities to the extent that they "imitate" or "participate" in beauty, the form of beauty itself is eternal, changeless and incorporeal. Plato regarded such forms as only being perceptible through pure reason or thought.

Plato's theory of "forms" assumes that everyone who fully utilizes their intellectual capabilities will eventually realize the same essences or forms constituting goodness and that they will all act accordingly. However, we are all aware of exceptions to this theory, such as other philosophers who have exhausted their intellectual capabilities only to come up with vastly disparate conclusions, or even those who continually choose to lie, cheat and steal despite fully knowing that such acts are wrong. Other thinkers, including Aristotle have had problems understanding how an independent world of forms can exist—claiming that the form and matter of entities are different aspects of the same object.

Without delving into other details of Plato's theory, perfectionism is also faced with a great deal of subjectivity in deciding not only what qualities are inherently worthy of pursuit, but also what activities, behaviors and thoughts they consist of. The virtue of benevolence, for example, can be taken to an extreme where fairness is compromised, just as justice can be followed so strictly that benevolence is compromised. Moreover, if justice is inherently worthy of pursuit, is capital punishment considered part of justice? Does the virtue of knowledge include "knowledge" of movie trivia? Eventually, we are forced to revert to the authority of human beings, whether individually or collectively, as the source of determining what constitutes goodness, and differentiating moral from immoral behavior.

5.3 Secular Humanism

In an age where vague notions of democracy, secularism, freedom, tolerance and independence have virtually attained the status of infallible deities, it is not surprising that many agnostics, atheists, secularists and even some "modern believers" feel that morality does not require God or religion. "Secular humanism" has emerged as a popular belief closely intertwined with a secular political outlook which holds that ethical and "humane" standards should be developed by the collective brain of society without interference from specific religious dictates. It is similar to ethical relativism in that it rejects any dependence of morality on God or religion, but is different in exalting particular societies or humanity as a whole as the source of moral values, as opposed to the individual. According to the Council for Secular Humanism, the core principles of its worldview include, but are not limited to:

(1) "A conviction that dogmas, ideologies, and traditions, whether religious, political or social, must be weighed and tested by each individual and not simply accepted on faith,

(2) Commitment to the use of critical reason, factual evidence, and scientific methods of inquiry, rather than faith and mysticism, in seeking solutions to human problems and answers to important human questions

(3) A conviction that with reason, an open marketplace of ideas, good will, and tolerance, progress can be made in building a better world for ourselves and our children."[10]

Common arguments used in support of secular humanism are that:
(a) secular humanism is superior because it is not motivated by rewards of an afterlife,

(b) human beings can lead moral and ethical lives without belief in God or religion,

(c) human beings can have purpose and meaning in life without belief in God or religion,

(d) a free, secular and democratic society requires tolerance and collective decision-making, and therefore must relinquish any notion of absolute truth or morality, and

(e) a diversity of religious moral ideas exists, which means that relativism already exists.

Let us briefly examine each of these arguments in turn:

(a) A popular argument of humanists is that secular humanism is somehow superior because it is not motivated by reward in heaven. It is argued that moral virtues are inherently worthy of pursuit without having to resort to heavenly rewards. As Kai Nielsen states:

> There is something to be said for a person who can hold steadily on a course without telling himself or herself fairy tales. Moral integrity, fraternity, and love of humankind are worth subscribing to without a thought of whether or not such virtues will be rewarded in heaven.[11]

While it is true that many religions consider heaven and hell an inevitable part of human destiny, it clearly is not true that the primary motivation for all religious followers lies therein. As discussed in Sections 5.7 and 5.9, the primary motivation for believers is the need to obey, love and submit to God as our Creator, with heaven being a secondary reward and blessing from God for doing so. What is so irrational about wanting to obey the Creator who is Infinite in Knowledge and Wisdom, and thereby, knows what is best for His creation? The fact is that all of human behavior is purposive or teleological in nature, and no moral values can be "inherently worthy of pursuit" unless they are considered universal forms or gods in and of themselves. In practice, acts that are considered moral or ethical are often motivated by selfishness with expectations of mutual compensation. Religion is the only force that truly promotes the importance of absolute moral behavior without ulterior selfish motives. Moral deeds should be pursued for the pleasure of God, and without further expectation. One cannot submit to God without fulfilling the rights of one's self as well as all other forms of creation.

> ... the primary motivation for believers is the need to obey, love and submit to God as our Creator, with heaven being a secondary reward and blessing from God for doing so.

(b) Secular humanists like to point to the fact that atheists, agnostics, secularists and the like can be "good" people who lead ethical lives, which is supposed to represent proof that morality does not require God. While it is acknowledged that those who do not believe in God can perform "good" deeds and have some semblance of moral standards, there are several reasons why it does not follow that morality does not require God.

Firstly, most theists would argue that the very reason atheists and agnostics can behave "morally" in the first place is because God is the Moral Law Giver who has imbued within each and every human being an inherent moral conscience. Not everyone necessarily or consistently follows their conscience, but the fact remains that this innate sense of morality exists, and is the reason why at least some moral principles have remained common across all ages and peoples. John Henry Newman (1801–1890) wrote "If, as is the case, we feel responsibility, are ashamed, are frightened, at transgressing the voice of conscience, this implies there is One to whom we are responsible, before whom we are ashamed, whose claim upon us we fear."[12] The skeptic's claim that such a moral conscience is merely an outgrowth of parental, societal and cultural influences does not hold weight given that there have been countless reformers, saints, and Prophets throughout history who have diametrically opposed external influences to follow their "calling within" and obliterate the evils of their times, such as slavery, racism, oppression, and paganism. In fact, it is this inherent moral conscience that has served to provide some semblance of ethics to societies and preserve and prolong the human race.

> ... the very reason atheists and agnostics can behave "morally" in the first place is because God is the Moral Law Giver who has imbued within each and every human being an inherent moral conscience.

Secondly, most theists would argue that if the goal is not merely being "good", but becoming virtuous in the highest sense, then God is, in fact, necessary to bestow this quality upon those who strive with sincerity to obey Him, without which neither atheist nor disingenuous theist has any hope of attaining it. In other words, God is necessary to exhibit "godly" character. While we all possess a moral conscience, God is still necessary to maximize the potential within it. History has proven that it is only the Prophets, Messengers, and select devotees of God who have truly attained the highest level of virtue. This highest level of virtue does not simply consist of occasional donations to charity and volunteer work, but tireless service to humanity, such that whatever one desires for one's self is wished for everyone else[13], and with no expectations in return. It is only the likes of Jesus (AS) who could have turned the other cheek to forgive his most ardent enemies. It is only the likes of Joseph (AS) who could have forgiven his jealous brothers who dropped him in the bottom of a well only to be taken away by a passing caravan. It is only the likes of Muhammad (SAW) who could have worried about the welfare of a Jewish woman who used to daily throw garbage on him, when one day she did not do so. While the Prophets and Saints of God are remembered by billions of people across the world, hundreds of years after the fact, for their magnanimous natures and extraordinary characters, there are no atheists or agnostics who are even remotely remembered in a similar fashion.

(c) The fact that many who do not believe in God or any religion have some semblance of purpose and meaning in life is also offered by some as proof that morality does not require God. To quote Kai Nielsen again:

If you have some life plan, if you want to be a doctor or a professor or a political radical, whatever you want to be, if there's something you want to do in this world, you can do that, God or no God...You can have all these purposes in life even though there is no purpose to life, so life doesn't become meaningless and pointless if you were not *made* for a purpose.[14]

This frail argument is analogous to the notion of a little girl who thinks she can do whatever she wants, with or without her parents. She is free to think as such, but this does not mean that she is correct in believing so or that she can prove such a belief. Rigorous proof of her point would require determining whether she could do as she pleases if her parents were not present or did not exist. Thus, in order for moral relativists to prove their point, they would have to argue that God does not exist, which we know cannot be proven from our discussion in Chapters 1 and 2.

Nonetheless, it is important to understand that there is no logical contradiction between a Supreme God and the material success of those who choose not to believe. By His Mercy, Love and Wisdom, God has left us to empirically determine the outcomes of exercising our free wills so that we may recognize our strengths and fallibilities and submit to a higher, infallible authority. God is not a vengeful being sitting on His Throne preventing those who do not believe in Him from fulfilling any worldly desires. In fact, God has gifted us with such intellectual capability and will-power that many who desire to become doctors will become doctors, many people who desire wealth will often get wealth, many who desire fame will often get fame, and many who desire power will often get power- regardless of belief or disbelief. Such is the Way of God.

However, it is those who realize that there is purpose to life who can transcend such worldly desires to realize what is truly important. Thus, the prince and pauper can be equal when they realize they were created for the same purpose of worshipping God, not worshipping wealth or fame. Those who suppose there can only be purpose in life cannot be equated with those who believe there is purpose to life, to borrow Nielsen's terms. There is surely a world of difference in the motivation behind actions in each of these cases.

Another major flaw in this argument is that it equates all purposes—as long as I see meaning in what I do, it is worthy and commendable of pursuit. But are not some purposes better than others? Is a thief equal to a saint? Is a bartender equal to a doctor? The fact is that when we realize the purpose and meaning of life as a whole, the career paths we take and the decisions we make can all be judged to the extent that they fulfill this overall purpose. It is not surprising that atheists and agnostics have resorted to arguments of altruistic egoism or the idea that it is better to live in harmony with others without "harming them" to further one's own interests (we will return to discuss the motivation behind behavior in Sections 5.7 and 5.9).

(d) Another popular argument is the notion that free, secular and democratic societies require moral relativism in order to properly function. Dogmatism and absolute morality are regarded as obstructive forces in a "progressive" society. Is it logically necessary, however, that there be a contradiction between a free society and moral absolutes?

The fact that I may believe in moral absolutes for the betterment of society does not mean that I also believe in coercion or that everyone has to agree with me.

Firstly, one can fully believe that there are moral absolutes and still believe that there is value in reaching conclusions through open discussion, dialogue and debate. Just as a relativist needs to present his or her case to reach consensus, so too can a theist use open discussion and debate. The fact that I may believe in moral absolutes for the betterment of society does not mean that I also believe in coercion or that everyone has to agree with me. While the exclusivists and extremists of various religions have helped create the perception of incompatibility between religious absolutes and freedom and tolerance, it must be remembered that there is no such inherent contradiction between the principles.

Secondly, it must be remembered that there is no such thing as a *completely free* society. There is no society on earth that does not have some form of binding laws and regulations, including the United States of America. Such laws do not simply involve the prevention of "harming others" as some suppose, but also considerably infringe upon personal and moral rights. In America, for example, you are not free to use recreational drugs; you are not free to obtain a driver's license without insurance; you are not free to build a home in a business-zoned district; you are not free to commit sodomy in your own home (in certain states); nor are you free to not pay taxes – and none of these prohibitions explicitly involves the "harming" of others. The legislation of federal laws encompasses almost every aspect of society, including morality. As introduced earlier, there are moral and ethical implications to every problem. While it is claimed that moral absolutes derived from religion infringe upon the rights of those who do not believe in a particular religion, do not the laws developed by slightly fallible, secular politicians infringe upon the rights of believers in God?

Yet another problem with the original argument is its implication that decisions reached by the majority will always be correct and binding. History, however, has provided numerous instances to the contrary. The majority can be wrong! Just because the majority of Americans at one time advocated and implemented the wholesale slavery of Africans does not make it right. Just because many people living under Nazi Germany supported genetics research to foster a "superior" race does not make it right. Just because a certain tribe likes to behead someone as a sacrifice to the gods does not mean that it is right. Just because a particular society condones gambling, drinking of alcohol, and night club dancing does not make it right. A related illusion of modern democracies is the idea that "the people" are responsible for policies and laws with everyone having an equal share in the decision-making process. Quite to the contrary, the extent of influence on policy is directly proportional to the magnitude of financial contributions and influence of special interest groups.

> *Just because the majority of Americans at one time advocated and implemented the wholesale slavery of Africans does not make it right.*

(e) This brings us to the next question of why is there no consensus among believers regarding moral principles if all of them acquire such principles from the same source, i.e. God. This question is similar to the question of why there is religious multiplicity if there is only one God addressed in Chapter 4. It should be recalled that this question boils down to a question of why there is disobedience since it is human beings who have evolved multiplicity in religion and ethics, not God.

> *... it is human beings who have evolved multiplicity in religion and ethics, not God.*

God has been fully consistent in the content of His Message to humanity, which includes moral principles. It is true that the application of principles has differed to some extent through the course of history, but the principles have remained the same.

Moreover, acknowledging that certain differences in religious ethical systems exist does not necessarily mean that all systems are correct. The existence of different views of biological evolution does not mean they are all correct. Diversity of answers on a multiple-choice test does not mean every answer is correct. We cannot abandon scholarly research in distinguishing what is "religiously human" from what is "religiously Divine", as discussed in Chapter 4. The point, however, is that even acknowledging the existence of moral diversity between and sometimes even within religions, does not invalidate the authority and reliability of God as the source of morality.

5.4 Religious Ethics

Judaism, Christianity and Islam are all in basic agreement regarding the fundamental and essential belief in God as the ultimate source of morality. God is believed to be the only objective source of a universal morality that can transcend the inherent human limitations of space, time and ego, and is considered the only Being that can provide complete justice and accountability for moral and immoral acts.[15] Just as children cannot be relied on to devise an optimal code of behavior without their parents, so too human beings must rely on God as the objective Creator whose Infinite Knowledge and Wisdom provide the ultimate moral authority. Within this general agreement, there are three kinds of theistic moralities with respect to how we actually acquire moral and ethical truths from God.

> *Just as children cannot be relied on to devise an optimal code of behavior without their parents, so too human beings must rely on God as the objective Creator whose Infinite Knowledge and Wisdom provide the ultimate moral authority.*

The first system, sometimes called the "Divine Command" theory, considers moral principles to be communicated by God to mankind through some form of Scripture or the teachings of a Messenger. Most believers of various faiths rely on at least some form of written Revelation or message of a Prophet for moral guidance. Here again, it is reasoned that God is the only objective source of morality that transcends human limitations, and must therefore be followed. Once this idea is accepted, one only has to determine where the genuine Message of God is to be found, and how to practically apply it.

Another theory is that of "natural law", developed most thoroughly by Thomas Aquinas. Aquinas believed that God has provided various moral principles through Revelation but that human reason can be used to discover moral standards in nature and can confirm and even provide supplementary details to Divine commandments. In this way human reason can participate and share in the eternal and perfect Reason of God in a manner prescribed by God.

Many religions also advocate that human beings possess an innate and inherent moral conscience that is part of human nature. Since human beings are considered created in God's image and imbued with His Spirit, they possess this innate moral sense. For example, it is claimed that every sane being knows intuitively that it is wrong to kill innocent children. Everyone knows what it is like to experience a sense of guilt or responsibility when one has done something wrong. Not all moral standards are necessarily considered inborn, but it is claimed that certain principles are.

Of course, several criticisms have been leveled at theistic moralities. Many, for instance, question why religion can sometimes sanction commandments that they consider morally questionable (according to human standards). Can God command something that is simply wrong, such as killing children or ordering oppression? Furthermore, how is one to evaluate the sometimes differing claims of various religions on ethical and moral issues? Skeptics also claim that "moral conscience" is merely an outcome of parental, societal and cultural influences. The atheist, Kai Nielsen, has leveled another criticism of religious ethics by arguing that everyone has pre-existing moral standards by which we judge whether God is Perfectly Good or not, and hence, feels that everyone's morality cyclically reverts back to their own human understanding.

Responses to such criticisms will be made from an Islamic point of view in the remainder of the chapter. In the meantime, it is necessary to understand certain fundamental principles of Islamic ethics.

5.5 The Foundation of Islamic Ethics

In order to answer the primary question posed as the heading of this Chapter and related questions from an Islamic point of view, the fundamental Islamic worldview concerning the nature of God and the nature and purpose of man must be recalled.

Islam does not simply regard God as a nebulous but powerful Being that created the Universe. In Chapter 1, we reviewed the Islamic principle of God having *Perfection and Unity of all Attributes described unto Himself* through Scripture and the Message of the Prophets. Everything begins and ends with God. Thus, God is not only the Creator, but is also Perfect in being the Merciful, the Knower, the Wise, the Just, the Sustainer, the Loving, the Forgiving, and the Righteous, etc. Among the Attributes of Allah that are immediately relevant are the attributes of *Al-Hadi*, the Perfect Guide, and *Ar-Rasheed*, the Guider to the Straight Path. With these Attributes in mind, it is blasphemous to regard God as having created human beings without providing some form of guidance to differentiate right from wrong. Furthermore, if God is truly *Al-Hakam*, the Judge, and *Al-Haseeb*, the Reckoner, then there cannot but be accountability and reckoning for our deeds in this life. The believer has firmly implanted in his or her heart the conviction that God will account for all actions and that there is no escaping or deceiving the Judgment of God.

> ...*it is blasphemous to regard God as having created human beings without providing some form of guidance to differentiate right from wrong.*

It is, thus, easy to understand why Islam considers God as not only the Master of the Natural, Physical, and Spiritual Orders, but also Master of the Moral Order. Indeed, most adherents of various religions throughout the world believe in God as the Moral Law-Giver and source and foundation for morality and ethics. It should not be surprising, then, that most detractors of Divine ethics are champions of atheism and agnosticism. Ultimately, the rejection of God as the source of morality in favor of human beings reverts to a disbelief in God; a reversion to the ultimate sin of Satan— arrogance. As long as human beings only recognize their own perceived authority and refuse to admit their limitations, any systems of ethics they devise are bound to fail. It is a peculiar aberration of modern societies that most "citizens" are proud to submit to the "rule of law" but not to the "rule of God". They willingly submit to ministers, prime-ministers, presidents and patriarchs, but not to God. Until there is reliance on the only Being who can transcend the limitation of space, time and ego, secular ethics will always be mired in social decay, unrest, and injustice. And they will keep on floundering as in the modern world.

5.6 Does God Command Immoral Acts?

What about the common criticism of skeptics that religious ethics or God can sometimes sanction what they consider immoral or morally questionable? The answer to such a question is muddled by the facts that certain religions have at times sanctioned morally questionable acts, and violence has been perpetrated in the name of all religions, including Islam. Skeptics often note that the Old Testament is replete with examples of commandments from God ordering the complete destruction of entire populations of men, women and children, and even animals.[16] In the Book of Joshua, we have that "he (Joshua) took it, and the king thereof, and all the cities thereof; and they smote them with the edge of the sword, and utterly destroyed all the souls that were therein, he left none remaining: as he had done to Hebron, so he did to Debir, and to the king thereof; as he had done also to Libnah, and to her king ... he left none remaining, but utterly destroyed all that breathed, as the Lord of God of Israel had commanded" (10:39-40). Without getting into the details or contexts of particular passages, the key is to differentiate between what human beings consider Divine commands and what truly are Divine commands. What is required is an objective analysis of the source of the teaching in question – if there is conviction in God as the source, then it must be followed, regardless of what is commanded.

At the same time, for a Muslim, there is absolutely no possibility of God sanctioning what is "immoral" since there is complete conviction that Allah is the Creator whose Infinite Love, Knowledge, Wisdom and Guidance make it blasphemous to think that Allah would command what is against our welfare, much less "immoral". Chapter 4 introduced some of the reasons for considering the Qur'an and Sunnah of Muhammad (SAW) as authentic and reliable primary sources of Divine Guidance.

It is worthwhile to consider two examples from the Qur'an, which include acts that would likely be considered "immoral" by the common skeptic. In the case of Prophet Ibrahim (Abraham), he saw in a vision that he was ordered to "offer thee (his son) in sacrifice" (Qur'an 37:102). Since he had no doubt that God had commanded him to sacrifice his son, he was obligated to act. In the end, of course, God through His Mercy replaced his son with a ram. The Divine order is not immoral because firstly, it is a specific order for Prophet Ibrahim as a test of faith, or *balaa'*, for someone who is going to be entrusted with the immense role of prophethood, which he obviously passes because of the strength of his conviction in God as the Source of Law, and secondly, because there is no actual sacrifice of Ismail (Ishmael).

Another relevant example, discussed earlier in Chapter 3 (Section 4) concerns an encounter between Prophet Moses (AS) and Khidr (AS), another Messenger of God, described at length in the Qur'an (18:60-82). The episode begins with an incident where Khidr (AS) cuts a hole in a boat, seemingly without reason, belonging to some honest workers or traders; a second incident involves the killing of a young man whom Moses (AS) perceives to be innocent; and a third tells of some inhabitants of a town who refuse to offer any food or hospitality to Khidr (AS) and Moses (AS), and yet Khidr (AS) helps the townsfolk by rebuilding and erecting a certain wall that was on the verge of collapse. Moses (AS) expresses his failure to understand Khidr's actions, after which Khidr (AS) proceeds to explain the Divine purpose behind each action he was ordered by God to carry out.

The first action was performed because there was an oppressive king who was unjustly seizing boats in the area the men were wishing to go towards. The simple act of making the boat un-seaworthy saved it from seizure. The second act of murder was carried out, not because Khidr disliked him, but because the young man was a constant source of obstinate rebellion and ingratitude towards his pious parents and God desired to "give them in exchange a son better in purity of conduct and closer in affection."[17] The last act of rebuilding the wall for their inhospitable hosts was intended to benefit two righteous youths who were orphans. Had the wall fallen, the other townsfolk would have looted the treasure that was buried beneath the wall by the pious father of the orphans. He had hidden it with the intent that his children would inherit the treasure when they had grown up.

Such incidents are conveyed to illustrate the Divine Order and purpose that continually works "behind the scenes", and which can easily be misunderstood by common human sensibilities. The human mind, with its inherent limitations, simply cannot fathom the infinitely complex web of phenomena, and their inter-relationships, throughout the universe. Thus, once again, the morality or immorality of any commandment is to be determined by God, not our own limited judgments. Nor does God ever will for His creation what is contrary to their well-being.

5.7 The Trust of Moral Responsibility

Despite our inherent limitations, there is a great deal we have to be thankful for. We are unique in a number of respects within the spectrum of creation. We have been blessed with the power of consciousness, the gift of free will, the ability to process emotions, and the discernment to know our Creator. We have been bestowed the ability to question who we are and where are we going. Such gifts, however, come at the cost of responsibility. Animals, plants, fungi and even angels do not have a choice in their affair-it is human beings who have the power of free will, and the consequent moral responsibility.

Moral responsibility is more than simply knowing right from wrong, however. Human beings have been created to serve and to submit to the Will of God.[18] In doing so, we have the potential to fulfill our cosmic roles as vicegerents of God on earth[19], thereby reflecting Divine Attributes in our own character and behavior. We are also indebted to God for having brought us into existence and for sustaining us. We were dissolved in the abyss of nothingness and now we are partaking of the treasure of existence. As Shaykh Fadhlalla Haeri states, "We were created to know the original love of the Creator, with Whom we were before creation, with Whom we are during the experience of existence, and with Whom we will be forever."[20] Prophet Muhammad (SAW) was once asked by a companion why he continuously prayed for so long that his feet became swollen while he is sinless and forgiven. He answered, "Should I not be a grateful servant?"[21]

> *We were dissolved in the abyss of nothingness and now we are partaking in the treasure of existence.*

Moral responsibility is, thus, not simply about knowing right from wrong, but is about gratefulness to our Lord and is part of the trust from the Lord to become His vicegerent on earth, thereby fulfilling the purpose with which we were created:

> We offered the Trust to the heavens and the earth and the mountains, but they drew back from bearing it and feared to do so. It is man who bore it...
> (33:72)

In this sense, morality is all about fulfilling our greater purpose on this earth. Thus, the magnitude of the importance of morality and ethics is reflected in Qur'anic statements like, "Allah will not change the condition of a people until they change what is within themselves,"[22] and the statements of Prophet Muhammad (SAW), "I was sent to perfect moral character"[23] and "Those who have perfect faith are those who have better moral character."[24]

To help us in this enormous mission, God has not only provided Guidance through the external messages of Scripture and the Prophets, but also through the internal faculties of spiritual intuition and unveiling. The endless debate over the nature of human nature has been answered clearly by Islam.

As noted on several occasions, Islam teaches that to follow the path of submission to God is to be faithful to one's very nature. Man is not "half good, half evil" as many presume. Our primordial nature is inherently inclined towards good, though we have the potential to sin (unlike the Christian belief in "original sin"). Islam considers all human beings to have acknowledged Allah as our Lord, or *rabb* in Arabic, before we were created:

> When your Lord drew forth from the children of Adam from their loins-their descendants and made them testify concerning themselves (saying), *'Am I not your rabb (Lord)'.* They said, *'Yes, we do testify!',* lest you should say on the Day of Judgment, 'Of this we were never mindful'. (7:172)
>
> And call in remembrance the favor of Allah unto you, and *His covenant, which He ratified with you when you said, 'We hear and we obey'*: and fear Allah for Allah knows well the secrets of your hearts. (5:7)
>
> By the soul and the proportion and order given to it, and *its enlightenment as to its wrong and its right,* truly he succeeds that purifies it and he fails that corrupts it... (91: 7-10)

Hence, we have already testified that Allah is our *Lord* and that we will obey Him before our physical existence in this world. Disbelief is a conscious denial of our original nature. Thus, regarding the purity of our creation, Prophet Muhammad (SAW) stated, "Every child is born according to primordial nature *(fitra),* then his parents make him a Jew, Christian, or Zoroastrian."[25] This primordial nature is a result of the spirit which was blown into every being by God Himself.[26] The greatest proof for God's existence, then, is already within us!

Of course, skeptics have long denied any aspect of human nature that could transcend its material nature. For them there is no spiritual intuition, insight or intellection, nor a universal conscience. In so believing, they fail to realize a number of points. If man were merely a creature of animal instinct in an evolutionary game of survival, there simply would not be any acts of utter selflessness or self-denial, such as firemen risking their lives to save unknown victims or monks taking vows of celibacy. The fact is that there is an undeniable facet of our nature that spans all peoples and all times which seeks to transcend corporeal limitation and return to our Origin, just as rain drops eventually return to immerse in the ocean. If man were merely an advanced byproduct of evolution, consciousness would never have arisen, for that which is immaterial cannot arise from pure material (see Chapter 1, Section 8). If man were merely a product of societal, cultural and environmental influences, there would never have arisen any reformers or Divine Messengers, like Abraham, Jesus (AS) and Muhammad (SAW), who radically challenged and strove to eradicate the deviance of their times.

> *If man were merely a product of societal, cultural and environmental influences, there would never have arisen any reformers or Divine Messengers, like Abraham, Jesus (AS) and Muhammad (SAW), who radically challenged and strived to eradicate the deviance of their times.*

Finally, it is important to reiterate the Islamic view of the motivation behind moral behavior. As noted earlier, the motivation is not, as many skeptics try to argue, promises of heavenly bliss and rewards. Rather, the primary motivation for morality is the pleasure and obedience of God, which is sought because of the Transcendence and Immanence of His Attributes. This is not to deny the reward and punishment of God and its role in the behavior of believers, but to state that it is secondary to the primary desire to obey God. Section 5.9 further discusses the importance of sincerity of intention in morality.

To summarize, it should be apparent from the recent discussion that the Islamic system of morality includes the following underlying principles:

(1) Allah is the Law-Giver or source of morality

(2) Moral behavior is part of fulfilling our purpose on earth, i.e. submission and obedience to the Will of God, and

(3) God has created us with an inherent tendency towards good and we have been imbued with both a material and a spiritual nature.

It is, thus, easy to understand that the Islamic definition of morality is a subset of the overall concept of submission and worship of God.

5.8 The Real World

For all the discussion of the merits and demerits of various ethical systems, the fact remains that what eventually concerns people most is how all these ideals are put into practice. To provide a comprehensive review of the specific moral teachings of Islam is beyond the scope of this work. However, concerning the primary issue of whether morality requires God, it is necessary to examine at least a few examples that highlight the significant gap that can exist between values commonly advocated by modern man and values ordained by God. Sometimes the wisdom of Divine ethics can only be appreciated by pondering its absence—i.e. by critically evaluating the systems of ethics devised by man.

Consider the use of alcohol, for example. While the God of Islam has unequivocally prohibited the use and promotion of intoxicating alcohol, much of the world considers so-called "moderate" or "responsible" alcohol consumption not only acceptable but even redeeming for its social value. Most Western societies regard "getting drunk" as an essential and inevitable rite of passage for teenagers to graduate to adulthood. The unabashed, shameless $100 billion alcohol industry proudly promotes the value of drinking as a means to endless fun, dancing, sexual encounters, and loss of inhibitions while hypocritically advertising meaningless slogans such as "Think before you drink" and "Don't drink and drive". Apparently they have intoxicated the masses to such an extent that they are unable to consider the value of "Don't drink—period". While the alcohol industry continues to boast about the "pleasures" of alcohol, even a remotely objective analysis of the situation would reveal a much more sinister side to the drug of alcohol.

The shameful truth is that alcohol is responsible for over 100,000 deaths per year in the U.S. alone,[27] at a cost to taxpayers and society of about $99 billion.[28] This annual death toll on average includes 19,000 who die due to alcohol-induced liver cirrhosis (not to mention the increased risk for cancer, heart disease, cerebro-vascular disease) and 2000 people killed by teenage drunk-drivers.[29] Coupled with the fact that 38% of all criminals were drinking at the time of their offenses,[30] each and every crime and death begs the resounding question as to why there is no serious effort to end such madness. While a "war on drugs" has raged for decades, a blind eye is turned to the significantly more lethal and costly epidemic of alcoholism. It is simply unacceptable to continue the failing argument for "moderation" in drinking while bodies are dropping—after all, why not argue for "moderation" in cocaine, heroin, and marijuana usage?

> *While a "war on drugs" has raged for decades, a blind eye is turned to the significantly more lethal and costly epidemic of alcoholism.*

The Wisdom of God recognizes the fact that the legalization of intoxicants inevitably leads to abuse and sin and hence; the Qur'an calls alcohol an "abomination of Satan's handiwork" (5:90). Until man recognizes the Divine Wisdom in the prohibition of alcohol and the fatal mistake he has made in its legalization, society will continue to suffer the dire consequences.

Another example relates to what is considered an "acceptable" dress code for women. The Islamic dress code has often been criticized for what some perceive as the subjugation and oppression of women based on their own cultural and societal biases. While contemporary Western views of dress are supposed to advocate personal freedom, including the option to barely dress at all, the commandment of God is for both men and women to dress in a modest and dignified way to garner the respect they deserve and righteousness. Thus, the Qur'an states:

> "And say to the believing women that they should lower their gaze and guard their modesty; that they should not display their beauty and ornaments except what (must ordinarily) appear thereof; that they should draw their veils over their bosoms..." (24:31)

This verse was implemented during the time of Prophet Muhammad (SAW) to include, at the very least, loose, full-length clothing from the nape to the ankles and a covering of the hair. While civilizations, nations, cultures and individuals have laid out a very broad range for what is considered "normal" dress, Islam argues that it is only God who can define such standards. The only way to overcome personal biases and limitations inherent within our confinements of space and time is to rely on the Wisdom of God. This Divine Wisdom knows that the only way to protect the dignity and respect of women is to encourage modesty in dress. While Islam does not try to deny or reject the natural beauty of women, it regards it as a valuable treasure or gem that is only to be displayed among family.

> *Divine Wisdom knows that the only way to protect the dignity and respect of women is to encourage modesty in dress.*

Contemporary societies have suffered the consequences of uninhibited dress through rape, sexual assault, sexual advances, sexual promiscuity and most of all, a lack of respect. In 1995, for example, there were over 350,000 cases of attempted or completed rape and sexual assault in the United States alone.[31] Feminists often complain about the monetary, sexual and technical injustices women suffer in the workplace and question when they will be taken seriously as equals with men in all pursuits. The fact is they will never be equals as long as society promotes the trivialization and debasement of women as sexual objects to fuel mass consumerism and quench male lust. In America alone, the $60 billion clothing industry, the $40 billion diet industry, the $20 billion cosmetic industry, and the $2 billion plastic surgery industry, to mention just a few, endlessly promote a debased image of women where an idealized image of beauty and body rules and occupies the common mind. The dirty truth is that while society gleefully gawks at such "Barbie-like" images, few people take them seriously when it comes to what matters most, i.e. their character and their ideas. The reason nuns dress the way they do is because they know they will not garner any respect if they were to dress otherwise. Similarly, Islam has emphasized modesty, dignity and respect for all women and men, and in doing so, provided true liberation and freedom.

The final example to be discussed highlighting the difference between human and Divine understanding concerns the concept of prayer. In an age of materialism fueled by industry, science, technology and mass consumerism, much of the world has precious little time for anything beyond earning the daily bread, much less prayer. Many regard prayer as a meaningless but convenient outlet for those in despair. Prayer is often viewed as a fleeting symbol of a religious past to be replaced by the certainty of the scientific present. Others, who at least recognize some value of prayer, merely resort to weekly, monthly, annual, or "as needed" sessions beseeching a Higher Power for help in their affairs.

Islam, on the other hand, recommends prayer as an essential link between the creation and the Creator, without which a gaping hole is left in the heart of the believer. Besides valuing personal and direct supplication to God, Islam has commanded the *salat*, a five-times daily, comprehensive form of prayer that is not only provides spiritual nourishment, but also moral uplifting and emotional and physical satisfaction. The *salat* represents a powerful and unparalleled combination of prayer, gratitude, meditation, discipline and physical exercise. It provides spiritual nourishment through the remembrance of God and recitation of His Word; moral uplifting through self-discipline and humility before a Higher Being; emotional stability through reliance on God and a calming of the central nervous system; and physical well-being through its frequent movements and stretches. As with other forms of worship in Islam, prayer is not only in the best interest of the individual, but also society. Prayer is said in the Qur'an to "prevent shameful and unjust deeds" (29:45), thereby supporting a righteous society, and is considered highly recommendable to be performed in congregation in mosques to foster unity and strengthen social bonds.

The physiological and psychological benefits of general prayer and meditation are also being increasingly supported by modern research. Prayer and meditation have been proven to heighten relaxation states by decreasing the heart rate, respiration rate, plasma cortisol (a major stress hormone), and pulse rate, while increasing EEG alpha, a brain wave associated with relaxation.[32] Other studies at UCLA found that meditation can enhance alertness, reduce reaction time, and even increase creativity.[33] Conditions for which meditation is currently being recommended as an adjunctive therapy include heart disease, hypertension, stress and anxiety, alcohol and drug addiction, chronic pain, cancer and AIDS. Besides personal benefits, a number of studies are pointing to the benefits of prayer in healing others. *The American Heart Journal*, for example, reported that among 150 patients scheduled for angioplasty, further heart complications were significantly less among those who were prayed for by various religious denominations.[34] Another study reported in the *Journal of Reproductive Medicine* included a double-blind, randomized study of 199 South Korean women with difficulty conceiving. Several Christian groups in the U.S., Canada and Australia prayed for them, with the result that the women who were prayed for had twice the pregnancy rate of those who were not prayed for.[35] Other studies have even proved that prayer can influence the growth of cells, bacteria, plants and animals.

At a time when modern lives are plagued by the financial, career, family stresses, the need for the counterbalancing force of prayer has arguably never been greater. No other religion has better implemented and institutionalized the importance of daily prayers than Islam. Thus, the five daily prayers of a Muslim must be performed regardless of how busy or where one may be. Work schedules cannot dictate when we "worship"—work schedules must fit into a way of life that acknowledges and follows the Wisdom of God.

5.9 What is Unique about Islamic Ethics?

Having introduced certain principles and examples of Islamic ethics, it remains to clarify what is unique or different about them. Although there are certainly more commonalities between ethical systems than differences, especially between the perspectives of various religions, the beauty of Islamic ethics can be appreciated when contrasted with other forms of ethics. Some of the unique features of the ethical system of Islam are as follows:

1. *Tawhid* as Basis.

The Islamic worldview of *Tawhid*, the Unity and Supremacy of Allah, provides the foundation for a successful ethical and moral system. Islam's view of God as the one and only Power necessitates God as the Source of Ethics. God cannot be considered the Master of the Natural and Physical Orders without being the Master of the Moral and Spiritual Orders. God has not left humanity at a loss with no guidance for how to conduct ourselves. To the contrary, God has invested man with His Trust and Covenant, which no other creature in the universe could bear, and whose fulfillment allows man to become the cosmic vicegerent of God on earth (as discussed above).

The Islamic view, firstly, stands in stark contrast to all secular ideologies. Many of the ancient Greek philosophies elevated and even deified man to the extent that the Greek gods and goddesses not only exemplified virtues, but also vices. The ancient Greek was not offended by cheating, conniving, jealous, vengeful, and incestuous deities because man was the ultimate criterion for all that is. Humanist ideologies also elevate humanity or society as the ultimate criterion for their worldview. However, the "majority" can be wrong—history testifies to the unimaginable atrocities that can occur when we are only accountable to society— the genocide of American Indians, the slavery and oppression of Africans, and the massacre of millions in Cambodia to name but a few instances. At a lesser level, the common societal acceptance of "norms" such as social drinking, drug abuse, gambling and sexual promiscuity does not make them "right". A truly relativist society can never promote genuine morality because they are inherently contradictory concepts. Relativism does not allow for any meaningful criticism, reform or progress of society since it must treat all forms of ethics as equal. Secular societies are facing a growing crisis of morality affecting all walks of life, which is becoming increasingly difficult to solve since it cannot resort to "religious ethics". Materialism's chaotic game of "survival of the wealthiest" is also at odds with morality, for it pits us against one another just as wolves scurrying for the last morsel of a carcass.

Ultimately all proponents of such secular ideologies fail most miserably in one area—in recognizing their own frailties and limitations. The debate of secularists over the source of ethics can be likened to the argument of paintings with their painter. While God has blessed us with remarkable capabilities of reason and discernment to discover aspects of "natural law", we cannot forget their inherent limitations within our particular space-time confinements and our dependence on God for ultimate guidance. As discussed at length in Chapter 2, our rational faculties can and should be used to complement, support and strengthen our understanding of the universe and God's existence, but we must ultimately depend on Divine guidance for understanding God and His Moral Ordering of the universe.

> *The debate of secularists over the source of ethics can be likened to the arguing of paintings with their painter.*

Any skepticism the secularists or agnostics have regarding an objective source of moral knowledge is answered in Islam through Divine Scriptures and Messengers. Skepticism regarding our ability to be moral is answered in Islam by affirming our inherent goodness and rejecting any notions of "original sin". Skepticism regarding the outcome of moral behavior is answered by the promise of Allah to reform society when we decide to reform ourselves[36] and the promise of complete Justice in the Hereafter. The endless search of philosophers for individual and collective "pleasure", "happiness", "virtue", and "freedom" is answered in Islam by obedience to God, which automatically encompasses and leads to all such treasures.

> *The endless search of philosophers for individual and collective "pleasure", "happiness", "virtue", and "freedom" is answered in Islam by obedience to God, which automatically encompasses and leads to all such treasures.*

As for the basis of other religious ethical systems, there is indeed a great deal in common with Islamic ethics, including the belief in God as the Moral Law-Giver, the importance of following His commandments, and the consideration of others' rights as importantly as our own. However, as discussed in Chapter 4, while other religions may have started with genuinely Divine origins, they have suffered from extensive and continual human intervention in the guidance from God. Thus, homosexual priests, adultery and pre-marital sex are tolerated or accepted in Modern Christianity; theft, lying, and cheating of gentiles is permitted in the Talmud of Judaism; and systematic discrimination against the "untouchables" is permitted and persists in Hinduism. Islam has, therefore, gone to great lengths in strictly prohibiting any modern innovations in its guiding principles—hence, the enormous difficulty in "reforming" Islam. The specific applications of principles may change with variables of time and place, but the principles themselves cannot be changed. While non-Muslims may initially disagree with certain Islamic teachings, it must be remembered that an objective evaluation of the truth of particular moral principles must revert to the authenticity and reliability of such teachings as commandments from God, and not our own biased opinions, beliefs, whims or fancies.

2. Understanding of Human Nature

Islam is the *religio naturalis* that affirms the purity of the primordial nature with which we have been created. Islam alone recognizes human nature as it is and promotes the attainable goal for morality as being the representative or vicegerent of God on earth. Although we have been created with free will to obey or disobey, our nature is inherently inclined towards good, stemming from the Divine Spirit that has been blown within us, and we have all acknowledged Allah as our Lord before being physically created (see Sec. 5.7 and Chapter 2). We have been created with a pure slate—it is only later that we learn to sin. According to Islamic belief, this is why it was possible for the most extraordinary individuals amongst us, i.e. the Prophets and Messengers to live infallible, sin-free lives.[37] Virtuous lives free of major sins are fully attainable, as documented and demonstrated not only by the Prophets, but also by the lives of countless believers or "friends of God", known as *awliya* in Islam.

Why, however, should a Muslim act morally? A true Muslim acts to obey Allah with the sincere intention of pleasing Him. And why does a Muslim desire to obey Allah? Ultimately, obedience to Allah is performed out of love for the Creator, gratefulness for the gift of existence, knowledge of human nature, and realization of His Wisdom in knowing what is best for the felicity and tranquility of His creation. Muslims have no nagging doubts about morality—they recognize the inherent goodness of the human spirit, they understand what constitutes moral behavior, and they know that goodness can be encouraged and is worth encouraging in the world.

Consider the beauty and uniqueness of the Islamic conception of human nature in relation to the Christian view. Modern Christian thinkers have sought to give the doctrine of "original sin" credibility by pointing to the undeniable sins and imperfections of man and this selfish and egoistic loci.

The Christian emphasis on an ontologically evil humanity is necessary to justify the death and blood atonement of the Divine incarnation. In the words of Faruqi, "there must be a predicament so absolute that only God could pull man out of it."[38] Islam rejects such notions outright.[39] While Islam acknowledges that *we can become* sinful, it is an altogether different matter to claim that we have been *created* sinful.

> *The Christian emphasis on an ontologically evil humanity is necessary to justify the death and blood atonement of the Divine Son.*

The doctrines of original sin and blood atonement of the "Son of God", which infer the idea that neither individual nor society can truly be "moral", and that moral behavior is irrelevant as long as one accepts Jesus as the Savior, have forced Christians who strive to be morally upright and philanthropic to violate their own doctrines. It is no wonder that there are some Christians who see no contradiction between their faith and habits such as alcoholism, gambling and sexual promiscuity. Unlike the Christian emphasis on faith over deeds, Islam maintains a perfect balance between the necessity of both faith and deeds, with each being insufficient without the other.

Besides Christian views of human nature, it is also important to address the earlier introduced criticism of atheists, which claims that everyone has pre-existing moral standards by which we judge whether God is Perfectly Good or not, and hence, argues that everyone's morality cyclically reverts to their own human understanding. In *Ethics Without God*, Kai Nielsen explains that:

> ...to understand that God, among other things, is a being worthy of worship and that God is said to be perfect, the perfect good, we need some logically prior understanding of those normative concepts. In order to understand that something is the perfect good, you have to understand what is good, and in order to understand that something is worthy of worship, you have to have at least some elementary criteria or understanding of what worthiness is, and that is not itself derived from a God.[40]

In this statement, Nielsen starts a logically valid argument but ends with a biased and un-provable conclusion, i.e. "and that is not itself derived from a God." Most Muslims would agree that in considering God to be the "Perfect Good", some prior normative understanding of good and worthiness is required—but that is precisely the point—God has created and imbued within us this inherent sense of good or what John Henry Newman called "moral conscience". In this sense, Nielsen starts with an argument that can actually be used to argue for the existence of God!

Yet another facet of Islamic ethics which recognizes the true nature of man is its maintenance of a harmonious balance between the physical and the spiritual, the worldliness and the non-worldliness. There is no contradiction between its promotion of worship (*'ibadah*) and the fulfillment of physical needs, for such fulfillment is itself considered worship when conducted with the sincere intention of pleasing Allah. Islam promotes the control of physical needs, not their renunciation. Thus, Prophet Muhammad (SAW) warned against celibacy, excessive seclusion, excessive fasting, pessimism, and cynicism, while encouraging the cleanliness of the body, brushing of the teeth, marriage, rest, and physical activities such as wrestling and horseback riding. The institutions of priesthood and monasticism are both unheard of in Islam. Muslims do not face a choice between being ascetic hermits and worldly, indulgent persons. A Muslim can fully engage in worship while simultaneously fulfilling all worldly or material responsibilities. At a time when non-Muslims are increasingly inclined towards either crass materialism or spiritual renunciation, it is especially worthwhile for non-Muslims to consider the beauty of the Islamic implementation of this principle.

> *Muslims do not face a choice between being an ascetic hermits and worldly, indulgent persons.*

3. Universalism

History confirms that, on the whole, it is only Islam that has been able to provide a truly universal civilization. Islam's conviction in the Unity of God and corresponding Unity of Truth and the universal human nature necessitates that moral and ethical obligation be equally incumbent upon all. As Faruqi stated, "Just as the patterns of God in nature apply to all of creation, thereby making creation an orderly cosmos, so His will for man applies to the whole of mankind."[41] The Qur'an is very clear that "We have not sent thee (Muhammad) save as a blessing for all mankind" (21:107). Unlike prior Messengers and Prophets whose messages were confined to their particular peoples, the message of Islam conveyed by Prophet Muhammad (SAW) has always been open to all of humanity, and never been limited to any particular people, nation, tribe, race or social class.

Not only does Islam not discriminate in the target of its message, but also in its application:

> O mankind! We created you from a single pair of a male and a female, and made you into nations and tribes, that you may know each other. Verily, the most honored of you in the sight of Allah is the most righteous of you (49:13)

A famous saying of Prophet Muhammad (SAW) proclaimed, "All men issue from Adam and Adam issued from dust. Therefore, no Arab may claim distinction over a non-Arab except in piety and righteousness."

While Islam has certainly had its share of racist and morally bankrupt followers, it nonetheless maintains the cleanest record of all religions in fairly applying its ethics to everyone, without regard to the common discriminants of race, color, social status, religion and national origin. The Qur'an, however, does speak of distinguishing between those who are *muttaqi*, God-conscious, and those who are not; which is necessarily so, for God must judge His creation to the extent that they fulfill their purpose of creation, i.e. obedience to Allah, which is inclusive of moral behavior. For ultimate justice to reign, the oppressor cannot be equal to the oppressed and the knower cannot be equal to the ignorant. In its application, Islam cannot discriminate based on mundane differences, since it does not recognize any modern notions of the "nation-state" or classifications based on race and color- it only considers one nation, or *Ummah*, all of whose members stand equally before God in sincere service. The early Caliphs of Islam, Abu Bakr, 'Umar, 'Uthman and 'Ali, led a vast cross-section of peoples, races and colors united simply in the common desire to follow Allah. Today, in the melting pot of American society, it is only Islam that is consistently able to bring together peoples from every corner of the globe in its place of worship, while the Church has altogether failed to reflect this feature of integration. Despite the deteriorated state of the Ummah, it is common for Muslims to feel a strong bond with other Muslims throughout the world and pray for and support their welfare, regardless of whether in Albania, Indonesia or Zambia.

Modern societies are still tainted with the evils of tribalism, nationalism, racism and aristocracy. Western norms of "etiquette" actually originated in the practices of the royal courts of Europe, which was used to distinguish the aristocratic elite from the masses. America faced 9730 confirmed reports of hate crimes in 2001, including crimes against people because of their race, religion, sex, ethnicity or disability.[42] Jewish history has never overcome a strand of elitism that not only considers Jews "the chosen people of God", but also attempts to bind and restrict God's favor to themselves. Similarly, Hindu history has always been plagued with the curse of the caste system, which still differentiates between Brahmin, Vaishya and Shudra in most aspects of society. Modern Muslim societies have also forgotten their religious teachings and fallen prey to ethnic and sectarian divisiveness. To cure such ills, people must overcome their misconceptions of Islam and realize that the world has much to gain from the principles and application of Islamic ethics.

4. Comprehensive Nature

Moral behavior in Islam is considered part and parcel of worship and submission to God, as discussed earlier. It is sometimes difficult for non-Muslims to understand the all-encompassing nature of Islam.

Unlike other religions, "worship" or more closely *'ibadah*, governs every aspect of life such that a Muslim's entire life can be spent in worship, 24 hours a day and 7 days a week. According to Faruqi, "In Islam, ethics is inseparable from religion and is entirely built upon it."[43] There are no artificial divides between the secular and the sacred or the Church and the State. Secular theories of ethics, such as hedonism, perfectionism, egoism and humanism, fall considerably short of providing clear moral guidance for many specific situations. Islamic law, on the other hand, provides concrete, specific guidance for all situations based on the Qur'an, traditions of Prophet Muhammad (SAW), or deductions from the principles therein. All actions are classified according to whether they are obligatory, permitted, recommended, prohibited, recommended-against, or neutral (the extent to which Islamic law applies to specific moral situations is considerably more detailed than Christianity but not to the extent of minutiae in Judaism).

The Islamic concept of worship is so comprehensive that Prophet Muhammad (SAW) advised: "Each person's every joint must perform a charity every day the sun arises: to act justly between two people is a charity; to help a man with his mount, lifting him onto it is a charity; a good word is a charity; every step you take to prayers is a charity; and removing a harmful thing from the road is a charity."[44] Thus, worship includes not only rituals like prayer and fasting but also everything from how to behave, eat, sleep, dress, and go to the bathroom. It not only seeks to establish harmonious relationships between human beings, but also with the natural world. Each deed or action also has a specific prayer, such as *bismillahir-rahman-ir-rahim* (In the name of Allah, the Most Beneficent, the Most Merciful), which should be recited before performing it so as to attain the blessing of God. In this manner, every action can be considered worship in Islam so long as there is a ·sincere desire to perform it for the sake of following God and according to the manner prescribed by Him.

Thus, unlike secular forms of ethics, such as hedonism and perfectionism, the comprehensive nature of Islamic ethics is such that a Muslim can confront any kind of moral dilemma with full confidence that he or she is doing the "right thing". For the Muslim there is no moral dilemma of abortion, capital punishment, euthanasia, cloning, or the like. There are no ambiguities concerning what constitutes "virtue", "pleasure", "happiness" or "freedom". The principles governing all moral problems have already been provided by the guidance of God through His Scripture and Messengers.

Another differentiating and essential feature of Islamic ethics is the concept of *al-amr bi'l-ma'ruf wa'l-nahi 'ani'l-munkar*, or encouraging righteousness and forbidding evil. The Qur'an clearly states, "Let there arise out of you a band of people inviting to all that is good, enjoining what is right and forbidding what is wrong: they are the ones to attain felicity" (3:104) and encourages this principle on numerous occasions.[45]

Unlike the secular promotion of "I'm OK, You're OK" relativism where no one supposedly has the authority to sanction anyone else, Islam promotes the idea that there must not only be "rule of law", but also civil encouragement of good and prevention of evil, to maintain a righteous society, reflective of the Kingdom of God on earth. Without this enforcement of Divine Law, communities deteriorate into moral, ethical and social decay, as witnessed in countless societies of the present day.

Chapter Summary

1. The fact that different individuals, cultures and societies have different codes of ethics does not provide legitimacy to ethical relativism. The fact that there have been differing theories throughout history regarding the laws of physics does not mean the world is without fixed, universal laws of physics; similarly, the diversity of ethical standards does not contradict the possibility of absolute and universal ethics. Another significant problem for relativism is its utter impracticality, for a truly relativist society cannot have any absolute good, absolute evil, or meaningful reform of ethics and morality.

2. All secular theories of ethics ultimately rely on individuals or collections of individuals as the only source and criterion for moral standards. Hedonism, for example, argues that maximizing "pleasure" (either individually or collectively) is the only criterion for right action. The theory of perfectionism maintains that goodness is inherently worthy of pursuit. Secular humanism is a popular modern movement, closely intertwined with a secular political outlook, which holds that ethical standards should be developed by the collective brain of humanity or a particular society without any interference from religious or Divine dictates. Each of these theories, particularly secular humanism, was critiqued in the chapter.

3. The faiths of Judaism, Christianity and Islam are in general agreement regarding the fundamental and essential belief in God as the Source of Morality. God is believed to be the only objective source of a universal morality that can transcend the inherent human limitations of space, time and ego and provide complete justice and accountability for both moral and immoral behavior. Just as children cannot be relied on to devise an optimal code of behavior without their parents, so too human beings must rely on God as the objective Creator whose Infinite Knowledge and Wisdom provide

the ultimate moral authority. Within this general agreement, however, there are various theories as to how we acquire moral and ethical truths from God, such as the Divine Command, natural law, and innate conscience theories.

4. Islam teaches that just as Allah is the Master of the Natural, Physical and Spiritual Orders, He is also the Master of the Moral Order. A Muslim cannot believe in Allah without believing that He has provided guidance concerning "right action" and that we will be called to account for not only our beliefs, but also our deeds.

5. Islam does not believe that Allah can command immoral acts, as skeptics often argue. Allah only commands what is in the best interest of His creation. It is critical to differentiate between what human beings consider as Divine commands and what truly are Divine commands, but once there is conviction in God as the source of a command, then it must be followed, even if limited human understanding may not always fully comprehend the wisdom behind it.

6. Moral behavior is regarded by Islam as part and parcel of fulfilling the purpose of creation, i.e. submission and obedience to God to become His vicegerents on earth. Moral behavior is also a responsibility and a trust from God, Who has bestowed upon man the gifts of life, consciousness and free will.

7. Islam not only affirms the idea that man possesses an inherent moral conscience, but also that he is created pure (unlike the Christian belief in "original sin") and inherently inclined towards "good", though we retain the potential to disobey and sin. Our innate moral sensibilities derive from the Divine Spirit that was blown into every one of us by God Himself.

8. In clarifying the question of whether morality requires God, a few practical examples were examined that highlight the significant gap that can exist between moral values commonly advocated by modern man and values ordained by God. These examples related to the use of

alcohol, the dress code of women, and the concept of prayer.

9 Certain unique features of Islamic ethics were presented as they compare to the views of other religions as well as secularism and agnosticism. These features relate to its reliance on Tawhid (supreme unity of God), understanding of human nature, universalism, and comprehensiveness.

Notes:

1 Global Policy Forum, www.igc.apc.org/globalpolicy/socecon/inequal/gates99.htm
2 Green Peace, www.greenpeace.org/~forests
3 See U.S. Dept. of Justice, Bureau of Justice Statistics, www.ojp.usdoj.gov/bjs/; National Institute of Mental Health, www.nimh.nih.gov/research/suifact.htm.
4 See U.S. Dept. of Health & Human Services, www.samhsa.gov/oas/NHSDA/2kNHSDA/highlights.htm; The Urban Institute, www.urban.org/new/pressrel/pr000201.html; U.S. Dept. of Justice, Bureau of Justice Statistics, www.ojp.usdoj.gov/bjs/; Center for Disease Control, www.cdc.gov/nchs/fastats/aids-hiv.htm; www.my.webmd.com; www.anxiety-disorder.net.
5 Joseph Runzo, *Global Philosophy of Religion—A Short Introduction* (Oxford: Oneworld Pub., 2001), p. 173.
6 Ed Miller, *Questions That Matter: An Invitation to Philosophy*, fourth ed. (New York: McGraw Hill Inc., 1984), p. 403.
7 B.F. Skinner, *Beyond Freedom and Dignity* (New York: Bantam Books, 1972), p. 122.
8 Greg Krehbiel, www.crowhill.net/atheists/html
9 Robert Audi, ed., *The Cambridge Dictionary of Philosophy* (Cambridge: Cambridge Univ. Press, 1995), p. 311.
10 See www.secularhumanism.org/intro/what.html
11 Kai Nielsen, "Ethics Without God" in *Does God Exist—The Debate Between Theists and Atheists* by J.P. Moreland and Kai Nielsen (Amherst, New York: Prometheus Books, 1993), p. 109.
12 J.H. Newman, *A Grammar of Assent*, ed. C.F. Harold (London and New York, 1947)
13 Prophet Muhammad (SAW) stated on the authority of Anas bin Malik that: "None of you truly believes until he wishes for his brother what he wishes for himself" (narrated in Sahih Al-Bukhari and Sahih Muslim).
14 Kai Nielsen op. cit., p. 104.
15 See Chap. 1 for Immanuel Kant's moral argument for the existence of God and Chap. 3 for elaboration on the concept of Divine Justice.
16 See Joshua, Chaps. 6, 8, 10, 11; Deuteronomy, Chaps. 2, 3, 21; Numbers, Chaps. 21, 25, 31; Genesis, 6, 7
17 Qur'an 18:81.
18 Qur'an, 51:56: "I have created jinns and mankind only that they may serve Me."
19 Qur'an, 2:30, 6:165: "Behold, your Lord said to the angels, 'I will create a vicegerent on earth'..."
20 Fadhlalla Haeri, *Decree and Destiny*, p. 5
21 *Sahih Muslim*, Book 39, No. 6773.
22 Qur'an 13:12
23 Narrated by Al-Bukhari in *Al-Adab al-mufrad*.

24 Narrated by Tirmidhi in *Al-Ruda' bab ma ja' fi haq al-mar'ah 'ala zawjaha*, no. 1162, and Abu Dawud, no. 4682.
25 Hadith narrated in *Sahih al-Bukhari*, Jana'iz, 80, 92, Tafsir 30:1; *Sahih Muslim*, Qadar 22–24.
26 See Qur'an 15:29, 32:9, and 38:72.
27 J. M. McGinnis and W. H. Foege. *Actual Causes of Death in the United States*, JAMA, 1993; 270 (18): 2207–12.
28 "A War on Drugs, But Only a Murmur on Booze," San Francisco *Examiner*, July 31, 1998.
29 See Center for Disease Control, www.cdc.gov/nchs/fastats/alcohol.htm
30 US Dept. of Justice, Bureau of Justice Statistics. *Alcohol and Crime: An Analysis of National Data on the Prevalence of Alcohol Involvement in Crime* (Washington: Dept. of Justice, 1998).
31 See U.S. Department of Justice, www.ojp.usdoj.gov/bjs/
32 The Burton Goldberg Group, *Alternative Medicine—The Definitive Guide* (Tiburon, CA: Future Medicine Publishing, 1997), p. 340–4.
33 Ibid, p. 341.
34 Krucoff, Mitchell et al., "Integrative noetic therapies as adjuncts to percutaneous intervention during unstable coronary syndromes: monitoring and actualization of noetic training feasibility pilot," *American Heart Journal*, Nov. 2001, Vol. 142, No.5.
35 Kuang Y. Cha et al., "Does Prayer Influence the Success of In-Vitro Fertilization Embryo Transfer?" *Journal of Reproductive Medicine*, Sep. 2001, Vol. 46, No. 9.
36 Qur'an 13:12- "Allah will not change the condition of a people unless and until they change what is within themselves."
37 Islamic doctrine holds that all genuine Prophets and Messengers of God (peace be upon them) are free of sin, though not necessarily minor mistakes.
38 Ismail Al-Faruqi, *Tawhid: Its Relevance for Thought and Life,* first ed. (Kuala Lumpur: IIFSO, 1983), p. 72.
39 See Qur'an 6:164 "…no soul will be charged except what it had wrought upon itself: no one is the bearer of guilt for another…"
40 Kai Nielsen, "Ethics Without God" in J.P. Moreland and Kai Nielsen, *Does God Exist: The Debate Between Theists and Atheists* (Amherst, NY: Prometheus Books, 1993), pp. 99–100.
41 Ismail Al-Faruqi, *Tawhid: Its Relevance for Thought and Life*, 1st ed. (Kuala Lumpur: IIFSO, 1983), p. 113.
42 See Federal Bureau of Investigations at www.fbi.gov/ucr/ucr.htm.
43 Ismail Al-Faruqi, *Tawhid: Its Relevance for Thought and Life*, 1st ed. (Kuala Lumpur: IIFSO, 1983), p. 73.
44 Hadith narrated by Al-Bukhari and Muslim.
45 See also Qur'an 3:110, 7:157, 9:71, and 22:41.

Appendix

"And to Allah belong the Most Beautiful Names, so call unto Him by them..." (7:180)

Ar-Rahman:	The Beneficent, The Gracious, The Compassionate
Ar-Raheem:	The Merciful
Al-Malik:	The King, The Sovereign Lord
Al-Quddoos:	The Holy
As-Salam:	The Peace
Al-Mu'min:	The Keeper of Faith; The Faithful, The Bestower of Security
Al-Muhaymin:	The Protector, The Guardian
Al-'Aziz:	The Mighty
Al-Jabbar:	The Compellor
Al-Mutakabbir:	The Majestic, The Superb
Al-Khaliq:	The Creator
Al-Bari':	The Maker-Out-Of-Naught
Al-Musawwir:	The Fashioner
Al-Ghaffar:	The Forgiver
Al-Qahhar:	The Subduer, The Conquering
Al-Wahhab:	The Bestower
Ar-Razzaq:	The Provider, The Sustainer
Al-Fattah:	The Opener, The Reliever
Al-'Aleem:	The All-Knowing, The Knower
Al-Qabid:	The Restrainer, The Withholder
Al-Basit:	The Extender, The Enlarger, The Spreader
Al-Khafid:	The Abaser
Ar-Rafi':	The Exalter
Al-Mu'izz:	The Honorer
Al-Mudhill:	The Abaser, The Dishonorer
As-Samee':	The All-Hearing, The Hearer

Al-Baseer:	The All-Seeing, The Perceiver
Al-Hakam:	The Judge
Al-'Adl:	The Just, The Equitable
Al-Lateef:	The Subtle, The Gracious
Al-Khabeer:	The Aware
Al-Haleem:	The Forbearing, The Clement
Al-Azeem:	The Magnificent, The Tremendous
Al-Ghafooor:	The All-Forgiving
Ash-Shakoor:	The Grateful, The Repayer of Good
Al-'Ali:	The High
Al-Kabeer:	The Great
Al-Hafeez:	The Preserver, The Protector, The Guardian
Al-Muqeet:	The Feeder, The Sustainer, The Strengthener
Al-Haseeb:	The Reckoner
Al-Jaleel:	The Majestic, The Sublime
Al-Kareem:	The Bountiful, The Generous
Ar-Raqeeb:	The Watcher, The Watchful
Al-Mujeeb:	The Responsive, The Hearkener (to prayer)
Al-Wasi':	The Vast, The All-Embracing
Al-Hakeem:	The Wise
Al-Wadood:	The Loving
Al-Majeed:	The Glorious
Al-Ba'ith:	The Raiser (from death)
Ash-Shaheed:	The Witness
Al-Haqq:	The Truth
Al-Wakeel:	The Trustee, The Advocate
Al-Qawi:	The Strong
Al-Mateen:	The Firm, The Steady
Al-Wali:	The Protecting Friend, The Patron
Al-Hameed:	The Praiseworthy
Al-Muhsee:	The Reckoner, The Accountant
Al-Mubdi':	The Originator, The Producer
Al-Mu'eed:	The Reproducer, The Restorer

Al-Muhyi:	The Giver of Life
Al-Mumeet:	The Causer of Death
Al-Hayy:	The Ever-Living, The Alive
Al-Qayyoom:	The Eternal, The Self-Subsisting
Al-Wajid:	The Illustrious, The Noble
Al-Majid:	The Glorious
Al-Wahid:	The Unique
Al-Ahad:	The One
As-Samad:	The Eternal Support of Creation
Al-Qadir:	The Capable
Al-Muqtadir:	The Prevailing, The Dominant
Al-Muqaddim:	The Promoter, The Expediter
Al-Mu'akhir:	The Deferrer, The Postponer
Al-Awwal:	The First
Al-Akhir:	The Last
Az-Zahir:	The Manifest, The Outward
Al-Batin:	The Hidden, The Inward
Al-Waali:	The Governor
Al-Muta'ali:	The Most Exalted
Al-Barr:	The Righteous
At-Tawwab:	The Acceptor of Repentance
Al-Muntaqim:	The Avenger
Al-'Afu:	The Pardoner, The Mild
Ar-Ra'oof:	The Compassionate, The Full of Pity
Malik-Al-Mulk:	The Owner of Sovereignty
Dhul-Jalali-Wal-Ikram-	The Lord of Majesty and Bounty
Al-Muqsit-	The Equitable
Al-Jami'-	The Gatherer, The Collector
Al-Ghani-	The Self-Sufficient, The Rich
Al-Mughni-	The Enricher
Al-Mani'-	The Withholder, The Preventer
Ad-Dar-	The Distresser
An-Nafi'-	The Profiter
An-Noor-	The Light
Al-Hadi-	The Guide
Al-Badi'-	The Inventor, The Originator,

	The Incomparable
Al-Baqi-	The Everlasting, The Enduring
Al-Warith-	The Heir, The Inheritor
Ar-Rasheed-	The Guide to the Straight Path
As-Saboor-	The Patient

Index

A
Abodah Zarah 145, 176
Abraham 53, 59, 66
Absolute truth 54, 75
Achieved virtue 88, 110, 118
Age of Enlightenment 182
Ahadith 19
Al-'Ali 100
Al-Farabi 9
Al-Ghazali 9, 39
Al-Hadi 198
Al-Hakam 198
Al-Haseeb 198
Al-Mutakabbir 100
Al-Qahhar 100
Analogical deduction 63
Ancient Sumeria 1
Anonymous Christians 129, 139
Anti-Semitic 153
Approaches to Religious Diversity 126
Aql 62, 63, 72, 73
Are My Actions Free or Determined 107
Argument from Consciousness 14
Aslama 130, 131
At-takhalluq bi akhlaq 99
Atman 57
Ayn al-yaqin 75

B
Baba Mezia 145, 153, 176
Babylonian Talmud 152, 176

Beauty of Islam 158
Berakhot 145, 176
Blind faith 45, 54, 55
Blind Reason 54
Blindness of Empiricism 42
Bogus science 44
Born homosexuals 44
Brahmins 155, 156
Buddhism 125, 131, 154, 156, 157, 159, 163, 173, 178

C
Chosen people 127, 144, 153
Christian 2, 20, 23, 29, 39, 40
Christian doctrine 127, 143
Christianity 196, 211, 217, 219
Comprehensive Nature 216, 217
Compromising Monotheism 141
Confucianism 154
Copernican theories 2
Cosmological Argument of Necessary Being 10
Cosmological First Cause Argument 6, 8, 11
Criticism 47, 54

D
Darwinian evolution 6
Darwin's theory 2
David Hume 5
Definitive truths 52
Denial of the Truth 148
Design Argument 3
Determinism and Omnipotence 108
Din 130, 134, 138
Dirham 141
Disbelief and Denial 71, 74

Distortion of Divine Scripture 146
Divine Command 196, 220
Divine Law 133, 150, 152, 164
DNA 5
Does God Command Immoral Acts 199

E
Eastern Religions 154, 173
Einstein's theories 43
Evolutionism 2
Experiencing God 15, 17, 24, 35
Experiential 32
Experiential knowledge 68
Extra sensory perception 54

F
Faith and Tranquility 72
Final Message 164
First Cause 7
Fitra 29
Foundation of Islamic Ethics 198
Free Thought 183
Free Will 84, 85, 87, 88, 89, 100, 103, 107, 108, 109, 110, 111, 113, 118, 119, 121, 123
Friends of God 212

G
Gemara 144
God According to God 19
God and Science 46, 51, 61
God-consciousness 60, 61
God-imposed 5, 6
God-incarnate 143
Gratuitous evil 103

H
Hadith qudsi 97, 106, 122
Hajj 75
Haqq al-yaqin 75
Heart of Certainty 71
Hedonism and Perfectionism 186, 217
Highest Good 13
Hinduism 125, 131, 154, 155, 156, 159, 163, 173, 177, 178, 211

I
Iblis 164
Ibn Rushd 9
Ihsan 75, 76
Ijma 63
Ilham 68
Ilm 59, 60, 75, 80
Iman 71, 75, 80
Immanuel Kant 5
Impartial theories 44
Indebtedness 130
Injeel 133
Innana 1
Insaan 132
Inspiration 55, 59, 65, 66, 67, 68, 73
Is Morality Relative or Absolute 183
Islam 183, 196, 198, 199, 202, 203, 205, 206, 207, 208, 209, 211, 212, 213, 214, 215, 216, 217, 218, 219, 220
Islam and Knowledge 59
Islam, Reason and Science 61
Islamic concept of worship 217
Islamic epistemology 61
Islamic perspective 82, 84, 86, 114

J

Jews 127, 137, 138, 139, 142, 144, 145, 146, 148, 149, 150, 153, 154, 172, 175
Jizya 141
John Henry Newman 14
John Locke 14
Juda Halevi 127
Justice for All 101, 119

K

Kalam Cosmological Argument 9, 10
Karen Armstrong 150, 177
Kashf 68
Key to Salvation 136, 137, 172
Khatam an-nabieen 165
Knowing of God in Islam 26
Knowledge 72
Koans 53, 79

L

Lack of tolerance 136
Lessons of Affliction 89

M

Mana 1
Manu Shastri 155
Materialism 2, 22, 23
Meiosis 5
Mesopotamia 1
Metaphysical 2
Mind-imposed 5, 6
Mishnah 144
Mitosis 5
Modern scientific 42, 43, 46, 63, 77

Monotheistic Judaeo-Christian 125
Moral Argument 13, 14, 32
Moral conscience 191, 197, 214, 220
Morality 202
Mother nature 4
Muhammad 53, 60, 63, 65, 66, 67, 68, 69, 70, 71, 73, 75, 78, 79, 80
Muttaqi 215

N
Nation-state 215
Natural Experience 16, 17
Natural law 197, 210, 220
Nebulous 2
Necessary being 3, 7, 10, 11, 13, 29, 32, 33, 35
Newtonian laws 43, 54

O
Objective truth 184
Observation 42, 44, 45, 46, 79
Occamís Razor 7, 22
Official creed 142, 143
Ontological argument 11, 12
Ontological argument of Anselm 11, 12
Ontological proof 52
Original sin 203, 211, 212, 213, 220
Osiris 1

P
Parameters 2
Peaceful Submission 130, 131, 134, 171
People of the Book 137, 138, 139, 140, 141, 146, 149, 151, 166, 170, 172, 173, 178
Perennialist School 128
Perfect Good 213, 214

Personal Experience 15, 18
Peter Plichta 50, 79
Plato's theory 188
Polytheistic monotheism 151
Prana 1
Preservation of Sources 158, 159
Prime Mover 8
Primordial Religion 130, 134, 136, 137, 153, 159, 161, 168, 170, 172, 178
Problem of evil 81, 85, 118
Pull the plug 110
Pure Monotheism 158, 162, 173
Purpose of Mankind in Relation to Evil 86

Q
Qalb 71
Qi 1
Qiyas 63
Quantum theory 49
Qur'an and Prophethood 64

R
Rabb 29
Rabbinic Judaism 144, 176
Radical doubt 45
Rationalism 41, 51, 52, 53
Real World 205
Reason 51
Relativism 210
Religious Ethics 183, 196, 197, 199, 210
Religious Experience 16, 19, 39
Rene Descartes 45, 52, 79
Revelation 41, 42, 51, 55, 56, 58, 59, 61, 63, 65, 66, 67, 68, 69, 70, 71, 73, 75, 77, 78
Richard Swinburne 3

RNA 5
Role of Satan 114, 116
Ruh 73
Rule of God 199
Rule of law 199, 218

S
Salahuddin Al-Ayyubi 140
Salat 75, 208
Sarswati 1
Sawm 75
Scientific proof 47
Scientific realism 47
Scientific studies 44
Scientism 2
Secular Ethics 186, 199
Secular Humanism 186, 188, 189, 190, 219
Secularism 2
Seeing is believing 42
Shahadah 75
Shiite law 63
Shudra 155
Skepticism 181, 211
Son of God 213
Spirit 73
Spiritual Certainty 54
Spiritual renunciation 214
Stiff-necked 144
Straight Path 90, 108
Submissiveness 130
Sunni law 63

T
Talmud of Judaism 211

Taoism 154
Taqwa 105, 120
Tasting belief 16
Tawhid 21, 22, 162, 209
The Bible 63, 65, 80
The Quran 63
Theological proofs 27
Theory of hedonism 186
Thermodynamics 10
Tolerance 136, 139, 140
Torah 133, 144, 145, 146, 152, 176
Touch God 17
Trinitarian monotheism 144
Trust of Moral Responsibility 201

U
Ummah 166, 215, 216
Understanding of Human Nature 212, 221
Unique about Islamic Ethics 209
Universalism 214, 221
Unmoved Mover 8
Untouchable 155
Untouchables 211
Unveiling 55, 56, 58, 61, 68

V
Vicegerent 75, 76, 80
Vicegerent on earth 81, 86, 87
View of Logic 84

W
Wahy 69, 70
Way of knowledge 17
Wisdom of Religious Diversity 168

Worship 3, 16, 17, 18, 19, 21, 23, 24, 25, 26, 35, 36

Y
Yathrib 150
Yin and yang 99

Z
Zakat 75
Zoroastrian 29